CW00688992

TEARS
of the
DAWN

by

JULES LINES

Shelterstone

www.shelterstone.co.uk

Acknowledgements

Thank you to:

David and Sal Hayes: for selflessly making me part of their family when I had nothing. Thank you for understanding me and for accepting me just as I am.

Dari Roberts and Joanne Apps: for always being there to listen to me, giving me sound advice and a roof over my head whenever needed.

Susannah Hume: for working tirelessly on my manuscript to make it flow and writing the Tears of the Dawn stanza, and for being a constant inspiration and creative force, especially at times when I doubt myself.

Thank you also to: **Dave 'Cubby' Cuthbertson** (www.cubbyimages.com) and **Mike Roberston** (www.mikerobertsonphotography.com) for allowing me free rein with their superb photographic portfolios; **Paul Higginson** (www.vimeo.com/paulhigginson) for trawling through my old photographs and slides and scanning them into format; **Inge Nic A'Bhraonaigh** (www.gaelicorbs.weebly.com), for original Gaelic orb poetry; **James Roberts**, for pointing the first draft manuscript in the right direction; **Peter Biggar**, for reading my early manuscripts and working selflessly on the final proof; **Edie Horton**, for gecko designs; **Eleanor Crow**, for illustrations, and **Julianne Irvine** (www.creativeowl.co.uk) for cover artwork and book set up.

Finally, to all those whose company I have enjoyed over the years – whether at school, on a mountain, a crag or an oil rig – thank you.

Copyright © Julian Lines 2013
Design & Typesetting: Creative Owl (Julianne Irvine)
Front cover photograph: Rhue, North West Highlands © Cubby Images
Back cover photograph © Dave Pickford

Printed in Scotland by J. Thomson Colour Printers, Glasgow

The right of Julian Lines to be identified as the author of this work has been asserted by him in accordance with the Copyright, Designs and Patents Act 1988.

All rights reserved. No part of this publication may be reproduced, stored in a retrieval system, or transmitted, in any form or by any means, electronic, mechanical, photocopying, recording or otherwise, without the prior permission of the copyright owner.

First published in Great Britain by Shelterstone Ltd 2013
A catalogue record for this book is available from the British Library

ISBN 978-0-9576817-0-5

Shelterstone Ltd: 3, The Steading, Aberdeen Road, Tarland, AB34 4UA
www.shelterstone.co.uk

For Jim Hayes

The Tears of the Dawn

For those with her eyes, nature now gives a sign

A window of opportunity, a shift of paradigm

It seems they are born of another race

The watchers, the seekers, imbued with her grace

And whilst nature awakes and stretches and yawns

They are setting themselves free

In the Tears of the Dawn

Contents

Prologue

The tide slowly ebbs away. A long, sunken beach is exposed against a rocky shore as barnacle-encrusted boulders steam and crackle in the afternoon sun. My eyes sweep along the beach towards a deep, parallel-sided zawn. In six hours time, the highest spring tide of the year will be punching its salty fist into this coastline. The zenith will arrive on the brink of darkness. Those are the rules dictated by the forces of attraction between the Moon and the Earth. The vertical walls of the zawn, rising 120ft straight up from the beach, will then be reduced to a mere 90ft above a 30ft cushion of water. It is a rare window of opportunity, and that is why I am here.

At twilight, I make my entrance at the top of the zawn, peering down into the gloom. Only the deep, booming sounds of the sloshing waves echo out. I throw my rope and abseil in, penduluming inches above the tideline. Grabbing on to the rock, I unhitch and let go of the rope, climbing earnestly. Two thirds of the way up, I can sense the back wall tilting, closing in behind me. To compensate, I move out towards a wider reach. The rock becomes smoother as the situation intensifies. Finally, I grasp an apple-sized handhold. It is enough on which to pause for reflection as the biggest tide of the year locks horns with the coast.

Without warning, I find myself in the air, juggling the Judas hold - frozen in space, portraying a cartoon character – before accelerating down the middle of this limestone vice. The feverish ocean groans as my arms begin to back-pedal in a subconscious attempt to maintain the upright. My feet break the surface tension, and I quietly slip into the obsidian room.

Walking on the Moon

The foot treads in the snow were deepening as the slope ascended towards the heart of a rigid, blue sky. Each step was a further foot of altitude, and with each one another mountain fell away on the horizon. This unforgettable feeling of elevation both exhilarated and fascinated my eleven-year-old mind.

After what felt like hours of trudging up the snowy highway, the slope flattened out, and around me a wintry vista of mountains radiated ad infinitum. I was on top of the world - or that was how I felt.

The year was 1980, and I was with friends from Prep school. We had just completed the ninety miles of the West Highland Way in the past week. We topped it all off by walking up Ben Nevis, Britain's highest mountain, the day after the race horse of the same name had won the Grand National.

Mountains began to intrigue me, and I wanted to be amongst them. I managed to get my hands on a coffee table book, 'The Love of Mountains', by Michael Crawford Poole. One double paged picture in particular seemed to me to be of unimaginable beauty. It both bewildered and enticed. To me, the mountains and hills of Britain simply could not compare.

I read the caption: 'El Capitan and Half Dome – Yosemite Valley.' Could a place like that really exist?

At that moment, I vowed to myself that one day I would go there. It was a promise that took more than thirty years to fulfil.

I have always been conscientious and had an innate work ethic, compounded by the influence of a disciplinarian father who indirectly discouraged me from travelling. For many years, my climbing destinations had been dictated by my work schedules around the globe, schedules that had unfortunately fallen short of delivering a contract in the Gulf of Mexico. By the autumn of 2011, I felt that I had enough financial stability to justify taking some time off, and to fulfil my long-held promise to travel to Yosemite.

Ben Nevis had been my first Munro, but within five years I had completed the entire list of (at the time) 277. The natural progression for me from that point was to rock climbing and then, perhaps unnaturally, I shed the ropes altogether, becoming ensconced in the most unforgiving discipline of them all: soloing (termed 'free soloing' in America). For me, soloing has been full of strict self-control, through which I have tried to harmonise with the natural surroundings. Being a little older, my fear threshold has receded, and I am now not perhaps feeling as immortal as my younger self might have taken for granted. With the lure of Yosemite's flawless granite walls and its history of ultimate free soloing, I was becoming very troubled . . .

I wasn't entirely sure what type of 'mind wars' might ensue in Yosemite. For me, the drive and determination of my 'conscious mind' are difficult to control. They never seem to want to obey the sensibility and discipline of my 'subconscious mind', with its inbuilt safety mechanism for bodily preservation. No matter what, it was going to prove interesting.

Four hours drive from San Francisco; another bend and the stage curtain opened. There, at last, she appeared in front of me: Yosemite – 'The Valley'. El Cap stood forward and stage left, draping gracefully into the trees on the valley floor. Far behind, centre stage, stood the fascinating Half Dome. It is all vectors and curves and looks as though it has quite simply fallen from space. Mid distant and stage right is the mind-opening, 600ft, silver hose of Bridalveil Falls, issuing from a coy cirque.

It doesn't take an inventive imagination to visualise and understand the geology that has formed this landscape. Glacial ice had scoured through 4,000ft of bedrock to produce the Yosemite Valley in the form that we see it today. Down in the valley, the Merced River is almost static, twisting and meandering through apathetic meadows. Giant sequoias and Douglas firs congregate and point towards the stars and waterfalls abound, feathering downwards in apparently supernatural white veils. It was autumn and the aspens were gold. The valley was supersaturated with vitality.

Not only is Yosemite the foremost climbing destination in the world, it also has a magnetic appeal to tourists. There is so much more to see than simply El Cap and Half Dome; a multitude of monstrous cliffs, a plentiful supply of waterfalls (including the Yosemite Falls, the highest waterfall in North America at 2,500ft) and unrivalled views that simply astound those that pass through the area.

In terms of climbing dosses, 'The Valley' also lays claim to the most famous postcode in the world. It was going to be my home for a while. CAMP 4 wasn't quite what I had expected, and I was surprised that I had to queue for a pitch. Log boundaries, dusty floors, cheeky squirrels, bear boxes, slack lines, lean torsos, haul bags, many languages, stories of derring-do and *Midnight Lightning* are all part of the furniture.

For the first few days, I felt tired and lazy, calculating the angle of the sun against the valley walls, like an expectant reptile. It was all about relaxation and warmth. As I hadn't bothered to pull on a climbing shoe since I had arrived, dinner consisted of two spoons of peanut butter. I didn't have a stove. I had decided to solo the easiest route in 'The Valley' the following morning. To get there was quite a trek, and I set out at 4 am, following the John Muir trail as it twisted through trees whose outlines were darker than the night skies. Stars flickered and hidden waterfalls hummed with a persistent decibel. An hour or two and the path angled away. I lost the subsidiary path and found myself blindly crunching through the undergrowth of a deep forest, alert and with a growing sense of fear, waiting for the sound of an approaching cougar or bear. My mind was playing all kinds of tricks in the shadows of the dark until the sky began to ripen. I finally arrived at the base of *Snake Dyke*. My senses came to life; El Cap now sat small and humbled way below. A peach-coloured hue drowned the eastern horizon, and the smell of fresh, cold granite ignited my desire to climb. Halfway up the dyke, its hold-friendly spine suddenly burst into flame, its warmth waking me from my trance, changing the dimension of my solace, a mere 600ft from the ground. The angle soon laid back, and I bounded up to the summit of Half Dome. It is flat and spacious, and meditation felt to be in order. The descent from the top of the dome via steel cables was rather less natural. A squirrel crossed my path – he was heading to the summit to check if I had left any food. An enchanting walk back followed, and I encountered pinecones the size of bears' fists as the path wiggled and wormed through a maze of sequoias under a deepening blue sky.

Back in the valley I couldn't resist a look at Washington Column, a 1,000ft high precipice. It had a finely cloven, clean symmetry. Voices could be heard, but they were lost to the human eye amidst a sea of granite. I had come for one reason - something that I tried to deny to myself – but that was to seek out the line of *Astroman*, a 1,000ft crack line, possibly the most coveted free climb in the world when it was first climbed free in the mid 1970s. In 1987, the impossible happened: the Canadian climber, Peter Croft, blew the imagination of the climbing world with a free solo of the route. In terms of achievement, it was far more than winning gold at the Olympics; it was on a par with being the first man to walk on the moon. I was only a teenager at the time, but I can recall a picture of him in the climbing press, sitting on top after his astonishing accomplishment, in white trousers, tanned with blonde locks, relaxed and stretching. That picture captured everything there is to know about the spirit of free soloing and a human's immensely fragile existence in the face of such unforgiving natural elements.

When I had finally deciphered the line of *Astroman*, I became dizzy and trembled at the idea of soloing up there. My own thoughts of a free solo lasted no more than a few seconds. I walked away happily and with a massive sense of relief.

Sitting in camp, I was doing little apart from reading and recovering from my long shifts of work. I had little motivation and I didn't have a guidebook from which to choose a route that I could get psyched about. I did have a printout of a climb in Tuolumne Meadows though: *Regular Route* on Fairview Dome was said to be in the 'top 50' climbs in North America. It wasn't too hard and was known to be incredibly popular, so 'expect queues'. Tuolumne is a high plateau bordering Yosemite to the north. It is an idyllic mix of ice-scoured granite domes, meadows, and lakes nestling in the lap of the Sierra Nevada mountain chain. The climbs in Tuolumne are much shorter than those in Yosemite . . . perhaps a better place for me to be?

At daybreak, I arrived at the layby for Fairview Dome. There wasn't one other car; I had beaten 'the queue'. The temperature gauge read 22F (-6C). Stuffing my boots and chalk bag into my down jacket, I stepped out into the perishing cold and weaved along the faint trail through the trees up to the crag. *Regular Route* is an obvious, 900ft flake line up the vague axis of the dome. The groove in the base of the route housed some snow, which was a comfort to me until I discovered that it was, in fact, solid ice. I changed into my boots, feet steaming in the frigid air, flung off my down jacket and set to the flake. Muscles cold, slow and sluggish, not fluent; move after move, repetitive; clean, honest climbing until I reached a small foot ledge at 150ft. My triceps had cramped in the cold; above, the moves were more complicated, perhaps the crux; the footholds were small, and the hand-crack would have been positive if it wasn't for the fact that a veneer of ice exited from it and swept down the rock in one long, frozen tear. I stood there, becoming colder, thinking, waiting, hoping that someone else was going to turn up and rescue me. Ten minutes, twenty minutes . . . I played with the holds. My hands didn't have much feeling left in them. I made the decision to descend, but I was too cold and stiff to reverse off the foot ledge.

Forty minutes, still nobody. The situation was fast becoming a serious one. My core temperature had dropped. I had to go up! With one hand stuck in the icy crack,

I put the other under my armpit in an attempt to gain core warmth. I alternated hands for fifteen minutes until I had finally melted enough ice in the crack to gain positive hand jams.

I pressed my feet onto the small holds and pulled up, gibbering without flexibility, sinews and muscles frozen. My movement was being coordinated only by my survival instinct. I continued shaking my way up the simplicity of the flake. At 200ft, a ledge on the left offered a rest; I declined it and immediately regretted my decision as 'hot aches' started to burn into my fingers. I jammed my foot into the crack, closed my eyes, and screamed with discontentment as I swapped my hands over and over, thumping them against the rock. I couldn't afford to stop for too long. I had to keep moving to regain warmth. Luckily the climb continued to relent and flowed beautifully. I pulled over onto the summit of the dome at 9,300ft. Tuolumne was bathed in sunshine, extending in all directions – an archaic battlefield of glaciers long since gone. There wasn't another soul in sight. If I had waited for a rescue, I would have certainly perished. Climbing on the Tuolumne domes was obviously not the norm in November.

The days drifted on in 'The Valley'. For once I didn't feel too perturbed that I wasn't doing much climbing. I was relaxed and happy that I wasn't hundreds, even thousands, of feet up without a rope. Perhaps common sense was beginning to win the day as I approached middle age. El Capitan soared – 3,000ft of unblemished, vertical granite pushing out, all brazen and bravado. It is the most popular piece of vertical real estate in the world; big wall climbing is all the rage here. It is all about 'living on the wall' for days or weeks; hauling, camping out on portaledges, and basically down and out blood, sweat and dehydration. It took a certain amount of personal sacrifice to climb a route on El Cap, sacrifice that I didn't have in me to give at that moment in time. I was happier to lie in the meadow, swim in the Merced and try my hand at the CAMP 4 boulders. Was it sacrilege to be climbing on boulders, surrounded by a plethora of fierce granite walls?

The boulders were glacially smooth, and it required a certain amount of adjustment in technique to become accustomed to the rock. I tried to work out if a hold was actually a hold, finding sequences, falling, trying again, falling and spraining an ankle on a tree root, limping off rather dejectedly. My conscience was eased when I met Alex Hannold on the boulders. He is considered to be the best free solo climber in the world at this time, not that free soloing should be any sort of competition. His recent solo ascent of the 2,000ft *Regular Route,* on the North West Face of Half Dome, pushed the standards up from *Astroman* and opened up the possibilities. He jibed at me about my hair . . .

'Is that a mullet you have?' I responded with only a laugh.

I began to wonder if he had designs on a free solo of one of the 'big' routes on El Cap. It will happen one day, someone will do it, and the achievement will be the equivalent of walking on Mars! There is such a fine line between the angstroms of attachment and the inevitable. The human body is so resilient and adaptable, yet so delicate; a soloist's mind so fascinating and complex, yet utterly natural. It is always such sad news when a soloist dies doing what they love. Do they have regrets? I don't think so. Phil 'Jimmy' Jewel (1987), 'Dirty' Derek Hersey (1993), and the legendary John Bachar (2009) all died in the pursuit of their goals, but they are remembered and revered and have inspired a generation of climbers, soloists and non soloists alike. In their own way, they have found immortality.

The Lure of the Tables

The motion of the bus was making me feel queasy as it rounded another bend. I sat huddled next to a slightly fogged up window, looking out across the broad expanse of Loch Lochy and the mountains disappearing into the mist on the far side. I was on edge - I had told my amicable housemaster, Ben Goss, I was going to stay with friends for the forthcoming half-term break. It was a little white lie, but one that I deemed absolutely necessary and, in truth, fairly harmless.

In general, I was a good pupil. I towed the line with regard to smoking and alcohol, apart from the odd tipple of gin on the eight hour train journey from Crewe to Inverness at the start and end of each term. I had crushes on a lot of girls, like any boy at that age, but my huge fear of rejection meant that I never actually asked anyone out. I very rarely listened in class – I was more likely to be daydreaming about my next expedition into the mountains.

When the bus reached Ballachulish, I stepped off, took my large rucksack from the underbelly of the bus, and heaved it onto my shoulders. It was mid afternoon, mid November; the sky was heavy and grey and the light levels were starting to fade. It was what the Scottish would only describe as 'dreich'.

I felt a little lonely and nervous, standing by the side of the road, watching the bus disappear towards Glencoe. I was dressed in my school uniform of black trousers, a white shirt, tie and a blazer. I needed to change into my hillwalking gear, so I nipped into someone's back garden and changed behind the garden shed. I stuffed my school uniform into the bottom of my rucksack, and on top I packed my sleeping bag, spare clothes, food, bivvi bag and waterproofs. Finally, I stuck my ice axe on the outside and set off up Beinn a Bheithir.

After a frantic few days in Glencoe, during which I had completed Beinn a Bheithir, the much lauded Aonach Eagach ridge and the majestic Bidean nam Bian, I caught a bus that was heading in the direction of Ullapool. I found myself waking up the following morning in an old, run-down, wooden bus shelter, 120 miles away at Braemore junction. I had a fever. Snowflakes were falling limply, and I wanted to get going along the Destitution Road towards An Teallach, but I was sweating and covered in a strange rash.

I first heard of Gordonstoun School, not because of its royal connections, but because Simon Roberts, one of the 'old boys' from my Preparatory School, Malsis, had gone there. Simon inadvertently gave me direction. He used to join us on our Easter-break walks. Stories of him joining the school Mountain Rescue team, rock climbing and having a large rucksack with an ice axe on the back, sealed my commitment to wanting to go to Gordonstoun. Simon, known as 'Silly' to his school friends, was well liked and extremely keen on climbing and the outdoors. After leaving school, he joined the RAF and became a helicopter pilot. On a tour of duty in Northern Ireland, his helicopter crashed, and he died in his mid twenties. A blanket of sadness spread over the lives of everybody that knew him.

The first term at Gordonstoun, in December of 1982, was a turning point in my life. On my 14th birthday, I donned appropriate 'going out' school uniform, took the bus into Elgin and with my pocket money bought 'Munro's Tables' for the princely sum of £5.95. In this book was the list of all of the mountains in Scotland of 3,000ft and above, as defined by Sir Hugh T Munro in 1891; there were 276 of them in the edition that I bought. I became so infatuated with Munro's Tables that I could recite the whole list and knew the heights of each and every one of them. At that time, I had completed only four Munros, which were duly ticked off in my book. The first two, Ben Nevis and Cairngorm, I had completed whilst on Malsis Easter walks.

Gordonstoun was renowned for outdoor pursuits; however, I couldn't join the Mountain Rescue team until the start of my third year at school. I had house and form expeditions to look forward to, but they were never enough for me. I was lucky enough to have a keen deputy housemaster (Tony Gabb) who loved the outdoors and was quite happy to organise some voluntary backpacking expeditions during the winter months. During the summer months, we were allowed to plan and go on our own voluntary expeditions without the accompaniment of a teacher.

There was now a small group of us that were keen on hillwalking. Paul Ewing, from Largs, almost always accompanied me. He was the cleverest in our year and went on to become a GP. Then there was John Forbes who lived on Westerfolds Farm, close to school. I often visited the farm. John's parents were welcoming; it was fun, and sometimes we used to get paid a little money for helping with the harvesting of the carrots or tatties. John went a little wayward, and we drifted apart. He was later expelled from school, along with Jim Hayes, for taking the school minibus during the middle of the night. They were caught by the police, jumping a red light thirty miles away in Nairn.

In May 1984, Paul, John and I, all now aged fifteen, went on our second voluntary expedition. Our first had been in the Monadh Liath the previous year. We alighted at Dalwhinnie Station on Friday night, and by Sunday afternoon we had walked forty-three miles and finished nine Munros in the Ben Alder region – one of the wildest tracts of land in Scotland.

At the end of the summer term, Jim Hayes invited me to his home near Aviemore in order to complete some Munros in the Cairngorms. Jim's father picked us up; I thought David was far too much fun and easy-going to be a father. An hour later we reached their home, Muir of Knock, where Jim's Mum, Sal, stood on the porch and gave me such a welcoming hug and a warm greeting that I almost melted in shyness. Jim and I roamed the Cairngorms and then Creag Megaidh. Sal gave us lifts: we swam in the Spey, taking advantage of the delightful weather, and we took Jim's polecat

Marlow out into the birch wood to catch rabbits. I met Jim's younger brothers, Joe and Ben, who were always out in the forest catching rabbits, picking mushrooms or smoking 'fungus fags'. After a memorable ten days, I had to go home. Sal put me on the train in Aviemore. I didn't want to leave, and I was in tears. It was the first time that I had felt that someone loved me, as an individual.

A decade later, when I became homeless and to all intents and purposes without family, David, Sal, Jim, Joe and Ben selflessly took me in and have treated me as one of their own family ever since. I sort of became the surrogate son and brother, and Muir of Knock became my home. I was incredibly fortunate.

During the remainder of that summer holiday, I worked on my father's building renovation project, doing demolition, labouring and landscaping, amongst other things. I hoped that my father would take me to Scotland for a week to do some Munros; he did. We stayed in a caravan in Tyndrum, and he drove Paul Ewing and me around. We took on arduous walks. Ben Cruachan was my 100th Munro at that time - our tallies were rising rapidly.

The following year after my O Levels, Paul, Jason Eker and I took the train to Achnashellach. I had a big walk planned to take in all fifteen of the Munros encircling Loch Monar. Paul wasn't that keen to accompany me, nor was Jason. It was to be the first time that I walked alone in the hills. The world was my oyster - I could go at my own pace and stop whenever I wanted, which was rarely. I left the tent at 2am and set off up Sgurr a' Chaorachain in the dark with a pound of wine gums and a handful of Mars Bars. It was daylight as I reached the remote peak of Lurg Mhor. I continued towards the Sgurr na Lapaich group and then into the deserted Glen Strathfarrar before starting to walk up the slopes of Sgurr na Ruaidhe with leaden legs and the Lionel Ritchie song – 'Hello' – going round and round my head. I didn't think I could go much further, so after twenty nine miles I slipped into my sleeping bag and my plastic, orange bivvi bag, scoffed a Mars Bar, and tried to sleep.

In the early hours of the morning, I felt something nudge the plastic of my outer bag: all jittery, I slowly unwrapped myself and peered out, and for a moment I was face to face with a stag's head. I'm not sure which of us was more bewildered. It trotted off, and I decided to get up and carry on walking. I was fatigued, but I just kept plodding on until I arrived back at the tent in the late afternoon, having walked forty-eight miles and 22,000ft of ascent in two days. I was invisibly driven by an obsession to tick off Munros. I discovered that my self-motivation was frighteningly powerful. I knew then that I was slightly unusual; most sixteen year olds would be hanging around the bike sheds, sneaking a cigarette, chatting up girls, getting 'a snog' or something a little more, but this was how I got my kicks.

Walking the Munros aside, my first few years at school were standard. I played rugby at first, but then I began to change and sought solitude away from team sports. Instead, I took up cross-country running in the winter and Mountain Rescue expeditions, sometimes snow holing and doing 500ft stretcher lowers in the mountains. In the summer term, I played golf and was on the school team. I liked golf because it had an element of freedom. Other ball sports were constrained to a court or a pitch. Sadly, over the years, it has gained the reputation of being 'classist'. I gave up golf and took up rock climbing. Right at this time, I ceased to see the point in being competitive, except with myself, and climbing was the perfect medium in which to fulfil that objective.

When I had first come into possession of Munro's Tables, it had never crossed my mind to do them all. I just ticked off as many as I could. I was always studying maps and trying to work out the most efficient ways to do as many as possible in one trip. After three years, it started to become harder as all the ridges with multiple Munros had been completed; now I concentrated on those that stood alone, or the outlying ones that I had missed on previous walks. Recently, Joe Hayes reminded me of a time when we were in Glen Affric, with Andrew Spark, to pick off some Munros. I had the idea that we should travel light and bivvi on top of Sgurr nan Ceathreamhnan. When they were lagging behind me, I supposedly left them a trail of wine gums to follow. It was slightly unorthodox, but it worked!

From my journal, I know that we reached the summit at 9.45pm. We had great views to the Cuillins of Skye and bivvied on the summit, resuming walking at 3.30am because no one slept. Later the following day, we met Tony Gabb and his 4th form expedition in Glen Affric. He asked if we wanted to join them at camp. We all looked somewhat hesitantly at each other, not knowing quite what to say, as we didn't want to let on that we did not, in fact, have any camping gear. I quickly answered that we had already planned on staying at the Camban bothy, two miles further down the glen. I was always pushing the boundaries of what was responsible and what I could get away with.

The following year, I joined a Duke of Edinburgh Gold expedition to the lonely peninsula of Knoydart. I wasn't doing the award, but some of my friends were. They needed to get a group of four people together to be able to carry out a fifty-mile walk over four days. I was keen as there were a number of Munros in Knoydart that I needed to do. Four miles into the walk, at Barrisdale Bay, we broke the rules and split into two groups. Ashley Bartlett and I wanted to go up Ladhar Beinn, whilst Cain Barnish and Jim Spark preferred to stay low and walk through the glens. So we made an arrangement to meet up at camp each night. Ashley and I scooped up seven Munros, with 40lb rucksacks, terrible midges morning and night, and perfect weather for the duration. We suffered from sunburn and dehydration – the temperatures were well over 80F (although my notes tell me actually 100F). I still have very fond memories of that particular expedition.

I coped with O levels, but I found A levels far more difficult. I was struggling - the results of my mock exams in the final year said as much. I somehow knew I was going to do poorly, so I just put more effort into finishing the Munros. At Easter break in 1987, my father drove me round to finish the final few. I spent a night alone in Shenavall bothy so I could get an early start to do the six Fisherfield Munros. I was woken at 3am by rustling noises and the tapping of feet on the floorboards. I was scared as I fumbled around for my torch, turned it on, and discovered a mouse scurrying by my face. It had eaten my Dairylea Cheese Triangles and left hundreds of tiny pieces of silver foil. I could not get back to sleep, so I lay and stared out of the window, watching the stars glinting above the pronounced silhouette of An Teallach. I completed the round of six Munros and the following day did An Teallach.

All that remained were nine of the eleven Munros in the Cuillins of Skye. I knew that I couldn't do the Inaccessible Pinnacle on my own in winter conditions, so I managed to persuade Joe (Hayes) to do some of the Cuillins with me. Being on the snow-coated Cuillin Ridge with the sun shining is a powerful experience. It is quite unlike anywhere else in Scotland. The peaks are steeper and fiercer, and it is considerably more treacherous. The Inaccessible Pinnacle is a spine of rock on the ridge and is in actual fact 25ft higher than the mountain it protrudes from. It is the only Munro that requires a level of climbing ability. There was a short, steep side and a long, exposed, scrambling side. Joe and I were capable of climbing the 'In-Pin' but perhaps not in winter. We had minimal climbing equipment; a walking-axe apiece, some crampons, a rope and a few slings. I set off up the groove at the start of the long side, but my crampons were a nuisance and so too were my boots – I took them off and tried in socks. 15ft up, I found my axe also to be of little use, so I hung it from a sling that was round my neck. It fell out and nearly hit Joe on the head. Joe had had enough and walked off, leaving me to make the decision to either carry on alone or go down. I retreated.

As the summer and my A levels approached, I had two Munros remaining. My father had driven up to take me over to Skye during my half-term break. I headed up to the In-Pin. I attempted the short side, rated 'difficult', but I failed to solo it in the wind and the rain, so I descended disappointedly back into Glen Brittle. My father told me to try the longer side, rated 'easy'. The following morning, I was back in the rain, mist and a 40 mph cross wind. I got organised, put some socks over my EB rock boots and went for it, clinging on for dear life, trailing a rope, not able to see the sheer drop on either side due to the mist. I finally made it and abseiled off, buffeted by the wind.

Sgurr nan Gillean (Peak of the Young Men) was to be my final Munro. On top, I simply lay by the cairn, almost emotionless, and said, 'You're my last Munro'. My father waited for me at the bottom. He seemed proud of me on that day - a first and probably a last. I think he saw my brother and I as disappointments after all of his financial input into our education. He had a bottle of champagne with him. I didn't like it, so he drank the bottle whilst I drove us the few miles back to the Sconser Lodge Hotel for a warm bath and a hearty homemade steak and kidney pie.

At school, we went to the chapel for assembly after breakfast every morning. The headmaster, Michael Mavor, took assembly on a Friday. On this particular morning, he strolled in with a book in his hands. I knew that book; it was Irvine Butterfield's tome called the 'High Mountains of Britain and Ireland'. I suddenly put two and two together and realised what was going to happen. I could feel my face heating up. I had to go up in front of the whole school to collect the book after the headmaster's announcement that I had completed all of the Munros. People started to clap and then there was a standing ovation; I had never witnessed a scene like this in assembly during my five years at school. I wanted to crawl into my shell and hide - my cheeks were burning up with embarrassment.

That summer, whilst waiting for my exam results, I was invited to the Alps for a couple of weeks with my friends, Peter and Angus Harper and their dad Fred, President of the British Mountain Guides. The Alps were so much bigger than the Munros, and the weather was so much better. I experienced many new things; altitude sickness, topless French girls, alpine huts, Fred's crazy driving, listening to Fleetwood Mac's 'Tango in the Night', and regrettably the way the French guides shout at, and barely tolerate, their clients. The climbs were brilliant; nice, clean granite towers above virgin, white glaciers - but they were busy, and queues formed if a team above was slow. When I had finished the list, I thought that the natural progression would be to start on the Alpine 4,000m peaks, of which there are over 50 major ones, including the likes of Mont Blanc and the Matterhorn. After that, perhaps the frozen giants of the Himalaya, pushing lucidly towards the stratosphere, would await me. However, Alpine mountaineering did not in the end take off for me, and it was purely down to logistics, travel and the costs for an eighteen year old. I looked closer to home for fulfilment, and my attention turned instead towards pure rock and ice climbing.

Precious Stones

A panic-stricken five year old charged through the forest, legs pedalling, feet pumping hard onto the forest floor. Occasionally, the odd branch hung in his path, its leaves whipping his face, but this did not deter him. He carried on faster and more blindly than before. He didn't dare to stop or look over his shoulder as he knew his pursuer was faster than him and was gaining rapidly. In blind fright, he launched onto a tree trunk, scratching at the rough, ridged textures of its bark, flailing for the lowest branch. He grabbed it, pulled hard and climbed as high as he dared up into the branches of the tree. He straddled a branch and shuffled out along it, cleverly calculating that the branch was strong enough to hold only his weight. He felt safe perched near the end, and now all he had to do was to get his breath back and wait until his pursuer got bored with waiting.

Crack!

The noise split the air like a whip. The branch sheared and tossed him into the air as though he were an inexperienced matador. He fell through the branches and landed in a pond thick with mud, rotting leaves and pond life. As he waded out, dripping with muck, he felt strangely excited - his older brother fell to the ground in hysterics. He laughed too, maybe because he thought that falling into the pond was enough punishment, or maybe he just loved getting dirty and the adventure of it all. It was tough being the younger sibling.

I enjoyed the forest and the fields behind our back garden in the village of Sutton on the Forest, ten miles north of York. Hours of my childhood were spent climbing trees, swinging in branches, making dens, hiding amongst the hay bales, shaping bows and arrows, finding conkers, falling 20ft into ponds, and even having a weeding fork stuck in my skull by my elder brother, Giles.

Twenty years later: once again I am at a fork in the forestry track. This time I had to consult my guidebook. One track led to the crag, the other into densely clad forest and a maze of footpaths. The forest reminded me of my childhood, albeit the memories were now long distant. My adventurous spirit had never waned – and I found myself wandering through this forest, searching for sandstone rocks hidden amongst trees. The deep foliage veiled the outside world; it felt secretive in there – no one could look in or out. I stumbled upon the rocks of *Kyloe in the Wood* quite by chance. The steep, honeycombed sandstone was textured in such a way that it seemed it had been deliberately formed as a test of human strength and prowess.

Northumberland is the quiet county, lost between England and Scotland. It doesn't quite belong to either – it is reclusive and has a fictitious feel, in parallel with the climbing and rocks there. Undulating waves of open countryside, the expansive quilt of fields, the small, inert forests and quaint, tight-knit villages make it refreshingly unique. Sporadically, speckled crests of sandstone appear, topping waves of rolling land, the rocks flashing with many colours on sunny evenings.

The northern extent of the Roman Empire, marked by Hadrian's Wall, fizzled out amongst this secluded countryside. Two thousand years later, I materialise! It was the summer of 1991. I was passing south from Scotland, in possession of the new climbing guidebook to Northumberland. The cover photo of the local climbing legend, Bob Smith, casually undercutting the brutal sandstone cornice of *Poseidon Adventure*, 30ft above the deck, *without* a rope, was scarily attractive. It had summoned me to visit and to solo these obscure and little-heralded crags.

I was excited when I stole into *Back Bowden Doors* at four in the morning, accompanied by the cooing noise of wood pigeons, wondering what climbs I might find. The crag was half-immersed in a wood – it was an enchanting place, a home for pixies and elves. The rocks themselves were exquisite: sandstone buttresses, subtle but strong, different shapes and dimensions, crowned with beautifully carved flutes of wind-eroded rock.

All of a sudden, underneath the large central roofs, I stumbled upon the pixies and elves – a random array of sleepers buried cosily in their sleeping bags. I wasn't sure who they were. I tiptoed past them along the pine-needled floor, hoping that I wasn't going to wake them.

After I had checked out all of the routes and had noted the ones that I wanted to climb, I was drawn to the smooth, central slab that hung in the air like a giant, inclined billboard, advertising: *Climb Here!* And that is exactly what I did. *On the Verge* became my first climb on Northumberland sandstone – an appealing, fat-rounded arête up the right edge of the slab. I had made an irreversible step-up move through a small overlap and spent a silent twenty minutes in contemplation, with my toes stubbed into a small seam below the main arête, trying to commit to its loneliness.

Nerves were twitching, and my balance felt precariously sluggish 20ft above hard ground. I stepped up and pulled tightly to the arête, the textures of the rock counterbalancing the tension of my limbs, channelling me into an instinctive sequence of brave, fluent moves.

I felt the rush of addiction and instantly wanted more, so I climbed the intriguing line of *The Arches*. This route cambers steeply out of the bowels of the crag and continues in a long, diagonal sweep to some final, hearty pulls on chunky flutes. I felt like an early morning elf floating through the forest. *The Witch, The Spell* and *Magic Flute* were sweet engagements as I began to warm up and move more fluidly.

Still the sleeping bodies lay below, silent and unmoving. I wanted to climb *The Wizard*, but there was a problem – there were sleepers right underneath it. Impatiently, I tiptoed between the sleeping bags to gain the starting holds. It was a rather reckless notion, climbing upside down along a horizontal flake line in the roof, 8ft above those sleeping. After a couple of hours, I had had my fill, so I hopped the fence and dissolved away over the fields as silently as I had arrived, unseen and invisible, leaving no trace apart from a possible footprint and the odd dab of chalk. My appreciation of Northumberland and its bijou stones of sand had been set and would never leave me. *Back Bowden Doors* is still my favourite Northumbrian crag because it has that strange, magical feel.

In January 1992, I was feeling low. I was in the midst of exams at University and revision had left no free time to climb. On top of that, I was still sore with injuries I had picked up three weeks previously when I had fallen from *Obsession Fatale* on the gritstone, meaning that I was in no fit state to climb, even if I had the time. My friends were making good use of the winter conditions, and all I heard of were their ascents of some of the best winter routes in Scotland. I was missing out and I was miffed. My girlfriend was bearing the brunt of my mood, so I decided to remedy the situation by driving down to Northumberland in the middle of the night, through thick fog, with the promise of a good forecast for the following few days.

I arrived at three in the morning in sub-zero temperatures. I curled up on the back seat of the car. When the sun rose, I pulled out of the car and tried to stretch. The sky was flawless; the ground was white and twinkled with frost. A wedge of dense fog nuzzled into the valley, like an imaginary glacier – it was a beautiful winter's morning. I could not appreciate it though as my core temperature had dipped close to hypothermic. With numb fingers, I managed to turn the ignition and run the engine to generate some warmth. After a few hours, I had defrosted. I packed my gear and limped over the fields towards the crag.

Over the last year, the possibility of a new route up the centre of the billboard slab at Back Bowden had been brewing in my mind, but my confidence was derailed when I arrived to see that the access to the centre of the slab was devoid of holds. Instead, I spied a solitary runnel, just left of centre, which could be accessed by the route: *Magic Flute*.

I was pleased with the discovery of a potential new route. In a way, I wish I hadn't found it, as my injuries, bruises and confidence probably weren't up to the rigours of another fall. The air was cold, and there was not a cloud in the sky. It was a perfect day for climbing and cooler rock meant better friction.

The branches of the larch trees drooped like petrified shelters, and the ground was locked tight with a strangling frost. There was silence – not even the customary summery voice of the wood pigeon. I sat on the frozen ground and pushed my numbed feet into stiff climbing boots and set off up *Magic Flute*. At 20ft a blind, energetic pull on some naturally carved holds landed me on the lip of the slab. There I stood, looking up earnestly at the solitary runnel, weighing up the moves and puzzling over the sequence to unlock them. I stepped right onto a smear and then another; my palms lay flat, fingers digging into the blank stone surface. I looked down to see the slab vanish 5ft beneath me, and I knew there was a further 20ft to the ground. My aches and pains started to intensify, and a sudden wave of nervous energy hit me. I wobbled down to the foothold on the lip and exited via *Magic Flute*.

Not wishing to fail, I limped back over the fields to fetch my rope, harness and some protection nuts from the car. Back at the crag, I put my harness on and climbed up to the base of the slab and placed a nut in a flute. I awkwardly measured out a length of rope with a knot in either end - one into the nut and the other to my harness. Feeling braver, I committed and began to rush, scratch and pray in an amalgam of uncontrolled hopelessness, all the while waiting for the slide . . . inevitably it happened, and I hurtled off the end of the slab . . . My feet hit the ground on the rope stretch before I sprung back on the elasticity, coming to rest with my feet raised and my backside a few feet from the ground. I waited for the pain to rush into my ankles, but strangely none arrived. I had forgotten to calculate the rope-stretch.

After something to eat and much mulling over, I shortened the rope further to account for the stretch before climbing back up onto the same lonely smears. I was slower this time, more calculating, and when I pushed onto the crucial smear and reached up, something made me look down. I saw to my horror that the nut had pulled out of the flute . . .

I had made the rope too short and it had become useless; I was soloing – fait accompli. I scrabbled for the top in a rubbery, gelatinous mess. I named *Bolder Lands* in honour of Northumberland's landscape and its climbing ethos.

It was January. The days were short, and the sun had started to threaten to drop below the Cheviot horizon. I sat on top, watching the last of the sun's orange, wintry shafts colour the landscape before they flickered out into the confines of a cold night sky.

I was in a much happier frame of mind when I returned to see my girlfriend. However, when my exams finished in the summer and I graduated with a degree in Geology, I plummeted into a depression, and it didn't help matters any when I broke up with her. I knew I had to go home to Cheshire and live and work with my father. It was the lowest point in my life. I didn't want to leave her; I didn't want to leave Aberdeen, and I didn't want to leave all of the friends I had grown with over the past four years, but I didn't have the strength at the time to cut the strings that were being pulled. I was being brainwashed into someone else's cruelly cynical world – a world where my life and my mind weren't my own. I just wanted to disappear, and if all else failed I just didn't want to exist.

A year passed by before my return to Scotland. I had been working continuously on my father's building sites in Cheshire, when I received word that two of my friends from University were to be married in Brechin. At the time, the housing market had been hard hit. Interest rates had practically doubled overnight, meaning that out of necessity I had become a jack of all trades; bricklaying, roofing, digging drainage systems, final fix joinery – basically everything. I was even the nightshift security guard, sleeping on the floors of the empty, doorless houses, guarding the copper pipe with none other than my hickory shafted ice axe as a weapon.

The wedding invitation was a godsend. It was an excuse to escape the shackles of labour and to head north for a bout of socialising.

At the wedding, I chatted with old friends and ended up overly drunk. I knew I had to stop drinking otherwise I would never be able to get up and drive south for some climbing in Northumberland. I was prone to hangovers that could last up to three days. When I awoke, it was noon. I bade Dave and Gillian goodbye, wished them luck, and turned south once more.

After a four-hour drive, I pulled up at Bowden Doors, jumped out and trotted briskly along the escarpment. The sandstone was infused with a welcoming plethora of colours. I followed the energetic movement offered by *Canada Crack, Overhanging Crack, Lorraine* and *Tiger Wall*. They were some of Bowden's best routes, and they stretched my tired and reluctant body back into working order. Further along the edge, I arrived at the classic route: *Poseidon Adventure*. Without any thought, I took hold of the appealing flake that led me blindly to a sudden impasse. I had to give myself a little reassurance before finding and pinching a wart of sand that unlocked the precarious move to reach the horizontal break. Above me reared the famous wave of the sandstone cornice, with a texture like whipped cream, looking steep and impossible. I began to weigh up the possibility of jumping off without breaking an ankle, but this simply wasn't an option, so with the picture of Bob Smith firmly lodged in my mind, I powered up through the overlap on undercuts with blind determination.

I sat on the heathery plateau above the edge, rather surprised. I was rewarded with a spacious view across a multi-coloured patchwork of fields towards the swelling of the Cheviot Hills in the distance. It was peaceful in the warm June air, and the countryside was green and fresh. I felt invigorated and revived.

After a few hours of soloing, meditating and dissolving my hangover, I decided to move on and visit another crag: Callerhues, an hour's drive to the southwest. As it was midsummer's day, it wouldn't be dark until well past ten o'clock, and I was convinced that the rocks would offer up a comfortable cave or niche for me to sleep in for the shortest night of the year. I rolled up at the farmhouse at eight o'clock, checked with the farmer that I might park the car, shouldered my rucksack and jogged with optimism through a rollercoaster of fields along the Pennine Way.

I passed a weary copse of trees on the left as I entered open moorland. The mottled, tranquil moor stretched out towards the eastern horizon, and I could see the rocks, visible splash marks on the crest of a greeny-brown wave.

I arrived at the cliff, eager and in a sweat as I had run across the bog and bracken clad moor to get there in the shortest time possible. On closer inspection, the silvery-white sentinels of rock were perfect for climbing – the pockets and nubbins were unnatural looking but were perfect beacons for grasping fingers and wandering toes. The height was amenable and the landings 'soft', so I started to climb at the northern end and soloed my way southwards, gradually wilting in accompaniment to the falling arc of the setting sun.

The shadows of dusk clawed over the moor, the air taking on a chill and the wildlife growing mute. Loneliness descended as I searched for a suitable bed for the night. It took me a while, but eventually I chose a dry patch of flat ground behind a boulder. I crawled into my sleeping bag, alert to my surroundings as darkness settled. Time rolled on passively . . . one hour . . . two hours . . . I calculated that I would have to endure a maximum of five hours of darkness. I tried to sleep, but I couldn't, and then I heard a faint and very distant noise. I thought nothing of it at first, but the noise increased, pulsing over the moor in waves. This was no dream. Flooded with adrenalin, I sat bolt upright and stared into the darkness of the moor, towards the source of the inexplicable sound. It was relentless, but there was only blackness . . . and then it appeared – a narrow shaft of light. It began to intensify and grow, shining on the cliff, sweeping towards me . . . two hundred metres . . . one hundred metres . . . fifty metres . . . ten metres . . . I was stone-cold petrified and rooted to the spot like a hunted animal. I stopped breathing altogether as the top edge of the beam shone over the boulder I was behind and caught the tip of my sleeping bag. I curled up more tensely, fingers clenched, eyelids shut tight, jaw muscles cramped.

The helicopter was barely twenty metres above me – I could have thrown a handful of sheep droppings into its fuselage. The noise was deafening; the downdraught from the rotors produced a miniature maelstrom that flattened the grass and the bracken around me. Then I heard the faint shift in engine pitch, signalling that the helicopter was moving away, continuing its search northwards.

Finally, the noise diminished into the vacuum of the night, and silence and darkness rolled back over the moor once again. For the remainder of the night I was far too nervous to sleep. Eventually I could sense the eastern sky brightening and I crawled out of my sleeping bag. I stretched, shoved my climbing boots on, and soloed a few more routes that I hadn't managed to complete the previous night. Tired and weary, and with the thought that another helicopter might appear unexpectedly, I raced back across the lonely moor. I sneaked quietly past the farm, trying not to arouse the farmyard dogs. There, I found a sleeve of paper slipped under my windscreen wiper with a note: *Please contact the Bellingham police!*

It was not yet 6am, but I drove down to the local village of Bellingham a couple of miles away and phoned the police from a local payphone. I explained the situation and waited to be lectured or charged with something, but a friendly voice explained simply that the farmer's wife had seen me leave on my own and had noticed that I hadn't returned by nightfall. From what I could make out, I had become the subject of a night exercise for the military who had a base nearby at Otterburn. They had failed to find me, and for that I was happy, although that wouldn't have been my view had I been lying on the floor of the crag with broken legs.

I became engrossed in these magical crags over the next few months – the long drives were a small price to pay for the ambience and solitude of the Northumbrian countryside. One July weekend in 1993, I made a 2am start from Cheshire – Howlerhirst was my destination. What a strange name for a crag – for some reason it brought to mind werewolves in medieval times. I had been to Howlerhirst the previous year to solo *Guardian Angel* – a brave encounter with a lovely flake and a distant pocket on a beautiful rib of silver-speckled sandstone.

It was a brisk, twenty-minute walk from the farm to the crag, through some fields and onto a bracken-clad hillside. The crag faced away from the valley and was all but hidden from the approach. I dropped down beneath it and sat on a flat boulder.

The morning air was tinged with dampness and the dew saturated the flora; the sky was a bleached-grey colour and the surrounding fells were draped with a saddening fog. I became nervous about soloing *Where Angels Fear to Tread;* to compensate, I started to embrace the surroundings and the tranquillity of the countryside. Then, in a more meditative state, I focused instinctively on a 'point' – a pearly dew-drop seated on the very pinnacle of a blade of grass. I closed my eyes to drain my thoughts, empty my mind and let go my nervousness, but I couldn't. I became totally fascinated that these 'tears of the dawn' could simply exist and undeniably defy the laws of gravity, something that no climber could ever do, however strong or light they might be. I mulled over the concept for some time before concluding that the silvery tears are natural indicators of possibilities for those purists who have the eyes to see them.

I stuffed my toes into my climbing boots, and without waiting to warm up, I started to climb. I felt lethargic; my movement wasn't fluent because my muscles were still cold. I persevered and had one more tenuous move before I could reach the flake on *Guardian Angel*. I bunched up, rigid . . .

My next conscious thought was one of shock as I began to untangle myself from some sharp boulders – I had fallen 20ft. A searing pain shot through my right ankle. I fumbled with my bootlaces, tore my boot off, and watched in astonishment as my ankle inflated instantaneously. I cursed myself for not having warmed up. I couldn't put any weight on my foot, so I had to crawl on my hands and knees through all the grass and bracken. On the way down the hill, I tried hopping, sliding on my backside, crawling on hands and knees - anything that might hold the pain in abeyance, all the while sensing that the 'tears of the dawn' were mocking me. Eventually I reached the car – a 350 mile round trip, to climb 20ft of rock, trash an ankle and get drenched, scratched and covered from head to toe in sheep shit.

I returned to Northumberland shortly afterwards and completed *Where Angels Fear to Tread*. I wanted to visit *Sandy Crag* because I had seen a photograph of a young Joe Webb soloing a dangerous arête in a recent climbing magazine. His face wore a mask of worry – his mouth open, oval-shaped like a goldfish, his concentration electric, his mind a mixture of calm and fear, with life hanging precariously in the balance on a gentle slice of sandstone. It had an addictive appeal.

Sandy Crag is tucked away on a grouse moor, right in the heart of Northumberland. Routes such as *Sandy Crack* and *Angel Fingers* are some of the county's most famous rock climbs. I decided to make my visit on a Sunday, a day in late August when the moors are safe from flying lead shot and smoking guns, and the grouse have peace to live another day. The walk took a little under an hour. Parts of the moor were scorched black. The smell of burned heather lingered in the air. Grouse moors are commonly set on fire in a controlled manner to kill off the older heather and to promote the growth of younger shoots, providing a more luscious habitat for young grouse to feed and grow, ultimately to be shot.

The crag loomed ahead with an appealing array of arêtes, cracks and chimneys, but the sandstone felt soft and grainy, which did not exactly instil confidence. Eventually I came upon *Time and Motion*. I looked at it in doubt; it was not greatly appealing, and I was more than a little disappointed. Then, when I looked at the landing below the arête, I stared in disbelief. A dilemma - I had to weigh up how badly I wanted to climb the route against how likely I was to fall off. Further complicating the equation was the fact that nobody knew where I was. If I fell, the best I could hope for would be a couple of broken bones. Having driven for over three hours, and having walked for almost an hour, it just wasn't in my nature to quit. I was here to test both my technique and the limits of my fear. I certainly wasn't going to walk away without even making an attempt.

I pulled tidily onto the rock and teetered to the subtle tune of the arête, soon realising that bravery and common sense were not altogether compatible. I shook intermittently as I climbed steadily higher. Typically, the holds started to become smaller and more discreet, balance and technique becoming more crucial than strength. I allowed the sight of the rocks below to frighten me to the extent that I froze at 20ft. I reversed meticulously, every move executed with painful precision and excess body torque, precisely to ensure that I didn't peel off.

Back on the ground, the tension released and I began to breathe normally again. I took my boots off and sat down. A macabre silence hovered over the moor, broken occasionally by the croaking of a distant, low-flying grouse. The scene was calming, but I was far from happy, humbled by my own cowardice and agitated that I had given in to my common sense. I craned my neck and gazed up at the arête, wondering how such a small obstacle could frighten me so much. After gazing over the moor, I became increasingly annoyed that the drive of my conscious mind could not override the safety mechanism of my subconscious in this instance. I was about to give up when an idea sprung into my head – an idea that would fool my subconscious into thinking there was no danger. With my penknife, I started to cut bracken from around the base of the crag. I then sprinkled the freshly cut fronds over the rocks until they were all hidden. Pleased with my handiwork, I excitedly pulled on my boots and climbed onto the arête. I reached my high point smoothly, looking down to see a lovely, soft carpet of bracken. The fear had been lifted, and I coolly climbed to the top, pleased with the way my conscious mind had fooled my subconscious in a dangerous game of self-deceit.

Many years had passed by before I returned to Northumberland – the rocks hadn't changed; they were more or less as I had left them, timeless and perpetual. I felt refreshed and vibrant and accepted the challenges with more vigour than before.

My first port of call was to my favourite haunt of *Back Bowden Doors*. Here, I had the urge to solo the popular test piece of *The Tube*. The line took a finger traverse under a cornice of fluted sandstone about 40ft above the ground. Its finale involved pulling through the cornice at its weakest point. But where was that? I didn't know, so I walked round the top and looked at the holds from above. Once satisfied, I committed to the route and accelerated along the finger traverse, not daring to go back or to look down. I reached the exit point and I pulled like fury, belly flopping over the top.

I was flowing well and felt confident; I continued on to solo *Bolder Lands*, thirteen years after my first ascent. Rather oddly it didn't seem to feel as difficult as it once had. I put it down to more years of experience and a more confident state of mind. Nine times out of ten, soloing is a 'state of the minds'.

The following day, I hiked up to the lofty escarpment of Ravensheugh that sits on a rural throne above the village of Rothbury. It was a fresh spring day, and I happened to be caught in a hailstorm whilst climbing the final concave scoop of *Candle in the Wind*, 40ft above the ground. The hail nipped the backs of my hands and bounced off the rock, stinging my eyes and face. All I could see was an infinite mass of tinkling, white ball bearings that danced around me like energetic springs. Within seconds, everything around me was white. In extremis, I tried to create as much friction as possible with everything I had at my disposal – forearms, knees, forehead . . . I had no faith in any of them, but in those tense few seconds I managed to scrape upwards whilst waiting for the inevitable slip into the white abyss . . .

Persistent as ever, and playing down my previous day's drama, I went in search of a hidden crag on Bewick Moor - Harehope Canyon. I walked for two miles across the moor before following a stream that trailed off through some reeds and grass into a small sandstone ravine, hidden from the moor itself. There were some half-dead rowan trees and a couple of buttresses of rock. One route required a scaffold plank to be placed over the stream in order to gain access to it. As I didn't have a plank, I tried to use a number of dead branches. On my first try, the branches swivelled and spun me into the knee-deep water. On my second try, I reached the rock, but I could not reach any holds. I gave up.

Instead, I climbed a route out of a rocky chasm, but a dinner plate sized foothold snapped at 10ft. Before I had time to think, I had smashed into the ground. Pain and swelling were intensifying, and in a mad, unconscious rush, I ran out of the chasm and through the stream before lying down on the grassy bank. I lay there banging my head on the ground, wondering why I had been so stupid as to trust the friable sandstone. I tore my boots off my burning feet and, with the realisation of a two mile crawl across the moor dawning, I decided to try submerging my feet in the cold water of the stream in the hope that it might reduce the heat of the swelling. I sat there until my feet had gone numb, and then began to limp back to the road.

Allowing myself no respite, I swallowed half a packet of Ibuprofen and drove on to Kyloe in the Wood. I climbed out of the car and started to walk once again through the enchanted forest. As I approached, I found emptiness, space, and tree stumps weeping with resin. Part of the forest had been felled and the rocks were bared - some of the magic was gone.

High T was possibly the finest climb in the woods, and that was the route I had come to do. Here, the rock was coated in a green veneer due to the proximity of the trees. I sat down under a huge larch, going to great lengths to ease my seemingly tight boots over my tender feet. I checked the landing, which was flat but hard sewn with roots, and I levitated, footless at first, on big holds that led up the wall via some long, faith-enduring stretches. I found myself at a large, dirty pocket, 30ft up. I stepped up to find that the rounded top was, agonisingly, inches away and was covered with decaying leaves and forest floor detritus. In a precarious position, I stretched up and tried to clean the top with my wire brush that hung from some elastic attached to my chalk bag cord. I snatched for the top, but my fingers slipped on the dirt . . .

My ankles screamed; my body tensed, expecting the inevitable. However, my fingers kept raking and tearing at the mulch in uncoordinated panic until I had managed to pedal and wriggle onto the damp forest floor. I lay there, out of breath, in a quagmire of sweat, with an acute pain in one of my fingertips. I checked it and somewhat bizarrely saw a small protrusion sticking out of the end. At first I thought it was a pine needle, but as I gripped it between my fingernails and began to pull, a complete length of wire from my wire brush slipped out. I felt queasy. This was obviously retribution for the sin of wire brushing Northumberland's precious stones.

I wandered out of the forest, content but limping, thinking about the meaning of it all – soloing *High T* was typical of many Northumbrian climbs, a fine line between the relief of success and the despair of breaking a bone. At the end of the day, all that I had to show tangibly for my efforts was a pencil tick beside the route in the guidebook. It doesn't really make sense; it never truly does. Northumberland will always be, for me, a place to lose myself in the countryside that reignites the memories of my childhood, charging around the forest with my elder brother.

The Hunted

Character, like a photograph, develops in darkness – Yousuf Karsh

Dark shadows slowly spiralled away in the valley. Ahead, the tarmac artery snaked its way onwards and westwards, vanishing into the tapestry of the landscape. The sky appeared infinitely grey, burdened with its own unwanted moisture as it moulded round the summits of Beinn Eighe and Liathach, two creatively carved and complex mountains, perhaps Scotland's finest. Gradually it descended further, smothering their naked profiles, transforming them into celestial ghosts.

Glen Torridon was desolate. Dull shades of green gasped for survival amidst swarms of brown and grey. It all looked so barren and it stank of infertility. Strange movement close by perplexed my rather lethargic mind. My sleep-glazed eyes took time to focus on a small herd of deer that were grazing, camouflaged against the valley floor. The snow-tattooed upper slopes were not the place for these otherwise reclusive creatures to be during the depths of a harsh winter.

Suddenly the brakes bit hard. I was thrown forward, my reactions thankfully quicker than my conscious thought as a stag appeared out of nowhere. He sauntered into the middle of the road and turned his head in my direction. I sensed his inquisitiveness; his nostrils twitched at the air, his black, opalescent eyes judging me with contempt and fear, apprehensive at my intrusion into his world. He stood still for a moment, alert, gauging my presence before turning his head, thinking . . . then with a sudden burst of energy he propelled himself effortlessly up the hillside. He dissolved into the stone-cold loneliness as though our chance encounter had never taken place.

I re-engaged the clutch and drifted back into autopilot, recollecting the sight of stags' heads peering down from the walls of hunting lodges around the Highlands. Their expressions of pain and humiliation were all too obvious. I began to imagine the hunter's crosshairs falling into focus and the bullet tearing across a remote glen, finding its target, ripping through flesh and organs, blood seeping into an acid-rich mountainside. A few years before, whilst carrying my paraglider up Rois Bheinn on the west coast of Scotland, the unmistakeable shockwave of air followed by the crack of a gunshot had ripped its way across my bow. Although I could see the stalkers to the north, I remained undeterred, and I continued to the summit. Flying down and following the contours of the mountain, I spotted two deer and swooped on them, shepherding them over the ridge into a distant glen and out of harm's way. I landed half an hour later in the tidal zone. Scooping up my glider, I ran to the car only to find a note stuck to the windscreen: 'Dear Hillwalker, You nearly ruined a day's stalking.' I threw it into the car and jumped in. As I drove off, I saw an estate Land Rover driving towards me. The occupants gestured to me to stop. I floored it. They turned around and gave chase for a few miles, but they failed to catch up with me and I got away, hopefully rather like the deer I had chased away earlier.

The abrupt appearance of a uniform copse of firs on my right interrupted my deliberations. I gazed at them - they seemed huddled together for survival in this stark glen. Muggy, warm air swirled around the car, making me feel drowsy, but the bend ahead was sharper than I had anticipated and jolted me sideways. Adrenalin rushed in and subsided as Upper Loch Torridon passed by. It was miserable, a day to go home and huddle up in front of a log fire and feel comforted by its glow and warmth.

The head of Loch Kishorn came into view. I stared out over the tidal flats where the River Kishorn meets the shoreline, and I felt the vacuum of depression that a midwinter coastline can generate. I climbed out of the car and shook with the chill as the cold air tore at my cheekbones. In the distance, the depleted arc of a washed out rainbow appeared. It was the only sign of colour; it rallied little morale. The mountain of Beinn Bhan, with its four gothic corries standing defiantly, should dominate this part of the Applecross peninsula; today the mountain simply did not exist.

It was purely down to my own stubbornness and stupidity that I hadn't made the decision to turn around and drive away. It had been a number of years since I had last hacked my way up some ice and I had become totally obsessed with finding some. I wanted to remember what it felt like to puncture this unrepentant element and to gaze at the beguiling shapes and textures that mysteriously form. So here I was, naively hoping to encounter a 1,000ft curtain of ice drooling down the back wall of Coire na Poite, the second of the mountain's four deeply-scooped coires.

I had bought my plastic ice-climbing boots second-hand years ago. They were three sizes too big, but I could not afford a new pair. Some lace hooks were stuck together with Araldite whilst bits of cord tied parts of the shell together where the rivets had fallen out. I had to wear three pairs of socks to stop my heels from slipping, and when I pulled the laces tight, they perished in my hand, so I ended up tying knots in them all. Eventually my feet were locked into the non-flexible boots, forcing me to walk robotically, adding to the misery of the approach towards the mountain. My axes were verging on relics, but I didn't have any money to buy a more modern pair, and my wrist leashes were made of thin tape that I had riveted together years ago. The final, glorious adjustment was a slice of garden hose used as a leash-tightener. This was simply yet another substandard modification to my shoddily - customised ice climbing equipment from which I was eager to hang my life.

I began to walk through a tiered sandstone landscape dusted with snow and patches of sorry vegetation. It was bleak and monotonous. Boulders strewn on the approach to the coire caused my ankle great pain, making me limp, reminding me that my last climbing accident had been only three months previously.

As I walked further into the coire, the cloud began to lift, gently unveiling a concave wall of terrifying verticality. The wind increased too and began to create miniature twisters that appeared and disappeared randomly along the ridges and down the slopes. By the time I had reached the semi-frozen lochan in the bosom of the coire, I felt small and pathetic. Very little ice had formed on the back wall where the long, icy daggers of *The Silver Tear* would be found pointing downwards during most winters. I was disappointed, but rather than contemplating retreat, I caught sight of a line of hope bisecting the left side of the coire. *March Hare's Gully* drew me in like a fool never knowing when to give up. I still wanted it all - to see, touch and climb ice - at any cost.

I carved a path through shallow powder snow to arrive at the base of the gully. Above me was a promising 100ft cascade of off-blue, vertical ice that excited me and banished any negative thoughts about the remaining 900ft of the route that wasn't in view. I fumbled with gloveless hands and frozen fingertips, trying to tighten my Neoprene crampon straps onto my boots. Once fixed, I armed myself with my axes and pulled onto the vertical cascade of ice.

It was poorer than I had anticipated. Plates of solid ice were latticed together with sugary snow. I hacked away at all the softer stuff, leaving tenuous patches of ice to climb. I was unfit and out of tune, and it took me ages to climb the pitch before being released into a lesser-angled, funnelled groove choked with deep powder snow. Above this, the gully tightened once more, into a 40ft vertical ice step.

Silky strands of white cloud started to condense and became greyer, licking down the menacing walls surrounding me. I thumped my axes into the start of the steep bottleneck – the mountain retorted with a deep, equatorial thunderstorm roar. My thoughts ricocheted around my head in alarm. I knew that sound . . .

Oh shit, avalanche!

Caught in the bottleneck with nowhere to hide, I recoiled into my shell like a hermit crab cringing from its predator, fearfully waiting to endure the brunt of the oncoming spindrift avalanche. It bellowed. The mountain seemed to shake, and then twenty tons of what could only be described as caster sugar poured onto me, burying me in my vertical world. It lasted ten seconds and then all went still. My arms were burning with the excess weight, but I hung on, shaking away the mounds of powder that had built up on me. I started to climb again, but it was only minutes before I heard another roar from above, and a second spindrift avalanche cascaded down. Nerves made me grip my axe shafts too tightly. My fingers cramped, and I began to lose the feeling in them.

The denseness of the powder made me close my mouth and eyes, and I held my breath for so long that I thought I was going to suffocate. I panicked and flung my head away, opening my mouth to suck on fresh air. Very quickly the torrent of powder began to build up, trying to prise me off. I took a few more breaths before I stuck my head back into the onslaught, trying to maintain balance. I hung on, gasping desperately, feeling as though I were cocooned in the centre of a 1,000ft hourglass egg timer, with *time* slowly slipping away.

The torrent slowly fizzled out, and I dared not move an inch, nor strike an axe, in case the egg timer inverted again. I had to move, and eventually I dared myself to do so, getting into an easier-angled section of deeper snow that soon led to another steep bottleneck. However, unlike before, this one was completely devoid of ice. It was quite literally a dead end.

The sight of the iceless section made me lose my composure; I wanted to go down, but I couldn't. I had no ropes with which to abseil off. There was nothing here apart from a hissing wind, a darkening mist and the ominous sound of dripping ice . . .

The bloody temperature's rising!

It was almost dark. How could I survive this? The only remaining option was to try to traverse left onto the unknown, snow-splattered buttress and return to the gully above the iceless section. This one slim chance of survival spurred me into action. I threaded my way between patches of unconsolidated snow. Occasionally my axes would hit rock, and the ringing of cold steel made me squirm. Getting stuck or lost on the buttress in the dark was becoming a reality. I climbed up and right, slowly and methodically, back towards my only remaining hope: the gully. When I came to the edge of the gully, it was bereft of ice and unreachable. I stayed with the buttress, trying to remain composed and strong. I felt marooned in a vicious world of melting ice, rock and complete darkness.

My eyes strained, trying to acclimatise to night vision. I was faced with a rocky overhang; my axes were flung over the top and sank through unconsolidated slush. I tentatively pulled on them, but I couldn't commit. I knew that if the axes ripped then I would bounce down the buttress for 500ft into the hollow depths of the coire floor. I searched for different paths - there were simply no options left.

Anxious and distraught, I knelt over my crampons, hunched in a niche underneath the bulge, reflecting on my predicament. At the moment I was warm, but the dripping of snowmelt and the cessation of movement would soon lead to hypothermia. The prospect of benightment began to destroy my will. Tears started to drool out of the corners of my eyes and mix with flakes of blown snow. I felt a deep emptiness. I thought of light, love, life, warmth, the chatting voices of friends and the colours and sounds of summer - in fact I thought of everything that I didn't have. I thought of Sal at home in front of the fire, reading, not worrying because I wasn't due back for four days. She didn't know where I was, no one did. It was just me and death in this gully. Those cold, supernatural hands started to tighten around my throat. I struggled and threw away my self-pity; there was nothing left to lose. I swung my axes blindly over the overhang again, tugging on them, both feet swinging free, eyes shut, stomach in knots. I hung there, frozen, not wanting to pull in case the axes ripped through the ice. I had to though - and quickly. I got my knees on and lashed out with a flailing axe, hoping for a placement in the snow above. I was over and weaving a blind traverse back into the gully and to another lifeline. I became excited when I saw the contrast between black rock and the thin, white line of the gully ascending before me like Ariadne's thread. I had returned to a vertical world of slushy ice and spindrift avalanches that continued to splutter in sporadic torrents. Suddenly, a ripping noise rang in my ears, with devastating effect; the sickening noise I just did not want to hear. My inertia built. I was off and free . . .

When the scramble of messages and the chaos subsided, I opened my eyes and found that I was still surrounded by rock and dripping ice. The pieces of the puzzle fell into place. I had dropped off before my crampon points and axes had re-engaged. One of my feet had caught on an icy boss, absorbing my momentum.

My body pulsed with the superhuman strength that manifests itself when self-preservation is the only thing that matters. The ice was fickle, and most of it had fallen away as a result of the rising temperatures. However, with the assistance of the rapid influx of adrenalin, I wedged a horizontal-press position across the iceless part. I reached the icier continuation and struck my way higher and higher up the gully. I was beyond caring about anything. Hundreds of vertical feet passed by – the route was endless. My mind was blank, for now I was absorbed in ice climbing in its rawest form. I could have been climbing in the afterlife for all I knew.

Time passed - minutes, hours, I wasn't really sure - but then the sky began to brighten. I wondered if I had actually been climbing all night and morning had arrived. No, it was the gully opening out and terminating in a fascinatingly destructive cornice that could quite easily collapse in these thawing conditions and engulf me in an embrace of icy dust. At that thought, I shuffled left at speed to avoid its treachery and onto a rocky rib where the angle relented and the crest had no cornice. On reaching the plateau, I was met with the firm conviction of a howling gale. Ice and snow particles stung my cheeks and eyes. The dangers of the climb were over; my adrenalin levels subsided, leaving a washed-up husk of a soul. I stumbled around in the blizzard that was abrading the plateau, trying to locate the summit. Eventually I found the cairn and huddled behind it for some shelter. I opened my rucksack and fumbled in the dark, discovering that I had brought no torch, no compass and no food. I had a map but not enough light by which to read it. I deduced that the prevailing winds were coming roughly from the west or southwest, and from what I could remember from the map, all of the cliffs faced in an easterly direction. I packed one axe and my crampons away before facing the wind head on, leaving the summit of the mountain in a state of bewilderment. The ground became ridiculously steep, and I began to lose confidence in my dead reckoning. I carried on in the hope that my memory of maps was better than I thought.

After the steep descent into an acutely tight gully, the gradient flattened, and the wind subsided too. I had no idea of distance or my whereabouts, but I had this strange feeling that the mountain of Sgurr a Chaorachain and its craggy sentries of cascading Torridonian sandstone were glowering down on me in the dark. I carried on over undulating ground, without an inkling of time until an incongruous ball of light appeared in the distance. Light meant life. It moved towards me, then away, snaking, my hopes rising and fading with its direction. It started to move away again, and I began to chase after it but then tumbled into a peat hag up to my knees, my momentum propelling me face first into it. I clawed my way out and continued more determinedly than before . . .

I stepped onto something uniform. I reached down and felt the rough, familiar texture of tarmac. Relief overcame me as I lay spread-eagled on the Bealach na Ba road in a sapped heap of emotion. I closed my eyes and contemplated the fine line between life and death and how it can all change in an instant. I thought back to my chance encounter with the stag, and I realised how easily we can all become The Hunted.

Spirits in the Rocks

Lakeland was just as I remembered – a miniature but tamer Scotland. Grey stone walls splattered with lime–green lichens lined the roads and fields. The mountainsides were littered with carefree Herdwick sheep that had little fear of walkers or cars on the twisting passes. Sheep ticks were rife amongst the dense, head–height fronds of bracken which had begun to corrode the fells under autumnal skies. Lakeland is what you would expect of it: passive, historic and toughly rural. It holds a special kind of ethos for me, unsurpassed elsewhere in England, because it was here on summer camp at Ullswater that I discovered how much I truly desired the freedom of the mountains. This deep-rooted feeling of wanting freedom came about because my home life was anything but free. We had moved from York to Harrogate, and my brother and I had gone from having nannies looking after us to the care of a guardian. Sometimes our guardian needed to go to work in an office, and we were left to our own devices playing Monopoly in the back of a Mini Clubman all day without being allowed out. It was those days that built into me the hunger to always strive for freedom. The lack of adventure, boredom and discontentment with life at that time drove me to steal some stationery from a shop, and I got caught. My brother and I might well have both received the riding crop; we usually did. It was discipline and it was meted out. We weren't perfect – we were unloved kids.

I found my solace whilst on summer camp in the Lake District, during which we did many activities. I had a go at fishing, but I was too impatient to wait to catch anything; kayaking, but I didn't like being trapped in something that could sink me; rock climbing, but I wasn't that interested in being tied into ropes. No, most of all I enjoyed the simple freedom of walking in the mountains. They were fascinating, and could be perplexing at times when the summits disappeared into the clouds, as was the case when I walked up Scafell Pike, the highest mountain in England, at the age of nine. It was energetic work and the feeling of elevation was a liberating experience, a world apart from being cooped in the back of a car for long periods of time.

My first ever walk in the Lake District was in the Langdales, where rustic slopes rise for 2,000ft from the green fertility of the valley floor to the auburn summits and the grey, volcanic sentinels of its Pikes. Hidden amongst this effervescent mountain topography is the sprawling crag of Pavey Arc. And now here I was, part way up the cliff, attached by ropes, looking down upon the ocular shape of Stickle Tarn, it in turn looking back with Cyclopic formality. Evening shafts of sunlight stroked across the mountainside, creating shadows that crept down into the valley, stealing the glorious colour. Above me towered the innocuous looking overhanging pod of *Fallen Angel*; without warning, a lanky creature dropped from it and the ropes went tight. The sight shocked me; this was not supposed to be in the script!

Paul 'The Stork' Thorburn is a Scottish climbing legend. With a six and a half foot frame and limbs like scaffolding tubes, he was merciless on the rock. Stories of him hanging from tiny holds on blank, unclimbed walls for hours on end were commonplace. Although thinly boned, not one of them is bad; he is the archetypal nice guy, academic but practical and terribly focused on climbing. And yet here he was, being spat out by the much-revered pod of *Fallen Angel;* a relatively straightforward climb by his standards. On reflection, I put this down to the virile growth of lichens and moss – some of the most prestigious rock climbs in the Lake District were returning to nature.

It was a further seven years before I returned to the Lake District, along with a different climbing partner, of fairer ilk. Vicci Chelton and I were good friends.

She was a stubborn wee sister to me and quite a tough, unique character. She loved the hardship of the mountain environment and the lifestyle of the outdoors, whether it was winter ice or summer rock climbing.

Her stories of becoming overweight on her last guiding trip to Venezuela were totally unfounded. She complained constantly for the next few days that she hadn't climbed for six weeks:

'I'm so weak!'

I shrugged off her ceaseless tide of complaints with . . .

'Don't talk rubbish, Vic!'

Within two days, I had become unhappy with the arrangement that she organised the food. We ate nothing but bananas, pears, apples and non-sulphurous dried apricots. Finally, after a few days, I persuaded her to add some cheese and nuts to the diet; I needed protein to repair my aching muscles, even if she deemed it unnecessary. Climbing again with a rope and harness was relaxing, enjoyable. It felt rather strange when I had to stop mid movement and lob a nut in a crack, as and when required, to safeguard the moves. Once a nut had been placed, I climbed through the sequences without thinking, feeling safe. It was even more relaxing when Vic led and I had the safety of the rope above me. It was a pleasant vacation from the intense concentration and rigours of soloing.

We enjoyed a good variety of climbing around Eskdale and Borrowdale; the weather was too unsettled for the mountains. After five days of climbing in Lakeland, Vic had to drive to Devon for some guiding work. She wasn't looking forward to leaving, but she could not afford to decline any work. When she departed, I grew lonely on my own. Being alone was always the unknown quantity: most of the time I craved it, but sometimes I feared it. Today it had rained heavily. I was feeling down, and I would have preferred some company. I decided to stay on for a few days in the hope that I might be able to solo a big mountain route or two if the weather cleared.

That night, I parked up above Langdale and drank a bottle of beer that I thought might help me to sleep, but the stagnant taste of hops made me feel sick. In the morning, I walked up to Black Crag above Wrynose Pass and spent the day on its multi-coloured rhyolite. It was a fascinating volcanic rock with remarkable textures that produced short walls, slabs and aretes, ideal for soloing if one had such an inclination . . . I soloed all the routes and then became apathetic. I lay in the grass and glanced southwards to the Old Man of Coniston, sitting underneath a sky afloat with quills of cirrus, relentlessly changing their shape before evaporating into a deep blue infinity.

When dusk fell, I was purring along the narrow, winding, blind, stonewalled roads of Eskdale, looking for somewhere to park up for the night. The full moon had risen above the dark silhouettes of the hills, radiating with a deep, yellow glow. I finally found a quiet place and curled up in the boot of the car, staring out towards the moon, nervous at which mountain route I might choose to solo the following morning. The night was an uncomfortable one, and by morning I had made up my mind. I searched in the footwell amongst yoghurt cartons and food wrappers for some paper, but there was none, so I searched in the glove box, finding only a mechanic's receipt for a new exhaust. I tore off a section and started to pencil down the *Central Pillar* route description, as if writing it down were my bond of commitment.

The *Central Pillar* was the climbing focus for the elite rock climbers of the 1960s. It was an obvious and formidable challenge that tackled a line up the centre of the famous Lakeland rock turret of Esk Buttress. I had read the literature and seen the pictures and for many years had wanted to climb on this legendary cliff. The idea of soloing a route on its much-coveted precipices, however, had never entered my head . . . until now.

I set to the slender, twisting roads towards my starting point, between Hardnott and Wrynose passes. I drove by a quaint little farmhouse with dilapidated outbuildings, all made of local square-cut stone and roofed with dark blue slate. An old, black and white sheepdog lay sprawled out on the road. As I drove carefully around him, I looked down into his skyward staring eye, which glinted like a blue marble. Deep in the centre was a black pupil, hollow and glazed in retirement, and he lay peacefully, taking in the familiar sounds and tranquil surroundings of his home. Perhaps one day I would find that same contentment and peace.

I set out with quiet optimism and headed northwards into mist-laden hills. After an hour's walk, the mists started to dispel and the Esk Buttress appeared in the middle-distance, a stout 400ft plinth of clean, volcanic rock that stooped down upon a soft valley floor scored by a silver meandering river. It felt remote, and I began to feel nervous at the prospect of climbing a 400ft route. However, clouds draped forlornly over the summit of Scafell Pike, putting a dampener on my spirits and my sense of commitment.

After negotiating both the river crossing and the slopes to the base of the cliff barefoot, the *Central Pillar* intimidated me. I skulked off to find an easier climb instead. The *Red Edge* was my next choice – but it was dribbling with water like a faulty tap. I was being manipulated by the uncertainty of the cliff. I felt gutless and considered retreat, when suddenly the clouds disappeared and sunlight tore through the coy Lakeland sky, reflecting my destination in the perfect stone in front of me.

I found a flat ledge amongst the slopes on which to organise my karma, absorb some sun and dry out wet, wrinkly feet. I tried to meditate, but I ended up nervously picking away wet skin from around my toes. I tried to stay calm, but my mind knew the perils that lay ahead and it wasn't going to be fooled. Turning to face the cliff, I tried to relate my paragraph of pencilled scrawl on my exhaust invoice to the 400ft pillar above. When I was happy with the whereabouts of the first section, I shoved the description into my pants, knowing that if I dropped it, I would be lost and, to be blunt, in the shit . . .

It was warm for an autumnal day in the hills, but I still opted to wear my grey fleece with holes in the cuffs. It is strange how one becomes attached to particular items of clothing when soloing; somehow, if they feel comfortable, they add an inner confidence to one's well being – a comfortable body is a comfortable mind. I cast one last glance down the broad, meandering valley. The browning bog-reeds and the white dots of sheep stamped authenticity on this typical Lakeland scene. I felt alone. I was alone.

I turned to the cliff that seemingly accelerated towards the sky above me and, trembling, lightly climbed onwards on good lichen imprinted jugs. The boulders below became more distant and fused into one. At 100ft, the holds gradually reduced in size but the rock was solid, sharing its secrets through touch, fingertip to rock - the reply was warm and positive.

I reached a small ledge and squeezed between a plinth and the cliff face. I made myself comfortable in my open-air coffin. I began to relax, breathing deeply through my stomach, emptying my fear. Lying there, hemmed in with my cheek close to the rock, I could see it aglow with a multitude of coloured lichens – whites, greys and lime greens. They were in irregular and complicated shapes, seemingly welded to the rock but entangled in a sort of pattern; it fascinated me. I became acutely conscious that I wasn't alone. I was surrounded by basic, living organisms. Like me, they were just breathing and fighting for survival.

Were they spirits in the rocks?

My gaze and thoughts floated past the lichens and up further still to a most appealing, slender groove that sliced elegantly up the overhanging wall. It flashed a smile, and I wanted to climb it, but hang on, this was the line of *The Cumbrian* – beautiful, volcanic architecture, but an absolutely suicidal prospect for any soloist. I didn't have the nerve to solo this route. Did anybody? I promised to return to climb Lakeland's most gracious climb with a rope and a partner. I closed my eyes to drain away such thoughts of disaster before gathering my concentration again. My line veered rightwards, away from the enticing groove, and I soon became absorbed. I adored the fragile harmony of fear and danger and the composure of soloing in the mountains. The spirit is free, and life is so angelic.

The pitch passed by in a dream-state, and conscious thought only re-engaged as my feet finally stood firm on a sloping ledge that was hemmed in by overhanging walls. My minds kicked in . . .

'Where to . . . ? It's a dead end.'

Read the description!

At that moment, the pen felt far mightier than the sword. I felt utterly deserted and afraid. Clouds started to swirl overhead too, their shadows scuttling across the walls around me. I began to despair, and the thought of rain began to terrify me.

'God . . . I really could die here!' I looked down and realised how elementarily simple it was to do just that . . .

Calm down and read the description!

I was the only human for miles around; there was no one coming to rescue me, so I carefully pulled my notes from my pants and read that the route traversed rightwards across the overhanging wall.

'That looks . . . impossible!'

It can't be as hard as it looks.

I tucked my notes away and stepped rightwards onto a small foot shelf with incredible exposure. The steep wall above pushed me outwards and I started to lose my balance . . . I didn't like it one bit, so I reversed to the security of the ledge to rethink and recompose.

I climbed out again, crouching low on the shelf whilst the impending rock was pushing me further backwards over the 300ft void. A tiny finger-hold was all I had to maintain balance as I made a *test-the-bath-water* poke with my right foot out onto a sloping foothold. Sinews strained; muscles flexed, and every nerve cell monitored any unwanted shift of balance that might accelerate me into a terminal vortex. My eyes squinted with precise focus, and then I saw it – 'the line' –between life and death, the molecular bond between the rock and a whirling vacuum of remorse . . .

. . . I bridged the void with pinpoint accuracy. There could be no mistakes. Time stood still. I dared not breathe as I reached upwards in one slow, yearning stretch and urgently gripped two large holds one after the other which gifted me upward passage to an old iron peg. There was no comfort for me in that small eye of metal – I had no rope to attach to it – I climbed on past its irrelevance. Soon I was prodding a loose block. I thumped it with my fist to test its firmness, but that was a futile action as I had no other option but to hang from it to reach the holds above. A couple of long lurches followed on blind, sloping holds, draining my arms of oxygen and energy. I emerged, emotionally and physically exhausted, onto a large shelf with only a 30ft chimney-crack above.

Sunlight sparkled on the summit of the buttress. At last I was empty of desire and urgency, at peace spiritually, and physically and mentally content – this was the elusive grail of soloing . . .

I was gazing blankly down the valley and into the distance when I became aware of a moving dot of colour – a hill-walker, who had unwittingly broken my magical isolation. It was over, and I could just sit there, wrapped up beneath the warm shoulders of England's highest mountain.

I ambled back down the valley. The river twisted and tumbled in caressing cascades as it swarmed over smooth, grey rocks, full of subtle power and nourishment. One area caught my attention; a tree with rich, yellow leaves overlooking some idyllic pools. The charm of the river almost lured me in for a swim, but the sun had gone in, and the dropping temperature curbed my desire. Just as I was busy with some highbrow romantic fantasy in my head, my foot kicked a rock that stuck proud in the path, and I nearly fell flat on my face.

Up ahead lay Heron Crag and a blatantly obvious line up the centre: *Gormenghast*. I crossed the river and scrambled up steep scree to the base of the cliff. I wasn't inspired, but with an inexplicable drive kicking me into action, I started to climb anyway, really as if it were my job. I am a climber who is attracted to the features, shapes and the cleanliness of a climb. But the first 80ft pitch of *Gormenghast* was anything but that – the rock was dirty, with wet, flat holds, and it wasn't fun. Above me hung a very steep pod, reminding me of the flying Stork seven years before. I didn't want to be there, tightening my body into a dirty, overhung crevice, 100ft above bone splintering scree. I wanted to close my eyes and wake up to find myself in the turbulent cascades 400ft beneath me, in amongst my fantasies, but there was no time for those in such grave circumstances. I found reverse gear and wobbled to the ground, my drive and commitment draining back into the riverbank. Weary, I sat there, looking across at the buff-coloured tone of a steep fell whose slopes were lapping down towards me. My car was on the other side of that. I felt totally weak - I had eaten only one banana all day, and I had nothing else. There was barely a calorie remaining in the tank. I knelt to the river, drank deeply, and set off up the cruel slopes of the fell . . .

Grit Years

Cure for an obsession: get another one. Mason Cooley

I was comfortably stuck. I was in a snug, overhung niche of rock, suspended from a fist jammed into the rough guts of a gritstone crack. To my left, in the distance, was the famous, four-mile long Stanage Edge dissolving into the High Peak of Derbyshire, and to my right was its continuation – Burbage Edge, followed by the escarpments of Froggatt and Curbar, melting away into the Derbyshire Dales. Together the escarpments traced a natural rampart that bore a resemblance to the Great Wall of China. Beneath me were 40ft of air and the crux of one of gritstone's finest climbs, *The Rasp.* Higgar Tor – the home of *The Rasp* – isn't an escarpment; it is more like a natural brick that has fallen from the Wall. The southwest face of the Tor was overhanging by ten degrees and was the reason why my forearms now burned - I had begun to climb without warming up. *The Rasp* was to be another tick closer to almost a thousand extreme, grit solos. It was a Joe Brown route, a classic climb delivered by a famous gritstone pioneer. It had bite, and near the top I was just beginning to discover how much - a 10ft traverse along a typical, gritstone rounded break, part-coated in veneers of ice. The south-westerly tore persistently at my trouser legs like a wayward terrier. I had to make a decision - and quickly - before I froze and turned into a fossil . . .

The reading of a book can shape our lives and futures, and that is exactly what the new *Staffordshire Gritstone* guidebook did for me at the Easter of 1989, for better or for worse. The front cover picture of John Perry climbing *Kicking Bird* inspired me – the trees, the technicalities of the grit and the snowy backdrop all portrayed a picture of an obscure, enchanted playground. I made eager visits to *The Roaches, Hen Cloud, the Five Clouds, the Skyline, the Baldstones* and *Ramshaw Rocks*. The texture of the rough-natured sandstone had such appealing frictional properties, it was liberating, and I soon began to gain experience and understand how best to move over this stone with as little effort as possible. Slabs required trust and courage; cracks required good jamming skills and a high pain threshold; arêtes required precise technique and balance. Each route I soloed became a parcel of fun – a mix of physical exercise wrapped in a little danger.

During the summer of 1989, Mike Francis and I were working as labourers in Manchester, carrying hods of mortar and breezeblocks up and down ladders all day. Mike was a fearless bear of a man with a sedate personality, impish smile and mole-grips for hands. He could flag his body horizontally from a lamp post, speaking volumes for his immense, natural strength. This was evident when, on only his second day on the grit, he nonchalantly soloed the mighty arête of *Archangel* at Stanage Edge - in his trainers. After a hard day's work, most labourers would finish at four and go straight to the pub, but not us teenagers – we jumped into the car, drove to the grit and climbed till dark. On this particular occasion, we were enjoying a typical, warm, summer's evening on Ramshaw rocks.

Ramshaw is a curious collection of natural sculptures that look like dinosaur's teeth piercing a benign countryside of stone farmhouses, nonchalantly grazing cows, ubiquitous sheep and a patchwork of fields hemmed in by miles of dry stone walls. One cannot help but gaze in wonder at such strange obelisks whilst driving along the Leek to Buxton road. For the rock climber, these sculptures provide many hours of fulfilling entertainment, although, on the flip side, the notorious crack climbing here can be excruciatingly painful. The cracks are lined with razor-sharp pebbles that puncture flesh, drawing blood and leaving hands forever marked with silky scars. Routes such as *Masochism* are exactly that . . .

We stopped at each buttress, soloed a few routes, and then moved on. This continued until we had reached the last buttress on the edge, where we were met with a compelling wall of the finest gritstone, engrained with a multitude of peanut-sized pebbles and a soft, grassy landing to boot. *Old Fogey Direct* was far too hard a route for us to try, but Mike, undeterred and ever optimistic, had different ideas and started to climb. Warmed by his courage, I prepared to follow like a lemming. We both fell. We had, however, surprised ourselves with our progress; tired and sore we retreated, inspired to return.

Mike had to catch a train to Scotland to re-sit an exam, leaving me to attempt the route on my own in the evenings after work. I found the climbing to be precarious and sequential – each move had to be performed in a specific order, like a puzzle. My feet pressed hard into the discreet scoops (smears) in the rough texture of the rock; my fingers pinched hard on the pebbles and my body seemed to be levitating in a form of anti-gravity. My feelings were of pure amazement, a type of awe that I had never felt before on easier climbs. I kept falling and then trying again, with sore muscles, battered joints and bleeding fingertips; such is the resilient vigour of youth. Finally, I fell and tore my ankle ligaments, leaving me with an awkward half-mile hop back to the car.

I was in too much pain to try again for a few weeks, but before my return to University I limped along the edge for one final attempt. I passed all the weather-beaten sculptures I knew so well and arrived beneath my nemesis. I pulled on with timid eagerness, pinching pebbles, terrified of falling and damaging my ankle further. On the last, hard move, from where I had fallen so many times, I pressed my left toe onto a pebble for balance and held on firmly, grimacing. The elation of success overrode all the pain that I had endured on the journey to get there.

The most favoured of all Staffordshire outcrops, The Roaches, sits a mile down the hill from Ramshaw. This crag has a certain charisma not found on other gritstone edges. Split into two tiers, the lower tier is host to a selection of antiquated towers and brazen faces, whilst the upper tier is more random and abounds with roofs. The two tiers are linked in the centre by an unobtrusive, ancient, stone staircase at the top of which is a hidden, stone seat with the inscription: *Visited by the Prince and Princess of Teck, August 23rd 1872*. In addition to this is *Rockhall*: a miniature castle with slim windows and squat turrets, built into the lower tier and overlooked by the classic grit routes of *Valkyrie, Mincer* and *Elegy,* all guarded by the winking eyes of the resident rooks. An eccentric named Doug lived there with his wife Annie for well over a decade. There was no power or running water. He was a legendary character amongst climbers. He sported a dirty, unshaven face, a black eyepatch, black cap, black donkey jacket, black trousers and boots, and spoke quickly in a raw, undeterminable accent. On first arrival in the late 1970s, he didn't take too kindly to climbers, and he used to chase after them with an axe. In later years, he became friendlier and would shout out encouragement and advice on how to climb the routes, even though he had never actually climbed them himself. Annie was more of a mystery. Nobody had seen her for years. Rumours were going around that he had dug a grave in the garden, crowned it with a cross, and told climbers that was where he had buried Annie. Another rumour has it that one winter it got so cold that he had cut the stairs out of the house and used it as firewood and Annie could not get down and was trapped upstairs for eternity. However, when the council finally managed to evict Doug in 1990, Annie certainly accompanied him. Rumour again has it that the deal to get him to go was only finally sealed when the council promised to fulfil Doug's explicit terms - that his new home must have a pink bathroom suite. It takes all sorts! Rockhall was renovated and is now the Don Whillans Memorial Hut. *The Roaches* wouldn't have such a seal of approval from me if it weren't for the larch trees that curtain it and the pine needles that carpet the ground with their luxurious bounce and softness. They add life and colour to what would otherwise be a bare, windswept facet of central England's moorland rocks.

For some reason I adopted the slab-climbing technique more so than the others, primarily because I felt more at home on them than on overhangs and I could control the fear that the slabs provided. I found it kind of harmonious. The slab test piece to do was *Chalkstorm*, on the right side of the lower tier. One evening I was halfway up, immersed in my own bubble of concentration, at the mercy of my climbing shoes as there were no handholds. I pieced it all together and sat down on the top with a certain amount of pride. I looked over towards two climbers who were trying an extremely blank looking slab next to the frightening, blunt rib of *Piece of Mind*. Johnny Woodward first climbed the rib without a rope or sticky rubber in 1977, years before hard, dangerous, gritstone routes were in vogue. To my knowledge, the blank slab had not yet been climbed without a rope.

I overheard their comments about the desperate crux at the top and 'death if you fall off'. I found *Chalkstorm* scary enough to solo. I sat down and visualised someone soloing up there, then shuddered at such an incomprehensible thought.

Two years had passed by, and for some inexplicable reason I was magnetically drawn to that dangerous, blank slab. I peered over the smooth, rounded top and shook at the sight of the boulders that rested below it, wondering if it were truly to be my destiny to unfurl amongst them. I threw down a rope and practised the possibilities. The final moves were smooth and hold-less, but the incline of the grit gave just enough friction for it to be climbable. A solo ascent, however, was bordering on unjustifiable and was a deathly challenge for the mind more than the body – one I instinctively began to relish. The seed had been sown.

I had little time before heading back to Scotland. With a high pressure forecast for the following day, I arrived early in the morning for preparation, but instead of the expected dry, frosty air, clear, blue skies and perfect friction, a mist hung with a heavy, damp odour. I was optimistic that the sun would soon appear and the mist would evaporate, but rather irritatingly it wasn't budging. Impatience won, and I began to climb the damp slab and reached a tiny foot ripple at 30ft below the final blankness. My head spun with indecisiveness as my subconscious mind once again repelled my conscious mind's determination.

My subconscious ripped in:

Go down. The rock is damp!

'This is my last chance before I return to Scotland.'

Don't be ridiculous!

'I'm going for it.'

My right foot lifted from the ripple onto the first, invisible smear - a damp, smooth grit incline to which my boot was hurriedly pressed. Then my left foot lifted from the ripple . . . my hands pressed hard against nothing, rubbing at the grains, my right toe on the limits of adhesion.

You fool!

'I'm committed.'

Climb down. It's damp!

'I can't!'

As my left foot wavered, my minds imploded in the chaos of uncertainty. Suddenly, the tension was broken by a strange noise that echoed . . . a scraping, sliding noise . . .

Falling from a rock climb is an incoherent experience. You no longer have any control over your faculties. Your last, subconscious words like *protect your head* are not your own: they belong to your inner Guardian Angel. Everything races in real time but it all passes in slow motion in virtual time. My body somehow rotated 180 degrees in the air, like a cat with the ability to spin on an axis and upright itself. Then I felt the air whip my face, and I caught a glimpse of a patchwork of fields in the distance, flying upwards at an alarming rate, as were the boulders I was destined for. I hit the first boulder like a bolt of lightning, feet first, before being hurled sideways, spinning into another. My knee punched into the next boulder, and my head was about to collide with another. I remembered *the words* and shot out my arm to protect my head. I spun off and tumbled to the bottom of a slope, 30ft from the base of the climb.

Alarmed, but wishing to appear nonchalant, I got up and started walking back up the slope just as someone came running over to ask if I was all right. By the look on his face, he had expected to find a corpse. Miraculously I was alive, although I was livid that I had fallen and began thumping myself in the face, shouting *'you useless piece of shit'*. In a rage, I tried to solo back up the route, but by the time I had climbed off the ground, my adrenalin had subsided, leaving me with severe body trauma. I lay down in agony. Later it took ages for me to make it the few hundred yards to the car. I got in and drove up to Scotland, in pain and subdued.

Within a month, I drove south with my good friend, Dari Roberts, to attempt the slab again. I had stuffed the mattress from my lodgings into the back of the car to use as a crash pad (it was well before the advent of bouldering mats). I quickly climbed up to the ripple from where the mattress below looked no bigger than an envelope. Dari shouted encouragement, but I still didn't feel prepared for the dangerous, mentally-scarring smears above.

Over the next few months, all I thought about was that dangerous plane of grit; I had become completely obsessed with it. I didn't care about the danger, I was driven by it, but why? I wasn't too sure. Perhaps it was a self-confidence test, to prove to myself that I could be good and succeed at something. Risking all and making the first solo ascent meant that I could name the route and earn a tiny slice of *The Roaches* climbing history for myself.

At Easter break, 1992, I turned up with complete determination, but my fears were all too obvious. Without rational thought and completely electrified, I smeared above the ripple as though I were tiptoeing barefoot across bottles, just waiting for the sound of splintering glass, the slicing of skin and the slow flow of thick blood. I dared not breathe; life stood still. Destruction was only a micron away, but I stuck to the roundness and luckily the cool, springtime friction held me firm . . .

After my ascent of *Obsession Fatale*, I was mentally worn out and spent time soloing routes that were far less dangerous and eminently more relaxing, until the autumn of the following year. I wandered through a dense, deciduous forest in the Upper Churnet Valley, searching for Harston Rock. Eventually, I found it bearing down upon me, partly hidden through the thick foliage of oak, beech, birch and sycamore. The slender buttress of gritstone stood out, fearless, to the elements, like a primitive fortress of stone. I traced the line; the striking left arête of *One Chromosome's Missing*, its height and swagger warning me:

Don't even consider it . . .

'The landing isn't too bad; it's a slope of soil, detritus and roots!'

45ft is a long way to fall, whatever the landing!

'I can leap into that tree if it all goes awry.'

For some unknown reason, knowing that a fall from 45ft was likely to inflict more than just a bruise or broken bone, my subconscious gave in, and my aspirations to solo *One Chromosome's Missing* began to take fruition. My mind was set, and all I could think about was this blunt edge of grit in the forest. I wanted to solo it at the next available opportunity because it was dangerous, esoteric and I felt 'safe' in the forest. The trees insulated me from the pressures of the outside world. I hated competition and rivalry; soloing distanced me from all of that.

It was a gentle, lazy, late September morning as I passed through the red-bricked mill town of Leek and south towards the Churnet. The Churnet Valley is pastoral country – a maze of rolling fields, incised by rather apathetic streams which have carved miniature valleys that are lined with ambient, leafy trees, bracken and the odd protruding obelisk of gritstone, of which Harston Rock is the finest. I was tense as I walked along the forest path, trying hard not to envisage what the final outcome might be. Finally, after a brisk fifteen-minute walk, I was on Harston's rocky summit. The view opened out to distant fields above a leafy canopy.

I threw down a rope to acquaint myself with the moves and chalk up some holds. Then I felt rather sick. Breakfast had made me lethargic and sleepy, so I lay down on the gently warming summit block and soaked up the autumn sunshine, listening to the chattering of birds before drifting off altogether. Some time must have passed before I awoke, as the sun had angled more obliquely in the sky. I descended to the base of the buttress and, after a few minutes of gathering my thoughts, I felt confident and had a real desire to solo. I have never understood where this desire originates from, but the process is at the heart of what makes me tick. Soloing gritstone routes is an adrenalin addiction; and adrenalin is a drug that can be found as readily on the grit escarpments as opium can be found in fields of poppies.

Without further hesitation, I pulled through the overhang and continued confidently to a good foothold and a vague rest at 30ft. I didn't want to stop too long lest fear got the better of me and my subconscious woke to ask distracting questions like: *What the hell are you doing?* I stuttered up to an undercut and twisted neatly on the outside edge of my left boot, a move that craftily gave me the right position and balance to reach for the more defined upper arête. I became absorbed with the spine of grit in front of me. My feet pressed onto blank rock as one hand at a time snatched for the next hold. I eased away higher above the forest floor until I could feel adrenalin trying to tear me open. I came out of autopilot 40ft up the arête, eyeing the final hold. It was one barn-door move for success; there was no other option now. I didn't rush at it. I took a deep breath and stared out over the canopy of trees, absorbing my surroundings for the first time with conscious thought. I relaxed and I felt great, even in a position of such danger. I composed myself and then let go with my right hand . . .

My body's axis spun outwards from the arête. I was momentarily out of control. My toes pushed down into rough grit, and with automated precision my hand landed on the final hold perfectly. It held . . . I was safe. The final 15ft up a groove was climbed with contented relief. Life, at that moment, felt fantastic, and for the remainder of the afternoon I sat on the summit, watching some cows in a nearby field chewing grass and swishing their tails at bothersome flies.

Soloing *One Chromosome's Missing* had given me confidence and now was a good time to take advantage of cooler, autumn temperatures and to attempt some further dangerous routes. I loved travelling to new gritstone venues - each one was a whole new adventure in itself. I made visits to Yorkshire and Derbyshire, soloing hundreds of extremes – each having its own quirks and foibles – and the scariest, or best, were not always the hardest. It led to many near-miss experiences. One such experience, burned into my memory, is that of climbing the classic route, *Valkyrie*, at the Roaches, barefoot on a hot day.

The Rasp on Higgar Tor was another such occasion; I was freezing cold and trying earnestly to make a decision on which again my fate rested. During these intense experiences coincidence can play a big part. Just before I set to slapping across the ice-coated holds, I heard a voice. It wasn't in my head, but came from below me. A climber was looking up and had enunciated the words that I thought weren't real . . .

'Do you want me to throw you a rope?'

The eastern gritstone edges, such as Stanage, Millstone and Froggat, were too busy for me with my reclusive tendencies. I didn't climb at those crags very often. I was, more often than not, drawn back to the Staffordshire area, and in particular to *Ramshaw Rocks*.

Halfway along *Ramshaw* sits a lone, slender buttress, home to a flying blade of grit that slices acutely through the air like an ancient artefact. The enticingly named *Dangerous Crocodile Snogging* was the first route to climb this feature. I had eyed the route many times, but the alarmingly rounded finish unnerved me. Then one day I decided to give it a go. I grappled with the overhang, followed by a powerful slap here and there, to attain a knee-lock at the base of the fin. I was in pre-programmed mode now, stretching leftwards from the fin to gain a hold in the sidewall. I couldn't reach it with my left hand; my minds bounced with confusion. I was jammed hard up against the fin.

I suddenly realised the problem; I needed to hook my right toe round the fin to gain the extra inches needed, but in a frozen state of panic all I could do was to stretch my arms further until my fingers eventually crept onto the top edge of the hold. Then I let go of my right hand on the fin, hoping to swing across onto the hold, but my inertia was too great. My fingers ripped away, and I spun from the rock like a sycamore seed helicoptering from the tree in late autumn. I hit the boulder on the incline, sending me bouncing down the slope with nothing more than two bruised ankles. Another life gone . . .

My friend, Paul Higginson, who had been watching from an adjacent sentinel of rock, just shook his head silently. He had mentioned once in passing that my obsession with dangerous gritstone routes was mostly to do with what he termed 'accidental suicide'. I thought that was a little harsh, but deep down he was closer to the mark than I would like to believe. Paul has been a good friend to me. He selflessly gave me shelter in his bedsit for a few months at the time in my life when I was homeless and penniless. He has a quiet demeanour until women are discussed - then he becomes far more jovial. He is a builder but keeps trying different avenues of work. He had a job as a life model once, at Bangor University, with a class full of female students. That was until he couldn't contain an arousal and the lecturer sent him away, P45 in hand. When it came to climbing, he loathed danger but enjoyed the physical aspects – bouldering especially. On a rare occasion, I held his ropes and watched incredulously as he utilised his bricklayer's strength and gymnast's power to overcome the *Elegy* roof. *A Little Peculiar* was the hardest move ever performed on a grit route, and remained that way for well over a decade.

Soon after I succeeded on *Dangerous Crocodile Snogging*, I turned my attention to soloing directly up the fin, one of the most distinctive features on gritstone. Seb Grieve had applied a little of his lunacy to solo the first ascent of this fin to give *Clipperty Clop, Clipperty Clop* in his legendary, out of control, verbal style. It's aptly named because the only imaginable way of climbing it is by riding forth into the sky with the fin firmly wedged between one's thighs. However, like most gritstone routes, being tall is certainly an advantage. It took me many attempts to devise a sequence that would enable me to reach, grab and then clamp it between my legs, before riding it with spasms of insanity to its termination, some 30ft above a hard slope.

Ironically, the hardest mental part of soloing a pre-practised, dangerous, gritstone route is the initial sowing of the seed in your mind, the idea that you are going to attempt it. Once this is done, the solo comes naturally – it's just a case of switching the mind off and memorising the moves in the manner that a dancer might learn critical choreography, the difference being that this is on a vertical stage rather than a horizontal one. This type of soloing became completely addictive to me. I looked in the guidebook for the climbs with the hardest grades, and the ones that had no protection, and then became obsessed with soloing them. I was in my early to mid twenties, a halcyon time when age, body ailments and hurting oneself were really of no concern to me. When I had soloed a dangerous route, it was never enough. I wanted to solo more and more; the routes were endless, and I had all the time in the world as you do at a young age, or so you believe . . .

It wasn't until October that the temperatures had cooled enough, psychologically at least, for me to attempt *Clipperty Clop* . . . Family affairs were coming to a head; I did not want to live at home anymore, which perhaps meant moving away from the grit, and that certainly contributed to my downward-spiralling mood. I wasn't going to let my moods cloud my infatuations and block the path to my goals. At that moment nothing else seemed to matter in life - I wanted to solo *Clipperty Clop* - and if I didn't have that opportunity then I just wanted to be dead anyway, it was as simple as that. It was an out and out obsession, and furthermore if my attempt failed, then it seemed likely that I wouldn't have a life to worry about anyway. That suited me.

One morning, Paul, Justin Critchlow, one of his mates called Billy and I took the short walk to the *Newstones* – a harsh, weathered outcrop situated on the moor behind *Ramshaw*. Justin was laid back and never seemed to have much care about anything, but he had an immense talent for climbing. In fact, he seemed to be talented at everything, even the hydroponics set up he had in his Dad's roof was making him good money until the police smelt the weed in the street and he got caught. He was inspiringly smooth and flowed naturally on the rock, and though he wasn't driven, he could perform effortlessly when he felt like it. I first met Justin at *The Roaches* when he was playing truant from school at the age of fourteen. I could see that he needed something to quench his youthful energy, so I became a sort of mentor. He started to outperform me within a year and began levitating up blank pieces of rock that I couldn't even grip on to. The blank arête of *Ultimate Sculpture* at Ramshaw said it all.

It was hazy, and I was rather lethargic and despondent due to the weather, although the boys were enjoying their bouldering. Billy, a little stocky for a climber, fell off one problem, creating a large cloud of chalk. Justin piped up and said, 'what's that in your chalk bag Billy, flour?' Paul quipped, 'yeah, he needs something to make him rise'. It broke the tension and lifted my mood immeasurably.

We walked over to *Ramshaw*, where I sat pensively amongst heather and tussocks of grass, thinking over the solo that lay ahead. I set up a top rope and practised the sequence a few times in order to gain greater confidence.

Finally, I took away the rope and stepped out of my harness. I felt vulnerable, my pulse quickened, and suddenly gravity began to feel heavy. Without a second thought, I swung through the lower overhang, my blood warming to the tune of my free weight. A small ledge above the overhang enabled me to stand a while and think. Above me, the improbable fin cut convincingly through the sky, luring me.

'Quick, lets go!'

Whoa, something doesn't feel right!

'Commit, it will be over in less than a minute!'

I'm not happy!

'No time like the present . . .'

The power of my conscious mind jerked me forwards, high stepping into a precarious crouch where the rock pushed my body outwards into an offset position.

I felt humbled now, alone with a stone-cold wedge of rock and gravity . . . deep breath . . . my left hand slapped energetically at the rough textures on the far side of the fin, whilst my chest bosomed the near side. It was a grotesque technique, but I grated upwards nonetheless, each hand in turn, stabbing blindly upwards for the better grips on the fin. My body was fully stretched, my feet on tiptoes. Then they lost adhesion and flew away, cutting a curve through the sky. I gripped hard, muscles tearing, tendons elastically pulled to their limits - they held my over-torqued body, but only just.

I was now dangling from two pinch grips, and all I needed to do was to pull up on them and clench the fin between my thighs and ride my way on a wave of euphoria to the top. Each time I pulled, I didn't move, I couldn't move, and then my hands began to slip with sweat. I couldn't take a hand off to chalk up; I couldn't do anything except just hang there uselessly. I was finished, but I just kept gripping on with an innate survival instinct, waiting for the oxygen in my bloodstream to run out, muscles to seize and fingers to open. Even so, I tried one last, desperate bid to leap for a better grip. It was a futile piece of heroism . . . I was met with only fresh air and acceleration as I was ripped from the rock. I felt sick; I could taste only bile, see only darkness, and silence fell now as softly as snow . . .

Time passed, I wasn't sure how long . . . minutes, seconds, microseconds, nanoseconds . . . bones impacting, humming, blackness . . . I waited for the pain to arrive, but it never came. I didn't understand. Then I heard voices, but I didn't know to which world they belonged.

Suddenly, the pain split me in two and I opened my eyes to see a sky drained of colour. I put my right hand up and slid my fingers across my face. My left eye wasn't there; instead, my fingers grazed over an egg-sized lump protruding from my eye socket. My left arm hung limp and throbbed in agony. I knew it was broken, and I began to feel faint as the shock finally set in. I lay down in the long, moorland grass, dizzy and cold. Justin ripped my left boot off my ever-bloating foot. My friends chatted, but I wasn't taking an interest. I just lay with closed eyes, listening to the background noise of the countryside and the engines of the cars. In the distance, I was aware of the familiar whine of an ambulance, but no paramedics arrived for a long time. They had first had to attend to a fatal car-crash half a mile down the hill before arriving to peel me from the base of the crag. I imagined the reaper's scythe cutting its way across the Staffordshire moors with intent to kill, missing me by a hair's breadth, and seconds later cutting down two poor motorists instead. It was the supernatural at its most potent . . .

The newspaper caption the following day read:

Climber escapes with his life
after falling 50ft at the Roaches.

It didn't quite ring true, but that is the beauty of the press – a little embellishment never goes amiss. My arm was in plaster for eight weeks. When it came off, my left arm was out of rotation and my wrist knuckle stuck up - a slight malformation I will have as a gritstone souvenir forever. Nursing my broken ulna and heavily bruised ankles was like being in drug rehabilitation - rehab from gritstone and its addictions. I needed to persuade myself now that the grit years were over before those nuggets of sand dismantled my life altogether.

For a number of years, I worked in South-East Asia, but I knew it was my destiny to return to the grit edges. I was never one to give up on my obsessions, and when I did return, in 1998, I went straight to Rylstone on the North York Moors and made a beeline for *Heart Beat City*. This route climbs a short but peerless arête. First climbed by Dave Pegg in 1989, he stated that it would never be congealed in chalk, along with something about death, earth and the soil . . . I was immediately sucked in. I knew the subtle countryside with its chameleon mix of colour and its rural flavour; it brought back memories, because Malsis Preparatory school, where I boarded from seven years of age, is at Cross Hills. I fell-ran on the golden, bracken-clad Embsay moors above Skipton, potholed near Dent, which I hated, and did my very first hill-walk at the age of nine: the Three Peaks, a twenty-five mile circuit that consisted of Penyghent, Whernside and Inglebrough.

The countryside and lifestyle were engrained in my memory; the Pennine Way, the people, the accents, the houses of stone, Malham Tarn, Bronte country, lazy becks and Fountains Abbey - it was all an integral part of my boyhood.

I knocked on the door of one of the houses in the village of Rylstone and asked the owner if he could keep an eye on my car, informing him that if the car were still to be there at nightfall then he should call the rescue services, and I told him exactly where I would be lying, unconscious or dead. I then set to the forty-minute walk onto the lofty escarpment. I felt relaxed and at peace until I saw the route looming ahead: a tilted block perched on the edge of the moor. I found to my horror, however, that the length of fall would be twice the length of the route and the landing was probably not survivable. The moves were desperately insecure, and any attempt at soloing it would be close to suicidal. I returned on numerous occasions to solo the route, but each time, much to my annoyance, I sided with common sense. Having recently spoken to 'Irish Si' Moore in San Francisco, I was incredulous to learn that he had tested this landing!

My other obsession lay at *Black Rocks* in Derbyshire, where there is a smooth, bulbous cube of grit that stands 25ft high, partially shaded by the boughs of a giant beech tree. On the shy side of the cube is an undercut slab, as coloured and smooth as baize. The centre of the slab stretches the imagination as to whether it is humanly possible to climb it. The myth was dispelled when Johnny Dawes, 'the' gritstone maestro, stepped up to the challenge and sensationally claimed *Angels' Share* in 1994. The name just said it all: the impossibility, the vanishing into nothingness and that variable state beyond reality.

Unlike *Heart Beat City*, *Angels' Share* wasn't potentially dangerous – the problem lay in the holds: there simply weren't any. How I tried to adhere to that impossible slab during the summer of 1994, eventually giving up and blaming it on the warm, summer temperatures. I meant to return in the winter, but by then I had broken my arm. In the meantime, Johnny had succeeded. I had been simply outclassed. As time went by I never gave up on the possibility of an ascent. It would eventually happen eight years later when I met up with Justin again. Justin could climb *Angels' Share* if he wanted to, but the question was could he be bothered!

We reached *Black Rocks* as the sun was at its zenith, pieced into an acutely crisp, midwinter sky. It had no heat but warmed the spirit if nothing else. The air was dry and the temperature was just below zero – perfect for gritstone climbing. Steam funnelled out of our mouths as we walked up to the cliff from the car park. We stopped and stared across at the infamous gritstone block, home to *Gaia* and *Curving Arête* – routes that were inexplicably absorbing with such minimalistic appeal. I had pulled onto *Curving Arête* once, only to fall instantaneously down the cleft, smacking my elbow in the process. I had never been back to try it since. We wandered past them and into the trees.

The boulder I had driven 400 miles to come and climb looked down upon me with its crooked smile (an ancient, chipped crease) and its hideously bald top.

Three routes utilized the crooked smile before going their separate ways. I warmed up on the two adjacent arête climbs: *Velvet Silence* and *Jumping on a Beetle*. I had soloed both of these routes a decade before, and it made me wonder where my life had disappeared to so quickly. The routes were faith and friction climbs and agonisingly tense in those few moments. That is why the memories of them were still so very fresh to me.

I turned my attention to the central slab of *The Angels' Share*. I sat under the boulder, trying to stretch, meditate, relax and summon up belief, but it was all too much. The anxiety, the frenetic excitement and the raw nerves overruled everything else. I put on my best pair of boots, making sure the soles were polished clean before fiddling with the laces. Finally, I inspected my right index finger that was holed and seeping blood; I doused it in chalk and stepped up to the rock. The initial overhang was immediate, and the ensuing struggle round it was undignified, leaving me stunned and a little breathless. I was now stable, standing on the inch-wide crease of 'the smile', feeling very vulnerable. My mind was disturbed; it wasn't the danger, but more the thought of attempting to climb something that felt impossible, even though rationality knew that it was possible. I soaked up the blood from my fingertip again with chalk, took a deep breath, and smeared up onto nothingness . . .

The following day, I met up with Johnny Dawes on the boulders at Stanage and we talked a little about *The Angels' Share*. I mentioned that I thought it was fourth dimensional slab climbing, which questions its very possibility as one's balance and centre of gravity have to be of the utmost precision for a successful ascent. Johnny looked at me deeply with his wide, inquisitive eyes, studying what I had just said. Possibly I had caught him on his wavelength – moving in a world on a hidden dimensional plane.

Or perhaps it was more fantastical than that, and we were fictional characters living amongst a playground of grit, playing out our dreams without destinies.

A Calm Sea Never Lies

Four miles south of Aberdeen; a fresh, cheeky-faced teenager is staring towards the camera, his mouth ajar, pouting. He wears baggy, white trousers and a red fleece jacket that hangs open from his shoulders giving him a middle-aged paunch. Leaning out from the rock face, straight-armed, his legs are almost horizontal. A mould-coloured sea slops a few feet beneath him and behind him is a dark sea cave, dank and devoid of life. The teenager's innocent face is the antithesis of the threatening backdrop that looms around him. The photo, portraying both darkness and light, is now long gone and so are the youthful features on that teenager's face. His memory of that cave did remain. Little did he know that his destiny was to return there, to tempt fate once more amongst its ugly chandeliers.

Ten years ago, the notion of soloing above a cold North Sea and falling in was unthinkable and also a little crazy. How attitudes have changed since the advent of 'deep water soloing', which entails climbing above the sea with a chalk bag, shorts, boots and very little else apart from a warped mind and a large set of *cojones*. This crazy concept was born on the south coast of England – specifically Dorset – created by a few adventurous visionaries. An insight into their shenanigans can be found within the pages of *Into the Blue*, a fun guidebook that bubbles with enthusiasm.

Deep water soloing isn't a sport, it is a passion; a passion fed by a drug that is only prescribed to those with adventurous blood and the will to be different. I became addicted, and when I returned to Scotland from the south coast, I felt like Drake or Magellan, returning from the South China Sea with a galleon laden with precious jade, incense and spices.

Destination: the Red Tower – twenty five miles north of Aberdeen. The wall of golden granite is mystical in its seclusion. Its routes are perplexing to find and even more so to climb. *Shere Khan* and *Bagheera* aren't just characters from 'The Jungle Book,' they are legendary climbing test pieces, aspirations to the best, mere illusions to the rest.

I arrived at the top of the wall and peered down the sheer, 50ft cascade of rock that dipped into the blue . . . I felt at ease. The water was placid and the rock was clean and honest . . . how I love the granite and the way it instils confidence in its intricacy. *Shere Khan* steals the left side of the wall via a pair of perfect parallel cracks that appear to have been clawed at by a mythical tiger, producing a minimalist masterpiece. Six years before, whilst at University, I had failed to tame the tiger with a rope, but now the idea of trying without one seemed immeasurably more exciting. A summer's afternoon was spent in assessing the sea conditions - the swell, the tides and the currents - before I climbed the arête between *Mowgli* and *Shere Khan*. I named him *Baloo* – the bear surely deserved a seat on the wall amongst his friends.

It was time to scale the tiger, but at sea level he stood formidable. I pounced on, soon realising my mistake; his stripes were so deceiving. He vanished suddenly, leaving no trace behind but a searing pain rippling through my fingertips. I desperately tried to cling on, but like a disobedient cub I was tossed away into the water for being found wanting. Although the tiger had beaten me, the myth of the sea had been dispelled – a fall into the North Sea was survivable. I began to feel more at ease attempting to play with these fictional creatures . . .

My body was weary, and it refused to challenge *Shere Khan* for a second time, so instead I turned my attention to *Hole in the Wall:* the original route, a classic, but out of touch with the other jungle beasts. Carefree, I passed by the eponymous hole, which didn't issue money but did issue brief finger respite. Up above, amidst the crux, I was glued flat to the wall, like a bank robber under arrest, restrained by the law of gravity. Nervous giggles welled from the depths of my stomach as I unwound and dropped into the cold embrace of the sea – a sanctuary where gravity has no jurisdiction.

Over a week passed before I could run wild and free again with the characters of the jungle. I had been recalled to work in Stavanger, Norway, dangling from hundreds of feet of rope to inspect the structural integrity of an oil rig's cylindrical legs with eddy current equipment. It goes without saying that I would rather have been climbing without ropes above the sea on golden granite. It was money though . . . just can't escape it in a world revolving on materialism and consumerism . . .

On my return to the vertical, granite jungle, I peered down the wall and gawped in surprise. *Hole in the Wall* was heavily coated in a trail of white chalk. The penny dropped, and I started to smile. Last week's conversation must have inspired my friend, Wilson Moir. He had obviously soloed *Hole in the Wall* whilst I had been away. I threw on my boots and followed the chalk. The crux glued me to the wall once again, in starfish mode until I managed to summon up all the power I had to reach the elusive hold.

Three long years passed by before my next visit. The air was fresh, quintessentially Scottish, quite unlike the equatorial humidity and dust of the oriental shipyard that had been my home. The sea twinkled; *Shere Khan* and *Bagheera* were pleased to see me. It was likely that no one had visited them for years, apart from the odd passing fisherman who might have thrown them an occasional glance as he tended to his pots.

I sat down and gazed along the coastline, appreciating the warm granite, the bright yellow lichens, the sea pink and the background chatter of the razorbills, guillemots and kittiwakes. More so than ever before, this place had the scent of freedom and felt insulated from the real world's hustle and bustle . . . I threw a glance seaward – the sea was calm, like a mirror without reflection, only disturbed by the silky wake of a small, wooden fishing boat that had rounded the headland. The boat glided towards a red buoy and tickled alongside. The fisherman leant over and hauled in his creel, before floating gently over to the next. An amiable feeling of peace filtered through the air; the day was tranquil and balmy. Rather apathetically I declined the ferocious challenge of *Shere Khan*, and instead I turned to *Bagheera* – sleek and agile, a line of undiminished beauty. The base of the wave-splashed wall is smooth and black just like the purring, velvet cat himself. I climbed on stealthily, with an apposite mix of cheek and nerves, soon finding the rhythm . . . suddenly and without warning, the holds became as fictitious as the panther itself. My sinews stretched, outstretched paw, outstretched claw, tantalising . . . the curvature of rock taught me free flow, lithe muscles pirouetting me up and away. The hunt was nearly over, but the cat turned vicious as the water grew shallower and more distant. I reached the top, ecstatic, encased in the silence of symbiosis, visible only to the flashing, coal-specked eye of the resident kittiwake nesting in the *Jungle Book* corner.

The approaching summer solstice was surely a good omen, a pertinent time to revisit *Shere Khan*. I returned with Dave 'Cubby' Cuthbertson – a climbing legend: a guru. His 'pièce de resistance' climb – *Requiem* – at Dumbarton Rock, climbed in 1983, is a national treasure and was perhaps the hardest climb in the world at the time. One would imagine that Cubby is a Scotsman of giant frame, an immortal being, but no . . . Cubby is remarkably slight of stature and quietly spoken. He is part humble climber, part elite athlete, and most definitely a perfectionist. He is also just a nice guy and an exceptionally gifted photographer. He was keen to capture me at play with the big, graceful cats of *Shere Khan* and *Bagheera*.

We found that the last wisps of haar had vanished, revealing a sun-drenched coastline above a perfect tide. The tension in the crisp, blue air was electric as I prepared – chalking holds and drinking Red Bull whilst Cubby checked his angles, film and lenses. Inches beneath me, the light danced like silver eels on the surface of the emerald-coloured sea. I cherished the colours, the life, the commitment and the perfect mixture of thoughts that gelled in my head. I launched on, pulling one way then the next, spinning a helix in haste. I held my breath in case the cat awoke and shredded my suspension of disbelief. Time stood still until I found myself on top, simultaneously sad and delighted with my success, whilst *Shere Khan* lay beneath me, unperturbed, snoozing in the noonday sun, oblivious . . .

The following year I had exhausted the supply of deep water solos on the Aberdeenshire coast, and I was looking for further opportunities. The memory of the photograph reappeared, beckoning me to return to the cave . . .

Destination: Bruin Cove – four miles south of Aberdeen. The cave hadn't changed apart from the added throng of nesting kittiwakes that chuckled away from their balconies hysterically, like childless witches.

On the straightforward traverse into the cave, hailstones of bird guano rained down, and the rock above me shone with a white patina, its stench burning deeply into my nostrils. I continued and the holds diminished as the traverse ended near the edge of the drooling cave mouth. Above me hung the arch – the gateway to hell . . .

Now where was Cerberus lurking?

Suddenly a hoarse, croaking noise echoed, repetitive, with a baritone voice like a broken woodwind instrument. It scared me . . .

What . . . is that?

I pulled up to face an angry shag with evil, sea-green eyes, who shook her javelin-like beak menacingly skywards, protesting at my intrusion. I tried to ignore it, but it wasn't easy when I was trying to summon the courage to embark on this ridiculous exploit. The rock ahead was a welded mess of porphyry, quartz and granite – geological carnage. I tried to make sense of a climbable passage through its maze. A blood-red, hanging slab led down to the edge of nowhere; the beginning of an inverted world. I hurried across the slab so that the shag would stop its protests. The roof became bigger, the shadows deeper, and the sound of the swell in the back of the cave became an orchestra of gloomy echoes. A hard move off a wet hold defined the point of no return . . . I was committed at the base of the cave mouth.

I wedged myself across a cleft, freed my arms, and hurriedly studied the 20ft long roof looking for clues and flaws . . . my legs started to tremble with the strain. I eased out of my body-wedge and began punching blindly into a crack; it was rougher than pumice stone and my knuckles bled. I hung on, squeezing and contorting my Houdini-like form into the roof. I threw a fist-jam behind my head. The rock was slimy and my jam just slipped . . . slipped . . . slipped again. My eyes were wide. I was failing; but gravity never does . . . down, down . . .

For a moment, there was calmness before an ocean full of pressure expelled my xenolith form back to the surface. I scraped out onto a barnacle-encrusted ledge just as the cold of the sea began to entwine around me. I tore off my clothes and shivered in spasms. Ten minutes of sunshine fired warmth back into me, and I was once again locked into the roof, powdering the wet fist-jam with a bag full of chalk. Eventually my fist stuck, and I rotated with inflexibility into the apex of the roof, cocooned in a three dimensional matrix, eyeing the lip and the daylight - a world away. I punched along the crack but then everything began to dwindle . . . holds, hope, energy . . . it was no use . . .

As my head turned down towards the sea, I caught sight of the rock behind me. I dropped backwards, hoping that my shoulders were going to wedge against it, knowing that if they didn't then I would slip and my head would hit the rock. I would be knocked unconscious and fall in . . .

My shoulders did lock, but they were lacerated in the process. I persevered towards the lip of the cave, blood dribbling down my back, droplets dispersing into the sea. I carried on, unaware if the route were possible at all . . .

I got to the lip, and my hand reached round from underneath into the sunlight. It wiped from side to side hoping to catch a hold . . . anxious moments . . . I felt one and tried to decide if it was positive enough for me to swing on. I decided that I had no other options, and with that I swung around the lip into the sunlight. Catching my breath, I glanced down at my watery safety net, which, to my astonishment, had now disappeared . . .

Where is the sea?

In that split second, there was utter confusion in my mind before I made sense of what I was looking at. An inflatable dinghy had silently drifted in, and six wide eyes were fixed on me with a sheen of amazement reflected in their pupils. They realised at the same time as I that if I fell off I would kill them, or myself, and sink the boat in the process . . . they quickly throttled the outboard and disappeared into the depths of the cave. It wasn't every day on the Aberdeen Riviera that one would encounter a lone lunatic hanging from a cliff, sporting a Mohican, beach shorts and an upper torso resembling road kill.

Later, I became intrigued with a counter-line on the other side of the cave. I traversed in and made an irreversible swing onto the daunting 100ft wall. I was committed . . . my journey ahead was uncharted and overhanging. I made my own rules, climbing across many avenues of deceit, feeling the true spirit of adventure. I began to lurch for holds, hoping that they were indeed holds, always conscious of the fact that I had to keep climbing rightwards in line with the sea. I reached a partial rest and shook with raw, nervous energy . . .

Which way?

The cliff looked unhelpful and devoid of grips; I had to make a decision quickly. I made a predatory leap rightwards into a groin-splitting bridge, my hands floundering for jams in the base of a hidden, overhanging crack. The crack was fair but relentless and, over 60ft above the sea, my body quivered with the fear of wild excitement. I struggled with an awkward jam. My arms were going numb with lactic acid; my body shook and time had run out . . . I made one final lunge for what looked like a good hold, but I knew it was pointless . . . I was airborne, pedalling towards a wicked surface tension . . .

In a millisecond, my senses returned, and I found that I was still attached to the wall. My fingers had uncurled, but part of my wrist had snagged over the hold, giving my forearms and fingers enough respite for me to re-grip. I clawed onto a ledge, with no finesse. I sat there catching my breath and wanting to vomit. The theatre full of kittiwakes was judging me with their virgin white faces and their eyes twinkling like beads of anthracite. The rocks were splashed with guano – a repulsive sight – the winged artists desecrating their own canvas.

I walked away through the thigh deep grass. I was happy with my work. Although ugly and imperfect, *Clash of the Titans* and *Last of the Mohicans* are energetic pieces of art, unknowingly inspired by that photograph of a teenager in a red fleece, fourteen years earlier . . .

My passion for deep water soloing exponentiated after *Clash of the Titans* and *Last of the Mohicans*. I was no longer content with *normal* deep water soloing, I wanted to find something close to my mental and physical climbing limit. I thought about an objective that would fulfil my requirements . . . but where? At this point some crazy ideas formed until a real solution resulted – *Cracks in Reality*.

Destination: the Red Hole – three miles south of Aberdeen. The Red Hole is host to the most adventurous sea cliff climbs on Scotland's east coast. The central, orange coloured wall is atmospheric. The *Black Sleep* climbs the left edge of the wall, *Cracks in Reality* takes the central line, and the two fluently engaging corner systems to the right are *Procrastination* and *Space Rats*. Almost all the best, hard routes on the north east coast were first climbed in the 1980s by the keenest and most tenacious climber of the day: Dougie Dinwoodie. The routes at the Red Hole are testaments to his ability and an integral part of his legacy.

On Christmas day, I wandered down to the Red Hole and I sat on the cliff top, peering down into a narrow inlet that thrashed with angry white horses, their spray galloping half way up the 120ft wall whilst the remainder cantered into the back of the cave, releasing a chorus of anguished echoes. The sky was without lustre, the rocks were cold and damp, the light levels low and dim; the sun hadn't bothered to show face for hours, days even. The whole mood was dire but I huddled, comfortable and pensive, contemplating the magnitude of this solo . . . after half an hour, I turned away uncertainly, with a desire to return at a later date, knowing that my fitness was the primary key to unlocking the insanity of my dream.

I returned to an empty cottage in the darkness to celebrate Christmas alone with a couple of bottles of red wine. I was in no mood to celebrate or socialise. One of my off-the-cuff misadventures in the Far East was causing me great concern. I had plugged money into the Singapore stock market in 1997, when the Asian economy had begun to flounder, and sold a year or so later when it was recovering. I became affluent. As usual I never spent anything, never had the urge to, but was always willing to speculate; and that is what I did – quite naively. My 'friend' led me to believe in investing in a high-return investment, which he termed a 'game', that was legalised through a bank in Papua New Guinea. After the three-month maturation period, my returns supposedly materialised, but I never got a sniff of them as they were now frozen in a holding account. All of Tony's accounts were frozen as he was under investigation by the monetary authority, so over the next six years I continued to shore up Tony and his family financially, all the while hoping that his accounts would be cleared and my initial investments retrieved.

Tony's stories became more incredulous: being shot in Hong Kong; kidnapped in Germany; his wife dying from black magic on a hospital bed in Canada. Then I heard from him that there was a 'hit' out on me from Singapore. I was the one who was keeping him financially afloat, and if they got rid of me, then he would ultimately be penniless and disclose all of his untraceable bank accounts to the Singapore government. I found it quite intriguing, but duly took note and spent the winter months partially on the run, camping on the North York Moors. It was a cold winter. The tent fabric was like cardboard some mornings and the streams were choked with ice. Washing was a hardship. All in all I was being morally blackmailed and I should have jumped ship at the first sniff of foul play, but I was living up to my given name of 'international man of mystery'. I was young and free, and taking on gambles was in my nature, regardless of the outcome. To my eyes, I was born with nothing, I was going to leave with nothing; riches are found in experiences and not in material wealth. However, Tony's deceitfulness and taking of liberties with my generosity and good nature were the real reason for my melancholy. I needed to clear my head of it.

On my next visit to the Red Hole, I crouched on my haunches at sea level on smooth wave-washed buttocks of rock, staring across the narrow inlet to the wall. I ascertained the depth of water, the line of fall, and my escape plan if I fell in; above all I needed to persuade my subconscious mind that a solo was justifiable. Then I discovered a traverse over a small cave that might provide a direct entry into the route. I became excited at the idea - my commitment was sealed.

I didn't feel ready in my heart of hearts to try *Cracks in Reality*, so I decided to solo *Black Sleep* first, to test the water. Firstly I made a rope ladder out of an old piece of rope by tying a number of alpine-butterfly knots in it before securing it and throwing it in the sea. Without this ladder, a deep water solo would be foolhardy – the inlet was lined with velvet smooth rock, from which escape would be impossible.

I abseiled to the lip of the 8ft roof that caps the wall; here, I had to kick out and swing in rhythm to my descent. Losing the pendulum effect would leave me dangling in space with no means of reaching the rock. I swung in and grabbed a hold on the belay 30ft above the water. Without considering the danger, I undressed from my harness, clipped it to the rope and let it go. The moment was electric as I watched my safety line spinning away into thin air, coming to rest a tantalising 10ft away from my grasp.

I turned and faced the rock. Its texture was strange – smooth, red porphyry sprinkled with crystals of mica and rivets of quartz. I hoped that it was going to be fair. I started to climb a vague arête in a nervous state, fumbling over every hold in a pathetic manner. I needed a more positive hold to help my upward progress and boost my confidence, but none materialised. The arête vanished, and I climbed rightwards on further discreet finger holds, always trying to work out the sequence of moves before I had reached them, to save strength.

I looked down at the sea to make sure it was there and could give me the confidence I needed to continue. I saw a positive foothold and climbed quickly onto it. At 60ft above the sea I could rest, surrounded by exits of varying difficulties, trying to absorb the experience, committed between hot sun and cold sea with a parched throat and dry lips.

The remaining 20ft of wall teased me . . . daring me. I felt like a lowly hyena challenging a lion over a carcass as I set to the wall, but the lion grew nasty and sent me scuttling down to my foothold sanctuary. My next attempt had more purpose as I hunted out all the hidden finger holds that granted me safe passage into a welcoming groove at 80ft.

The psychological barrier of deep water soloing in the Red Hole had been broken, and now I was totally addicted to these solo adventures. Next was *Cracks in Reality*.

I had aspirations to climb *Cracks in Reality* whilst at university, but they had not been realised. On one occasion, I went down to hold Matt 'The Cat' Ingham's ropes on the route. I hung on the belay, holding his 30ft fall in astonishment; we both jumared out. Eight years later, I abseiled onto the belay just as a passing rainstorm unleashed havoc, but on that occasion I had no jumars with which to escape. My friend Charlie Ord, my climbing partner on that day, luckily hadn't abseiled, so he threw me a rope from the other side of the inlet. I swung around frantically trying to grab the smooth, tilting slabs on the opposite side . . . what a circus! Looking back, I realised that it was so fateful; it seemed to have been my destiny to solo the route, and success would be far more pleasurable than I could have anticipated. Furthermore, the direct entry would produce a better route; perhaps the finest on the whole Aberdeen coast . . . this alone was driving the cogs of my own obsession. Two days after soloing the *Black Sleep*, I returned with Cubby, who had driven from Glen Coe to capture the moment on camera. Apathy set in when we found the coast covered in cloud, but when the cloud soon evaporated it left me with no further excuses . . .

The rock architecture at the start is weird and obtusely dimensional – a smooth hanging wall suspends above a water-worn slab angling into the sea; their relationship is awkward and not favourable to human ergonomics. I linked the two with a vulnerable and precarious splits position; a slip here would be embarrassing . . . I pulled on and gulped at the sight of no water beneath me. My anxiety rode high, hands slipping on the ultra smooth rock; the holds were blind and the path indeterminable, but this was the adventure I was here for. I reached a hanging rib of rock and looked round the corner . . . suddenly I was a fathom deep in cold water. I surfaced and trod water, squeaking: 'Can you throw the rope in?'

My heart was ripping at my chest like a caged rat whilst Cubby was fiddling with his camera. I was frustrated, and I just wanted to get out. Finally the rope snaked into the water. I pulled up eagerly, the smooth rock making me slip and slide, my knees bashing against the slab, and my blood spilling down the rock and into the sea. I dried off, changed chalk bag and returned. I passed my falling point, trying earnestly to piece a sequence together. I found one, but my hands were the wrong way round . . . splash! This time my feet just hit the slab of rock under the water. I pulled out, convulsing with the cold. I tried again for a third time, and this time I dropped down to the lip of the arch, jammed my body in and pulled over onto a smooth, black slab at the base of the orange wall. I just happened to glance up at the fearsome, 120ft cliff above me, knowing that I was in no physical state to attempt it; I jumped in and retreated for the day.

The next morning was fine, and the sea was calm with a number of moon jellyfish now apparent. I tried not to focus on them. The sunshine lifted my morale as it revealed the wall in a morning glow set against the darker shadows of the overhangs that framed it. This time the traverse passed fluently, and I continued upwards on chunky holds until they ran out. The rock became awkward, and the connection with the original line was still 20ft away. Looking down, I realised that I needed to jump back 4ft to hit water, and lactic acid began to rip through my forearms turning them into a solid mass. I barely held on to reach the *Procrastination* belay ledge and respite.

I was dwarfed and held spellbound by the powers of the intense walls and overhanging corners that incarcerated me. I traced the 100ft, overhanging corner of *Procrastination*, curving insanely above my head. I could hear myself asking the question:

'Is there water below the corner?'

NO . . . don't even think about it!

'I guess not then.'

The sun was intense, the rock was radiating heat furiously, and I was perspiring like a sumo in a sauna. In a dehydrated state, I climbed down to a small ledge just above sea level. Cubby's voice broke the silence . . .

'What are you thinking Jules?'

'It is too hot; I'm going to wait for the sun to leave the face!' I replied. I had a deep suspicion that he thought I was going to give up and swim back across the inlet.

The wall was getting the better of me mentally; my mortality was being bared, and the reality of it all was that I had to climb a 100ft, vertical wall, capped by an overhang, with fingers and arms that hadn't enough strength left to peel an orange. My forearms were swollen and I needed them to subside. I rested for as long as it took for the wall to go into the shade, and by then my arms had depleted and my strength had returned. My tenacity surprised me as I climbed upwards to join the parent route. Then, at 60ft, I hit the psychological barrier – the point where deep water is no longer 'safe'. I was only halfway!

Above was the zone where danger increases and strength decreases exponentially – I was being cleaved in two by a double-edged sword. I started to grip harder as my safety net disappeared. My arms began to tire; my mind began to overload with risk assessments – subconscious calculations being performed at break-neck speed. I had to down climb into the safety zone, or climb higher and risk all. Indecision made me look up instinctively, and I spotted a good hold way above. I dashed for it with committed eagerness, and then up to a small foothold at 80ft, which was just enough to rest my arms and recollect. I looked down towards that lonely strip of surface tension, ready to snap me, before looking up at the roof, which had grown substantially. I felt very fragile and studious, trying to read the intricacies of the rock's literature, the hidden story leading me off the wall and onto a hanging slab under the mighty roof.

The rock under the roof was damp, and I had run out of chalk. My left foot was blistering in its boot, so I untied my lace and pulled my heel out, forgetting that I had no chance of taking both hands off to re-tie. I stretched into the jaw of the roof and swung out on hand-jams and guano-coated holds, 100ft above the water. In these circumstances, gravity feels as though it grows stronger, and I intuitively pulled harder, acutely aware of the penalty of letting go . . .

The neatly cut, final groove was easy. I took one last look down before pulling into the horizontal world. I stretched out and let the poisons of fear drain into the deep, deep, green grass.

Skye is the Limit

At 100ft, I was stuck to the wall, straining to hold on, surrounded by a vast amphitheatre of black, disintegrating rock. I had climbed the initial sustained crackline of *Dilemma* into a world of subtleties above. I needed to move left in order to gain the thin, snaking crack of *Cling On*, but by following the most positive holds, I had become stranded off route. My minds were in turmoil. I tried to focus elsewhere, thinking of a girl I had just met and trying to dilute the intensity by entertaining thoughts of where that relationship might take me - but such thoughts dissolve in the depths of an apparently chaotic, and yet paradoxically coherent soloist's mind. I closed my eyes, breathed deeply for ten seconds and, when I opened them again, looked down into a humbling and destitute gully of potential destruction. I swallowed hard and turned my head to scan the invasive cliff, the ozone and a poker playing sky. They were all vectors connecting to a single point in space and time - one of human catastrophe.

The Cuillins were growing dark and ugly. Sinister shadows crept across the wall. On the verge of cranial meltdown, I stuttered into action - tensed up, body trembling, utterly dependent on the micro-textures of rock in front of me. My left hand was by my left foot; the cliff was bullying me into an unnatural position. With my head stuck in a sideways counterbalance, my right hand swept upwards over the rock, fingers touching, rubbing in a blind arc of extremis, praying for a hold. Then, with horror, I felt a casual spit of rain . . .

Eighteen years earlier: 10pm, midsummer 1987. The sun is burnishing the mountain. An incandescent face of gabbro radiates with a fabulous, blood-orange hue whilst a dark, animated shadow slowly nibbles across the valley like a tide rising towards the impenetrable bastion. I was in awe of the moment as my ropes spilt between my legs, 900ft above that darkening valley floor.

My A-Levels had just finished and, now liberated, I felt full of fascination and inspiration, climbing amongst such thrilling mountains. I pulled over the top and set a belay. It was warm and uncannily silent as I sat on my rocky perch, pulling in the ropes to Andrew Spark (Sparky), my sixteen-year-old climbing partner. I began to relax contentedly as my gaze fixed to the north west, towards the Outer Hebrides. The distant islands appeared to be timeless as they floated upon the last patch of a shimmering, golden sea.

The power of emotion and the raw romanticism of that forever-fading sunset, together with the completion of *Integrity* – one of Scotland's finest rock climbs – had left an everlasting impression on my youthful mind. Her sister route - *Trophy Crack* - had toyed with my subconscious ever since. In 1987, the idea of attempting a route rated *Extreme* was ridiculous, but as my strength and confidence grew over the years, the idea of soloing *Trophy Crack* started to take shape. I knew the sheer audacity required to achieve such a solo would leave me with both a reckless sense of pleasure and another eternal memory.

Further visits to Skye became infrequent, due mainly to the unsettled weather that the Cuillins attract. I did not want any adverse weather to ruin the memories and dreams gleaned in my youth. During a pleasant spell of weather in the spring of 2003, I started out on my five-hour journey from Deeside. It was a tedious one, especially along the shores of Loch Ness, busy with slow moving tourists looking for a glimpse of 'the monster'. At Invermoriston, the road turns west and soon opens up into longer bends and straights as it coils through the mountainous panorama of Glen Shiel. The Five Sisters of Kintail flash by on the right and, soon afterwards, the romantic, slender walled castle of Eilean Donan on the left. Then on to the Kyle of Lochalsh, where a small car ferry once crossed to Skye, making the adventure more authentic, but where now in its place the sleek, if controversial, Skye Bridge carries the road directly onto the island. Up ahead, the steep profiles of the Red Cuillins show stage presence as the road meanders beneath them along the kelp-ridden shoreline.

Only at Sligachan do the Black Cuillins first come into view. They are mightier than the Red Cuillins, and their menacing molars grimace darkly at the tourists who pass by on their way to Portree. I turned into Glen Brittle, and the final stretch of road soon passed by the youth hostel, the mountain rescue post and a homely farm shrouded amongst alder, oak and sycamore trees, enclosed by moss and lichen-clad drystone walls. It was more reminiscent of the Lake District than Scotland. Finally, the road bent sharply, petering out at the campsite, the beach and Loch Brittle.

I had little incentive to do anything. The mist was well down and dusk crept guilefully in. I sat in the car, motionless, procrastinating idly, my thoughts stewing in their own pessimism. Then, without warning, I jumped up and tore some equipment from the boot of the car and punched it all awkwardly into my rucksack, slung it on my shoulders, and took to the rocky path that led into Coire Lagan and the night.

Coire Lagan is a magical spot on a fine day, when the lochan, nestling serenely in between the mountains, radiates a mixture of blue and turquoise against the dark, chocolate-coloured spires. The shore is hemmed in with smooth lumps of ice-carved rock and a small, gravel beach on which it is possible to pitch a tent. An array of boulders are strewn randomly, their features tempting you to climb, but for that the price to be paid is bloodied fingertips. Bouldering in the Cuillins is comparable to playing catch with angle grinders.

On the approach, darkness aside, the visibility was down to zero due to a thick, cooling fog that had rolled in and stuck to the landscape like Velcro, making me walk into the lochan unaware. I blindly homed in on the only tent spot available: a flat piece of shaly ground by the water's edge. Within minutes, I lay wrapped up in my sleeping bag, staring at the inner walls of my tent, wondering what the morning might bring. I dozed off lightly, but the tinkling of rain on the flysheet during the night sank my hopes of climbing in the morning.

Morning light filtered through the tent, and I stuck my head out of my nylon shell like an optimistic tortoise. Visibility was down to 100ft. I shot my head back inside with disgust, cursing lamely before curling back into my cosy sleeping bag. I must have slept for a while, but then I became impatient. I started to jot down some route descriptions from the guidebook onto a scrap of paper. Eventually, a ray of sunlight made contact with the tent, energising my cold-blooded reptile state. I dropped the guidebook and scuttled out on all fours into the great arena that is Coire Lagan. I was surrounded on three sides by dark, abrasive mountains, by screes and precipices that made me feel weak. I could sense the fire in the rock, for gabbro is a coarsely crystalline, plagioclase-rich, igneous rock. On the fourth side was an open window that had an unforgettable view westward, down towards a distant coastline.

The serrated summits of Sgurr Alasdair and Sgurr Dearg – the Cuillins' highest peaks – were still sheathed in their scabbards of mist. The clouds were constantly changing their shape and density, allowing blue patches to develop, and this heralded sunshine, heat and hope. My eagerness to climb began to increase as the sun warmed the air. It was still too cold to climb out of the sun, but I knew that the South Buttress of Sgurr Dearg receives the sun in the morning, and I remembered that there was an unclimbed arête up there, something I had noticed some years previously. I turned round and looked up towards the buttress - there it was; a beautifully clean blade of gabbro, with the morning light casting its shadow onto the wall behind, sharpening its edge.

I started to grow uncontrollably excited about the prospect of soloing such a fine arête, but I was nervous too, asking myself many questions that I didn't have the answers to. That was always the way when I was about to solo into the realms of the unknown. I began walking towards the buttress, climbing up over loose, aggravating scree. Reaching the base of the cliff, I stumbled upon a strange, lime-green patch of springy moss. Once I'd caught my breath, I could hear the soothing sound of a spring burbling beneath my feet. Somewhat ominously the adjacent route is called *Styx:* the river separating this world from the underworld.

I wasn't wholly convinced about ancient mythology, but could it be that the arête was my line between the living and the dead? I didn't really care because the magnetic appeal of climbing this was far greater than the risk of the consequences if it all went wrong; that was just how my mindset was fixed. I sat down, prepared myself, and began to feel humble; a rock *hobo* with nothing apart from two sticky rubber shoes and a chalk bag full of quite possibly the wrong sort of white powder for the adventure ahead. Without further ado, I pulled on and followed a slender basaltic dyke for 30ft until I was able to stop on a toehold and collect my thoughts. I looked around and absorbed the cruelly-jagged amphitheatre of mountains surrounding me, uncaring and oblivious to my amoebic form's mortality.

I stepped off the friendly toehold and onto an intricate wall of rough, miniscule holds. I read and performed the sequences carefully, moving slowly, edging ever closer to the salvation of a fat hold on the arête. I grabbed it and clung on like a mariner clutching the mast of his sinking ship. The arête soared upwards; I was now committed to it, but I had no idea if there were enough positive holds up there. The little, green oasis of moss crept further away as I climbed on . . . the gods were obviously looking down favourably from their rocky precipices - positive hold followed positive hold until I reached a sit-down ledge at 100ft. The remaining 100ft were fluent on slabs of warm, rough rock.

On the descent, I began to run down over the surface of the scree, causing a turbulent river of rock. Its grinding echo broke the silence of the mountains. My ankles were battered and blood spilled into my socks; I didn't stop, however, until my momentum had receded at the lochan. By then the sky had ripened into a deep shade of blue. I found a sheltered spot on a glaciated lump and I lay down, gazing at the textures of the gabbro and the quartz veins that ran through it. It wasn't long before the keen edge of the April wind brought my geological deliberation to a halt, waking my body from spiralling lethargy.

I urged myself to move on to Sron na Ciche even though the sun still hadn't arced sufficiently across the western sky to animate the expansive, 1,000ft high cliff. In the late afternoon, this cliff, riddled with history, reveals its age through the shadows that are cast on it, highlighting the routes like wrinkles: *Cioch Direct* (1907) was the first wrinkle to appear and nearly fifty years later, *Trophy Crack* (1956) appeared. The face has many wrinkles and many more yet to come.

I sat down in a sheltered spot to soak up the afternoon sun, but I soon grew impatient with the Earth's slow rotation. I picked myself up and started to climb *Cioch Grooves:* a 500ft route that would lead onto the rock terrace below the Cioch and ultimately to *Trophy Crack*. The first pitch was wet in places; it was, however, easy movement on clean rock up a gradually steepening slab scored with cracks. The thin traverse on the second pitch was more positive than expected, after which I climbed with speed and confidence, although a couple of rough jams tore at my knuckles, ripping skin and leaving some bloody mementos in the cracks' innards. The cracks disappeared, and the slab tapered off onto the flatter terrace beneath the Cioch: a 60ft high 'breast' of gabbro piercing out of the cliff, 600ft above the valley floor.

Arrow Route lies between the terrace and the Cioch, suspended like a giant gothic mural. It is a perfect piece of low-angled rock that instils fear in all climbers who can operate at the given grade of 'very difficult'. This grade in the modern day idiom means 'straightforward', but this is patently not the case. Back in the summer of 1987, Sparky and I stood beneath this route, quavering at the thought of leading up there - exposed, with no protection and no holds. It looked insane. We were adamant that the guidebook must have been misprinted, and we shelved it for *Slab Corner* because it looked a far safer way to summit the Cioch.

I chose my own path up the slab, climbing between dimples and contours of finest gabbro. Even though the holds were positive and the tilt of the slab compassionate, I felt exposed and very aware of the rocky carnage that surrounded me. At the top, there was an airy scramble along a narrow spine of rock leading to the summit of the Cioch. It was here that Sir Sean Connery and Christopher Lambert had been sword fighting in the atmospherically filmed 'Highlander'. I lay down and took a short rest to absorb the atmosphere on what must be one of the most exposed, coveted and regal summits in the British Isles. It is a place to romanticise, one where dreams are won and lost. I wavered, trying to embrace concepts of happiness, to harmonise peacefulness with the geological landscape.

Sunshine glanced over my skin, but it wasn't warm enough to send me to sleep.

Instead my eye was drawn straight up the line of *Trophy Crack*. The route was still in the shade, but I could not control my anxiety any longer. It was time to climb. I slid from the smooth summit contours and scrambled over to a pleasant, grass platform that lay at the base of the route; weirdly it gave me peace of mind - a haven amongst hostilities. The start was steep and powerful, and after 50ft of sustained, positive climbing it was clear that it was far more strenuous than I had expected. A wry smile stole across my face as I recalled that this was a Pat Walsh route.

I had met Pat Walsh at Richard McHardy's home on the Black Isle. I had first got to know Richard when he had taught me Rope Access up at the 'shed'. I barely had two pennies to rub together, and turned up for my five-day course with the intention of sleeping in my car and eating muesli, bread and tuna for the week. I chatted vigorously about climbing, and Richard and his wife Barbara had enjoyed my company and gave me board and lodgings for the week. They are incredibly caring and welcoming towards me. Richard and Barbara were hosting a party for Paul Ross who was emigrating to the United States, and the house was full of climbing gurus from the sixties, including Pat. Paul was ranting about my generation, making it clear that in his day climbers were braver, as they had very little rock protection and sub-standard gear on their climbs. Richard was probably the strongest and bravest of them all with solos of *Carnivore* in Glencoe, *Vector* at Tremadog, and *Chartreuse* on Scafell, amongst many others. These absolutely heroic feats of audacity and ability in the 1960s and 1970s would still be substantial solo challenges forty years on. Tales of a 130ft leader fall from the top of *T.Rex* at Gogarth and a ground fall from *Ribstone Crack* in Llanberis pass when his belayer had to push his brains back into his holed skull were casual gossip to Richard. He recounted the first ascent of his über gritstone route at Millstone: *Edge Lane*. Unprotected and gripped, 50ft above the quarry floor, he demonstrated how he crazily slung his legs over the holds . . . I shook my head at the madness of it all. Those were the days of unsung bravery, when diets consisted of brews, alcohol and fags. In our more mollycoddled, modern climbing world, our biggest worry is missing the bouldering pad during a session on the boulders, or catching pleurisy at the indoor climbing wall.

Richard introduced me to Pat, who was sitting quietly in the corner drinking whisky. He seemed to be a jovial sort; stocky, with grey hair, an old school chequered shirt and thick glasses. He looked really strong, particularly for a seventy year old, and I could imagine him arm wrestling and breaking ulnas, using his malt as a general anaesthetic to ease their pain. Although short, he was larger than life, and if I had had more nerve to ask questions, I am sure that a river laden with sagas would have flowed from him. However, *Trophy Crack* seemed to reflect his squat, muscular build - a little deceiving and traditionally powerful.

I climbed past an old piece of white tat, possibly a sign of a previous retreat, and I looked down to place my feet on some fine scoops in the rock just as the glare from the sun reflected back off the *Arrow Route* slab, now sheathed in sunlight 150ft below me. I soaked in the atmosphere and the space around me before leisurely engaging in the exposed top pitch, nearly 1,000ft above the valley floor.

My happiness on completion was curtailed by the persistence of an icy wind that had become relentless and that was stopping me from becoming too lazy. I moved on to the west face of Sgurr Sgumain, which glinted in the afternoon light. The guidebook's recommended route is called *The Klondyker*. It is five pitches long. I slipped my handwritten description into my trousers and set off.

The rock, so atypical of Skye, was impeccably solid, and I climbed free of worry until halfway through the second pitch. Things started to go wrong. I wasn't able to decipher my notes and relate them to the rock in front of me, and the line in which I was supposed to climb looked devoid of any holds. I heard voices echoing around the Coire and it took me some time to locate five people at the lochan, all looking up at me. To them, I was a mere blot of colour amidst a dark, 700ft face of rock. To me, they were irrelevant. Not wishing to give them any cause for concern and scare them witless, I shuffled down onto a small shelf of rock and meditated for a while. I was in no apparent rush. I stared down over the gliding slopes of the Eilean and watched how they diffused into the glimmering sea and then on to infinity. No finer country in the world than Scotland, when the weather is good, I mused.

Ten minutes later, it was back to reality. The line of holds that I had initially thought was the way trailed out left and blanked out; but another set of holds dictated my movement straight up. I had lost my rhythm and had grown a little ruffled. A roof felt awkward and unhelpful. A poor hand jam wobbled insecurely in its seat and caused tension in my stomach; my footholds were positive, curbing my fears a little. One move at a time - I reached out to clasp some loving laybacks and I pulled onto a terrace before fumbling in my pocket for my description. I memorised the last three pitches (250ft) before swinging off the terrace and onto the edge of a massive void. The exposure held me in a motionless trance for a number of seconds. I felt very mortal, clinging there on the edge of an incredibly fragile world. Big holds materialized one after another, making for the most exposed 'very severe' pitch I had ever climbed in the mountains. At the top of the climb, my feet were swimming inside my boots. I sat on some warm, angular boulders, took my boots off, and using a small nugget of rock, I scraped all the sweat and dead skin out of both boots before rubbing my feet appreciatively over some pumice textured rock.

I gazed across the rocky mountainside to a 250ft high, rectangular shaped, pristine face, partly in sunlight and partly shaded at its right hand edge as it blended into an acute line of grooves. The face seemed unique for the Cuillins – it was positively smooth and glowing with a dull, silvery hue. Now I was in a dilemma; I was exhausted and worn out from climbing, but the beautiful evening was leaving me with no option other than to climb more.

A vague line of cracks up the left side of the wall was nagging at my subconscious: *Vulcan Wall*. Sixteen years previously, the mention of this route had put the fear of god into both Sparky and me; we both wanted to climb it but at the time we had neither the confidence nor the ability to attempt such a route. This route was first climbed in 1957 by Hamish MacInnes. To us, he was a Scottish climbing legend whose mountaineering and mountain rescue feats were famous. So *Vulcan Wall* didn't bode well for a couple of teenagers still learning the ropes.

I wanted to solo *Vulcan Wall*. I started to walk towards the buttress, eyeing the stunning line. I had only climbed one route on the wall, four years before in a lovely 9pm glow, and that was the central line of *Uhuru* with Hui Li. Hui Li was a quiet, sweet and discreetly tenacious Singaporean girl who had never seen snow, had never been in a mountain environment, nor had she climbed on traditional gear prior to her visit to Scotland. She climbed cat-like, smooth and precisely, dressed in pink lycra shorts and a white T shirt, competently moving up one of the finest wall climbs in Scotland, whilst two more traditional types watched in admiration from the confines of the *Vulcan Wall* belay ledge.

It took me ten minutes to reach the base of the Vulcan wall, and I felt so free and excited about soloing it. The rock radiated with comfort and it looked and felt trustworthy. I cherished the moment, wiped my boots with the palm of my hand, pulled on and was immediately sucked upwards. The ground fell away with ease and shortly I returned into a horizontal world wanting more. It was over all too soon. My stomach began to groan with neglect and emptiness, and I felt faint as my blood sugar lowered, so I descended the gully and returned to my tent for food.

Cheese, oatcakes, beetroot and tuna were on my *à la carte* menu for my ailing body. It deserved better, but I tended not to bother with cutlery, stoves or hot meals on these short trips in the mountains, and I didn't drink tea or coffee. It was a great way to force myself into a detox for a few days. I lay with the tent door open, staring up and gazing at the stars and constellations – Ursa Major, Ursa Minor . . . Ursula Andress; that was about my limited knowledge of the heavens – until the wind picked up, buffeted the tent, and rendered me sleepless.

After a night that dragged on forever, the darkness eventually gave way to more defined shapes with the approaching dawn. It was time to get up and head over the ridge to the Coireachan Ruahda face. The Rotten Gully descent lived up to its name, but I found it calm and sheltered over on the east face of the Cuillin Ridge. I stood there, very silent, sizing up the massive cliffs and the blatantly obvious unclimbed lines; it looked like the cliff that time had forgotten. I traversed round to the foot of *King Cobra* and *Dawn Grooves*, and here the cliff looked menacing, far more so than I had ever anticipated. I was drawn more to *King Cobra* because it was heralded as one of Skye's best routes.

The mountains felt eerily quiet; only the squawk of a distant raven – the guardians of the Cuillins - and the faint murmuring of distant streams made any sound. The morning had a melancholic feel as wafer-thin cloud had partially blotted out the weak morning sunshine. I didn't know the time; I had no need to know, but it could not have been much past six. The sun had barely risen above the peaks of the distant

Red Cuillins - I was barely awake, and my legs felt like pulp. I needed a reprieve, but I knew I wasn't going to give myself one. I was tough on myself, always had been. It was the way I had been brought up, to feel that I was never good enough or tough enough. My school motto was *Plus est en Vous* ('there is more in you'); that sort of summed it up. So, without much hesitation, I shoved the route description into my pants, tied my laces, and chalked my hands in a kind of pre soloing ritual. I started to climb into a mass of spooky-looking, shattered basalt for 150ft, feeling like a soldier on the front line, ordered to run into the enemy's line of fire without a gun.

At 150ft, the line started to take more shape as the loose nonsense gelled into a square-cut corner with large holds. The vastness of the cliff, its remoteness, and my predicament dictated a level of fear in me that made me shake and lurch for holds. I felt humbled and pathetic, and it was probably going to get worse. I persuaded myself to get a grip; otherwise I would lose it, lose it all . . .

At the top of the square-cut corner, I swung right around a rib and onto the infamous ledge at the base of the crux groove, described by Tom Patey in *One Man's Mountains* as, 'a sloping foothold, large enough for a roosting seagull.' I perched there, quite aware of the 200ft of free space beneath my feet, shaking uncontrollably. I tried to breathe slowly through my stomach to calm myself, trying to deduce the easiest sequence up the smooth, open book corner of rock. There were two rust-coloured stains in the thin crack that lined the corner – perhaps the site of the original pegs used by Tom Patey and Sir Chris Bonington (1960). I began to build a picture in my head of the two stalwarts hammering home those long lost relics, before doing battle with the groove – an impressive climb for its time.

My imagination was running riot - my subconscious snapped me back to reality. I had to negotiate a blank groove over 200ft up with no ropes, no back up plan and a body akin to a sapling blowing in a force eight gale. Aware that retreat was no longer a sane option, I decided to shuffle down to a ledge, twenty feet below. Here I could sit down, take my boots off and calm down. This ledge was where I learned that yoga meditation methods did not work when one was shaking with uncontrollable fear . . .

Presently I climbed back up to the groove and became somewhat flummoxed - I didn't want to trust pressing the soles of my feet directly onto the glass-smooth rock.

I wouldn't have thought twice about it had I been attached to a rope. I needed to build up confidence, and that took a little time and calmness. Eventually I committed and pressed into the corner, secured by body tension rather than positive holds. The exposure was indescribable, as were the potential consequences . . . I went into slow motion, and my breathing seemed to stop entirely. I wanted to climb down to the security of the ledge, but I just couldn't. I had lost all of my faculties apart from that of basic survival. My left hand slapped at an outward side pull ('gaston') in the wall of the groove. This move enabled my legs to flex into a higher position, allowing me to reach some better holds. Suddenly my rhythm cut in, like a turbo-charger sucking in air, and I fired up the groove in a rush, leaving behind me a wake of fear.

To my dismay, the groove fused out into another soul-humbling shattered basalt ledge. If I had been tied on with ropes, I could have relaxed in safety now and enjoyed the exposure, the atmosphere, the views to the rugged profile of Blaven and the finely tapered hills of the Red Cuillins. With no security though, my senses were ultra alert. I had no time to relax, and my mind was too overwrought to appreciate the scenery. I inhaled deeply and took a look down at the once car-sized boulders at the base of the cliff, which now looked to be the size of pebbles on a storm beach.

An overhang loomed menacingly above. I took out my notes, hoping that my pencilled scrawl wasn't going to direct me to go up through there. If it did, I wasn't sure that I would make it. Thankfully my notes informed me that I should traverse under the overhang and round the corner into another system of hidden grooves. I climbed on, not dwelling too much on what lay above.

For a further 300ft, I treated every hold with tenderness; one loose hold would spell disaster. Eventually the cliff lay back as I reached the safety of the main Cuillin Ridge. My relief overrode any sense of achievement. No one had warned me about soloing *King Cobra*, possibly because I didn't know of anyone who had done it, and maybe also because I hadn't asked anyone. But one thing was for sure; the term 'classic' certainly took on a whole new meaning.

I sat on the spine of the Cuillin Ridge and glanced along the length and over to Sgurr nan Gillean, the ridge's most northern tooth, and my last Munro some sixteen years previously. The fresh wind didn't entice me to hang around. I quickly threaded my way down ledge systems and loose gullies, eventually regaining the base of the route. I sat down on a huge boulder, took my sweaty boots off and stared incredulously at the 600ft cliff of tottering rock. The mid morning light revealed its true nature. I followed the line I had just soloed and shook my head, muttering the word *lunatic* . . .

I scrambled around to the infamous Thearlaich Dubh gap - one of the technical sections on the main Cuillin Ridge traverse. I passed through the gap to reach the southern flanks of Sgurr Alasdair. I came upon a buttress with a handful of recommended, short routes; I dug out a few boulders to make a flattish patch, enough to squeeze out of the wind, catch some sun and give my body half an hour of peace.

The Asp is a chimney crack-line that I found appealing. Jamming and weird body contortions encouraged . . . then at 50ft my fleece caught on a loose spike of rock on the back wall of the chimney. It broke off and went splintering to the ground. I'd had enough scary moments that morning to last me a lifetime, so I descended and sloped off in the direction of my tent. It was time for a siesta and some food before committing to one final adventure.

For most of the afternoon, I lazed about and spent time watching the sun suspending itself over the western horizon. I half expected it to lose its orbit and plummet directly down into the ocean. Even though the orb was ninety three million miles away with a temperature that didn't bear thinking about, I still felt I could pluck it from the sky like a satsuma. After some time, I tied my chalk bag round my waist, stuffed my rock boots down the front of my jacket, creating my own pair of *ciochs*, and then made haste for the Eastern Buttress and *Spock*. The wall came into view, glowing weakly in the spring sunshine. I leapt across the scree slope, only the crunching of boulders rubbing against one another breaking the silence. At the base of the cliff, feeling quite tense, I slowly stuffed my feet into my overly tight boots, tied my laces, untied and then tied again. Once this rigmarole had been completed, I stepped up to face the challenge.

An overhanging flake in the arête bulged down towards me with distantly enticing holds. I grabbed onto the familiar, rough surface and powered upwards into another world of unknown destinies. The steepness of the rock made my blood flow suddenly and urgently. The wall relented and became more delicate. It was clean and honest; as near to perfection as rock climbing could be in Scotland. At 120ft, I reached a foothold beneath a small overlap, and here the deep void beneath my feet made its presence felt. I had to negotiate an awkward rockover, but instead of experiencing fear, I experienced an odd inner happiness.

I brought my foot up to my waist and poked my toe onto a minute kerb of rock. As I began to push my weight onto it, my thoughts were of a gazelle bounding through the long, golden grass of the savannah, being chased by a lion: both creatures' muscles rippling like finely tuned biomechanical pistons until the gazelle faltered between the lion's two hydraulic paws, crumpling and dying gracefully. In my dangerous world of rock, I was well aware that my predator was invisible, odourless and equally unforgiving. Then I heard the eerie noise of the distinct squawk of a raven – the opportunist. My thoughts made me teeter as I visualized myself lying on the ground, broken but conscious, an opportunity for the raven to swoop down beside me and mock me with its funny dance before scooping my eyes out with its beak.

With as much concentration as I could muster, I moved slowly upwards in a state of relief. The final 80ft were comfortable, and I enjoyed the spoils of my audacity. I didn't linger for long on the top though and the voracity of the scree descent angered my toes. I wanted to sit at the base of that wall forever and just coexist peacefully with the amphitheatre and the timeless view, but hunger finally drove me home to the tent. On the way there, I made the fatal mistake of glancing back at the wall one last time. And there I saw it, the *perfect* line up the centre: the lower crack of *Dilemma* linked by the spidery cracks *(Cling On)* into the top crack of *Uhuru*.

As dusk settled and I was lying belly up in the tent, it felt strange to be watching someone climbing upside down in near darkness on *Slab Corner*. But the can of worms inside my head could think only about soloing the link of *Dilemma* and *Uhuru* . . . *'Diuru'* . . . I had already inadvertently planned my return.

Although it was just a few spits, the rain wasn't imaginary - it was very real. I knew that within seconds my world would fall apart - the rock would be useless, my mind would implode, my body would begin to flail and slip . . .

My right hand was arcing blindly for a finger hold. I had reached no-man's land, staring down 100ft into a black hole of my own creation. Suddenly, my fingers brushed over a cusp. It wasn't positive, but that was all there was, so I pulled hard on its intricacies, and I played out the craziest foot manoeuvres. It was theatrical, more desperate than balletic, but somehow the sequence moved me into balance.

I wished it was over; I wasn't halfway up the wall yet, and it wasn't relenting. I just couldn't see myself surviving the next hour; it would be a miracle if I did. I tried to see Cubby, who had come along to photograph my ascent, but even he was invisible amongst the talus, nonchalantly twisting his lens in and out of focus, unaware of what I was going through. I felt guilty because if I fell he was the one who was going to have to deal with the detritus and the long, lonely walk to 'call the chiropractor!' . . . nightmares, flashbacks . . .

There was no rope, no chance of rescue. He was an innocent party, and I was glad he was too far away to realise that I was on the edge of meltdown. There was no point in scaring him unnecessarily by shouting for help; what could he do anyway? No, I was on my own, and that was the best way; it had always been that way . . .

I frantically hunted out the next sequence of holds. Then a small ledge appeared where I rested my heels and could at least breathe again, but it was false security. The spits of rain had ceased, but the skies still held a threat. Some holds led leftwards to beneath the final finger crack of *Uhuru*. With a sense of renewed hope, I moved into the crack, but it was wet! For fifteen minutes, I tried futilely to powder the wet sections with copious quantities of chalk, but again demoralising and dangerous spits of rain fell from the skies in random spirals.

My subconscious threw it all in, and I climbed fast and decisively for the final 30ft. I reached the top with a profound feeling of shock and relief, empty at the damaged sense of achievement. I had passed the realms of the aesthetics and began to have distinct concerns about the point of it all, in such a beautiful and wild place.

Icon of Lust

Failing my A levels was inevitable, so I went on to resit them at South Cheshire College in Crewe. In between my studies, I climbed a little in the Peak District, the Lake District and North Wales, with the South Cheshire Climbing Club. I managed to lead up to HVS ('hard very severe') standard. I wanted to return to Scotland because, having read about it in Ken Wilson's book, 'Hard Rock', I had become characteristically obsessive about one particular route - *The Needle* on the Shelterstone. Climbed in 1962 by the very talented Robin Smith, it was the first route in the Cairngorms to receive a rating of Extreme. It forged a way straight up the front of the 800ft high Bastion on the Shelterstone Crag. It was harder than anything I had done before; the challenge would be a formidable one and one that I would relish.

I passed my exams and made the trip to Scotland, teaming up with Robin Whitworth, a friend from school. We camped near Loch Avon, waiting for our chance to climb *The Needle*. We were there for a week, and the Shelterstone Crag drooped, grey and destitute in the mist. We lay in the tent with the rain beating down on the flysheet. Having only one guidebook between us for reading material, we played a game of guess the route. One of us would read part of a route description and the other would have to guess what it was. One morning there was a break in the weather, simply a patch of blue sky, but enough for us to reach halfway up the 2nd pitch before it rained again. We headed out, bedraggled and defeated - the romance had somewhat gone.

A year later: 'Hard Rock' was out and 'Extreme Rock' was in, and especially the picture of Murray Hamilton stepping delicately out onto the blank granite of *Missing Link*, hands on insignificant features and ropes spilling in gentle arcs. I wanted to be there - on those same smears - feeling the fear, controlling it, playing a game of nerves on such beautiful rock. And I did get my chance, with Mike Francis. We had no right to be there. The climb was too hard for us, but we were both young and brave. The next lead was mine; moving out from the belay there were no holds or gear - it was where Murray had been in that picture. Stay cool, step up, trust, step, step, the rock is clean, sweeping away in two dimensions. I clipped a couple of pitons and continued . . . and then it all started to go wrong. Ahead, the smooth sheet of crystalline granite steepened into a foiling awkwardness, giving away none of its secrets and unforgivingly tossing me down its cruel, rough surface. I yelped and closed my eyes until I felt the twine-like security of my two ropes tugging at my harness, rendering me safe. With some concern, I shot a glance up the line of ropey tension to the downward pointing piton from which I was suspended. I pulled up the rope and tried again . . . and again . . . the piton still holding firm.

Sunlight had disappeared from the surrounding plateau; shadows crept in as my confidence leaked out. I glanced down to Mike on the belay. His expression wasn't one of worry but rather of amusement at my cloth ripping falls.

'Are you ok?' he asked with a grin.

'Yeah, I'm fine,' I replied, reluctant to relinquish the lead. I pulled hand-over-hand up the rope to the piton again, for a fourth time, determined to succeed.

Sighing heavily, I looked around, absorbing the darkening arena, authenticated by the perpetual echo of tumbling melt water. On the one hand, I felt demoralised, but on the other I felt free and happy, testing my limited technique on the unorthodox granite of the Shelterstone's Central Slabs.

Back again; 15ft above the security of the piton, my body was being channelled into the same compulsory sequence as before. I half froze, anticipating another skin-tearing arc down the slab, but this time I was still on and reached better holds. I secured a big nut before scampering youthfully along a hollow flake, followed with an awkward pull to the belay. I hauled in the ropes with both relief and contentment, having secured my first route on the Shelterstone. Mike followed rapidly and we abseiled off into the gathering gloom.

We bivvied on the beach at the head of Loch Avon under a clear sky: it was windless and the midges were becoming a nuisance. At an early hour, I propped myself up on my elbows and gazed at the charcoal shapes of the mountains silhouetted against the dawning-hue, their reflection varnished onto the surface of the loch.

Daylight slowly intensified, and the heat of the morning sun induced apathy. We sunbathed and swam. It was cold. I kept looking up at the turret of the Shelterstone, standing as a loyal sentry, and I became fascinated with the vertical potency of the Bastion, and even more so with the smooth, seductive features of the Central Slabs.

Later that afternoon, when the shadows had drifted over the beach, we gathered our ropes and harnesses and headed for *Steeple* – an 800ft line of corners up the main Bastion. It is the sister route to *The Needle* - a notch harder perhaps and possibly a touch better quality too.

It was late evening when Mike set off up the final open-book corner. Rays of sunshine emerged out of nowhere and bathed us in gentle warmth, illuminating us out of the surrounding shadows. Mike made effortless work as I struggled to pay out the disobedient ropes in rhythm with his upward movement. Within minutes he was out of sight, the ropes snaked out and pulled tightly. It was my turn. We both sat on top, spellbound. The view down the loch, the peace of the mountains, the company, the fun and the freedom of youth made for a memory that will last my lifetime. In total contrast to the previous year of constant rain, the Shelterstone had now stoked my desire for many return visits, and it became my favourite spiritual home.

Three years later: My finals exams at Aberdeen University were to start in the morning. If only I could revise Geochemistry as well as I did the guidebook, then I would surely attain a first class degree. I was on course to barely scrape a two-two. Instead of revising, I was on the Shelterstone starting the main pitch of *Run of the Arrow*, originally climbed by the bold and legendary Pete Whillance. A head crammed full of Basin Analysis and Paleontology didn't leave much commitment for a route described in the guidebook as 'a modern desperate'. My head was minced, and I duly backed off.

Matt 'The Cat' Ingham and I returned to *Run of the Arrow* for another attempt, after my finals. Matt tried first - with his agility and easy-going flair he climbed fluently up to the flake, 70ft above the belay. The crux followed and, not finding the large nut to protect this section, he somewhat casually took some 20ft falls. On reaching the belay, he abseiled down, stripped the gear and pulled the rope for me. His chalked holds instilled confidence as I committed to the tricky lower section to reach a natural line of steps in the granite – easy for 40ft. The steps petered out at a flat handhold where, once home to the infamous 'welded nuts', a tiny parallel-sided slot hoodwinked me. Now nothing fitted. A slab of moderate difficulty had to be crossed to reach the flake. A slip here meant a 100ft fall; it was truly frightening. My mental state was poor, possibly due to my time at University coming to an end and not knowing where my life was going – a period of uncertainty. My commitment slowly drained away, as did the contents of my chalk bag. My only option was to climb down the steps and fall the remaining 30ft onto my assortment of RPs (tiny, soldered brass wedges, roughly the size of a pine nut).

Once I had reached the point where I could no longer down-climb, the idea of 'just' falling frightened me. I felt humiliated and stuck. Somehow I found a dubious looking crack in the granite that took a tiny nut. I repeatedly tugged it to make sure it was firm. Matt took up the tension in the rope; I spread-eagled myself on the rock, closed my eyes, let go and shouted . . . 'lower!' I slid down the rock, waiting for the nut to pop. It held and I escaped, thoroughly traumatised. When I returned four years later to climb *Run of the Arrow* with Sue Harper, I couldn't even find that nut placement - an illusion found in desperation perhaps.

Ever since I had seen the picture of Murray climbing the *Missing Link,* my eyes had been drawn to the beautifully curving, sickle-shaped groove behind him. Without a doubt, it is the most gracious line in the mountains of Scotland, if not in the whole of the UK. It curved into *Missing Link* and ended up adrift in the middle of the slabs. I couldn't understand why it hadn't been climbed.

I left Scotland after University, but I constantly referred to the photos in 'Extreme Rock' in order to link the sickle-shaped groove with a blank slab above *Thor*. I soon read in the climbing press that Rick 'The Stick' Campbell had succeeded in climbing the sickle-shaped groove and named it *Realm of the Senses*. I felt rather homesick, and this news urged me to return to the Shelterstone. The following year, Rick climbed the blank slab above *Thor*, and rumour has it he scared himself stupid on the ascent. When he returned to his tent in the meadow, he proposed to his now wife, Sarah, and gave up bold slab climbing. *L'Elisir d'Amore* was a fitting romantic ending to Rick's involvement with the Shelterstone.

It was hard for me to find climbing partners to accompany me. It was quite a big commitment, and it entailed a two-hour walk from the Cairngorm ski lift car park. Additionally, being at an altitude of 3,000ft in the middle of the Cairngorm massif, the crag was frequently enveloped in mist. The two keenest Shelterstone devotees were Rick and his main climbing partner over the years, Paul 'The Stork' Thorburn. Known as Sticky and Storky, their climbing partnership gelled into a Scottish *tour-de-force* in the mid 1990s. Their spoils covered Scotland, and when one failed, the other would succeed - it was symbiosis and harmony.

On this occasion, I met up with Rick in the meadow at the base of the crag. He had climbed everything on the slabs, but was quite keen to hold my ropes on one of his climbs.

'Which of the three routes do you want to climb today, Julian?' Rick asked in his well-spoken tongue - like me, Rick had gone to public (or is that private?) school.

'Err . . . I'm keen to try *Realm* . . . and link it with *L'Elisir* . . . '. Rick was a little disappointed with my decision; he had hoped I was going to try his most coveted route: *Aphrodite*.

With Rick on belay, I set to the beautiful groove of *Realm* . . . I felt unfit and a little intimidated by the fact that Rick was obediently holding my ropes. I struggled with the puzzling dynamics and angles of the groove. Rick's fresh wit mellowed the moment as he made a jocular comment about my ballooning forearms. Higher up, the groove almost dissolves away - my body tension needed to be precise to equalise the geometry. Rick was shouting something . . . my centre of gravity was wrong. I fought it, but the moment had gone; I peeled off onto some RPs.

'Julian, your rock boots are falling apart; you can't climb in those.' Rick laughed.

'But they are my favourites.' I said defensively, even though there was fresh air circulating around my toes. On my second attempt, I got the body tension right and moved up under the overlap and a brief rest.

'Pinch the lip of the overlap and traverse left onto a foothold', Rick advised, trying to be helpful. This doesn't actually work for me as I am not 6' 2" like Rick. Instead, I tried to climb entirely on the slab's crystalline surface, falling numerous times, and eventually retreating. To console ourselves, we decided to climb the 800ft *Stone Bastion*. Only the top two pitches were supposedly of worth, so we raced up the lower pitches of *The Needle*. I was sitting on a ledge 500ft up, below 'the crack for thin fingers', pulling in the ropes, when in the distance I heard the familiar deep-bass roar of a Sea King. It emerged at the head of the glen and headed straight for us.

The helicopter pulled broadside, opposite Rick down below - the door was pulled open, and the winch man was smiling and clapping his hands. The door then pulled closed, and the helicopter disappeared down the glen and was gone. I was baffled. What was all that about?

When Rick climbed up to the stance, I asked . . . 'What was all the clapping for?'

'The helicopter flew in close to see if we were in trouble, so I entertained them with the Highland fling on the belay ledge,' Rick said with a grin, rather pleased with his performance.

The next opportunity I had to climb on the Shelterstone was the following summer. I had a four-week break from working in the shipyards in Singapore. I was generally fit, but worn out and hadn't been climbing for months. Stork was available to climb, so we set our sights on linking *Realm* . . . and *L'Elisir* . . . Stork had been climbing loads and was very much in tune with the technicalities of the granite. He climbed *Realm* . . . with only one fall. Then the onus was on me to lead the bold slab pitch above. Some water streaks striped the slab and ended our attempt.

The day before my departure to Singapore, we decided to try *Aphrodite*. It was climbed by Rick in 1990 and became the hardest climb in the Cairngorms. Essentially it goes through a big overlap into *Run of the Arrow* and continues directly and boldly up the slab above. The stories that circulated of Rick - climbing into the unknown, his rope being too short, and additionally a very thin 60ft run-out - sort of persuaded everyone to stay clear. We had come to the arrangement that Stork was to lead the short, overlap pitch at the start, and I was to lead the big slab pitch. This time I had an air of confidence as I spent little time dwelling on the consequences of the 100ft fall on the *Run of the Arrow* section. I grabbed the flake and fumbled in the gear. *Aphrodite* now led straight up through a steepening in the slab on discreet edges and seams. I took a deep breath and committed to a sustained sequence on tiny, positive holds that all fitted neatly together, and then, to my surprise, I found myself eyeballing the slender ledge that marks the end of the hard section. I reached up for the hold. My fingers curled onto it. The excitement of success was unbearable - the tension drained from my legs; my feet slipped, and I was ripped from it, denied. I rattled down the slab for 35ft until I bounced to a stop. I was so annoyed with myself. On the second attempt I made no mistakes. Standing in balance, there was nothing but a sea of granite, albeit covered with positive edges, but it was so hard to commit to them. It took twenty minutes for me to gather the required mental kinetic energy to leave the hospitality of the slender ledge and climb, way, way from the gear. Involuntary shaking increased as I approached the good holds and gear, looking at an 80ft fall. Stork and I both thought *Aphrodite* wasn't too hard, although we both felt it to be a very prestigious piece of very bold slab climbing, now sadly neglected.

I didn't return to the Shelterstone for two years. Some years the weather can be dreadful in the Cairngorms, not only for a day, but for a whole season, and it is demoralising. However, on this particular day as I crept out of the tent, I found, to my delight, full sun. I knew that this *was* the day. The sky did not have a cloud in it, the boulders radiated heat and the alpine flowers in the meadow were vibrant with colour. I looked up to see the slabs soaked in sunlight. Now all I had to do was awaken Stork - easier said than done.

Somehow the tables had been reversed since I had last climbed with Stork. He had found himself a girlfriend, had a haircut, taken up paddling and now had regular work. So when Stork led the introductory pitch to *Realm*... he was climbing slowly and nervously.

'Come on Stork, if you don't hurry up I will untie the ropes,' I called over, jibing him. Maybe he thought I was serious because he twitched and gibbered to the belay. I set to the sickle-shaped groove of *Realm*... with confidence. The moves required to solve it, for a short person, were subtle and purely exquisite. Stork followed, tied into the assortment of pitons at the belay. The white streak above *Thor* looked blank. I dabbed chalk on what I thought were the most reliant crystals and clawed up to a flat hold that offered a perfect nut. I pulled at the ropes to make sure they were running smoothly, and without hesitation launched into my own self-inflicted environment of crystals, shallow pockets and nervous tension. High up, my foot slipped... I dramatised the inevitable 60ft fall, but my hands had found the good hold moments before. It still wasn't over - a line of holds curved to a final impasse where a nut was just out of reach. I started to break down under the duress, and in desperation I began bashing an RP into a poor slot with my nut key as tears began to flow. In one last moment of conviction, I focused hard and climbed out onto the turfy finishing ledges, empty of all emotion.

Two years after the link-up - which I nicknamed *Athene* - I was back and toying with the idea of a possible direct line up the slabs – a paragraph of Shelterstone history for myself. I managed to talk Lawrence Hughes into a trip to the Shelterstone.

He was more than keen to accompany me to attempt this line. Lawrence managed the climbing shop in Aviemore. He was young, fun and relaxing to be around; he loved to drive fast, party and play music at full volume - and he called me 'Judge'.

My knees were burning under the sheer mass of two climbing ropes, climbing gear, camping gear and food for a few days as I descended from the summits into the secluded Loch Avon basin. It all seemed worthwhile when I reached my idyllic camping spot down the far side of the loch. It is a tight pitch by a small strip of beach with an adjacent boulder in the water, *the diving board*.

Lawrence was working and said he would turn up later. It was getting dark, and I began to wonder if he had written off his car. Finally, there were footsteps and a voice . . .

'How's it going Judge?'

'Hey man, glad you have turned up.'

'I've brought something for you to help to release your stress.' A couple of Mayfair type magazines were pushed through the flap of the tent. I shook my head and laughed.

The morning was calm, and the Central Slabs glistened like a stone, circular shield. I took a swim, trying to free myself of all inhibitions. I felt ready.

All geared up, I tried an unclimbed pitch straight into the belay on *Realm* . . . finding myself at the final crux move; my position was inescapable, so I rolled onto a high foot, knowing that if I fell I would go 50ft and break my legs. Confidence won through. When Lawrence reached the belay he said . . .

'Judge you're mad. That was awesome!'

I laughed sheepishly, knowing that the outcome could quite easily have been different. Lawrence supplied the snacks before I set to the *Realm* . . . groove. The overlap above was improbable, although strangely there were a couple of tiny holds in the blank slab above, enough to tempt a challenge. I laid siege to it, falling, trying a different position, falling, falling . . . frustration mounting after I had fallen fifteen times. *It must be possible? It must be* . . . I lowered off, humbled, and we climbed *Pin*. Whilst abseiling, I had a look at the overlap and found an easier solution a few feet to the right of where I had been trying. My inspiration had returned, although typically the next day the rain did too.

Lawrence and I returned a few weeks later; however, there were wet streaks on the top slab, so we climbed *Thor*. It is the visible, lucid route on the slabs, and probably the most coveted mountain rock climb of its standard in Scotland. It follows a long, sweeping line of diagonal corners making for a perfect granite experience. First climbed on aid with many pitons, and even a bolt, by Mike Rennie and Greg Strange, it took twenty years until the free ascent by Rick. It provided us with a continually interesting, sometimes awkward, but never too bold route.

Within two days I was back at the overlap, with left foot high and right hand on a crystal; I committed to a heinous move that left me stranded on the upper slab, feeling very scared and lonely. And then, to my astonishment, spits of rain tinkled around me. With curses mixing with fears, I sketched up to the hidden slot 15ft. above, deadly focused on fixing my lifeline (in the form of a tiny cam) into a weird slot. Just as I clipped the rope through the karabiner, rendering myself safe, the clouds unleashed havoc. I hung from the cam as waves of water rippled their way down the granite-plane.

'Why ... why ... ?' I shouted out in anguish. The thought of another failed attempt started to sink in. Then in a moment of utter vexation, I repeatedly banged my head on the slab, shouting . . . 'I hate ******* Scotland!' Blood started to drip from my forehead, mingling with the torrents as it flushed away into the void below.

There was a strange case of trading places going on. Lawrence departed and Richard Biggar turned up. Rich worked in the climbing shop too. He was well to do, reserved, intellectual and difficult to fathom. On the outside, he didn't show much energy towards climbing, but on the inside he was subtly passionate about it.

The wet streaks emerged on the upper slabs after the heavy bout of rain, and I knew that it wouldn't dry out for a few days. So we decided on climbing *The Needle*. Neither of us had done it - ironically, the first route I had attempted on the Shelterstone was going to be one of the last. This was probably because I had it in mind to solo *The Needle*. I had tried to do so once, but it rained, luckily when I was only 80ft up on the first pitch. Rich would obviously enjoy climbing *The Needle*, so we took it at a leisurely pace, enjoying the increasing atmosphere with every pitch. It was a fun mountain climb experience and would have been a severe test if I had had that chance to climb it thirteen years earlier with Robin.

Finally, a few years later there seemed to be a prolonged spell of good weather. Climbing the big routes on the Central Slabs was like playing poker with the Cairngorm Mountain gods. Good weather was the ace in the deck - Stork, keen to hold my ropes, was the King. I suppose Lawrence was the Jack, Rick the self-proclaimed Joker, and I can only hazard a guess at who the Queen was. Anyway, I was ready to play my hand and win.

Back up at the overlap, the tension became unbearable. The thought of failing flooded in. I had been practising one-legged squats for the last two years to ensure I had the ability to get through the overlap. I moved into position, built my feet high, and then left toe by left hand, right hand on a crystal. Push, quadriceps searing under the duress . . . I was on the upper slab awash with bewilderment. I coolly climbed to the cam slot and then set to the blank granite with a mind full of faith. I relaxed as the climbing eased considerably when I reached holds on *Missing Link*, at the exact point where I had fallen three times, fourteen years ago. *No substitute for experience*, I smiled. I made further out of balance moves to reach the *Thor* belay before spinning a web amongst the pitons.

'Climb when ready,' I shouted down to the ever patient Stork.

I wanted to relax now after my success on such a rewarding pitch, but the belay was painfully awkward and didn't inspire relaxation; and still I was only halfway there. Above was a 180ft pitch of dangerous slab climbing. When Stork reached the belay, it was cramped and untidy until we sorted the ropes and gear. I didn't want to leave the security of that tiny alcove, but words rolled round my head . . .

It is now or never.

Sometimes the toughest mental part of a multiple pitch climb is not the crux, but leaving the belay. Leaving the Thor belay was mental; it was also awkward and tenuous. I climbed quickly to a crescent-shaped crack complete with a bull's nose ring piton. I clipped it and momentarily felt safe - this was the last place I would have safety until I reached the belay 150ft above. With my toes stubbed in the crack, I leaned my forehead against the rock, dropped my hands to my sides, closed my eyes and tried to summon calmness. After a number of deep breaths, I engaged clutch and smeared into a selection of vague pockets that soon ran out. I was then staring at a blank slab - it looked impossible, but as with all hard slab climbing, attention to detail is the key to success. I had to study every kerb, every crystal, their dimensions and orientations, chalk them and read a plausible sequence of moves that would work. I set to my braille, shuddering and praying that my body was suited to the sequences I had predicted. It was. I reached a hidden, flat hold, 30ft above the piton. From the temporary comfort of this hold, I stretched blindly to push a tiny cam into a flake. It was worthless but gave me confidence as there was no more gear for 50ft. The red streak was now the line. I cautiously followed it to a foothold at its top. I stood there for eternity, weighing up my mortality, gazing down the slab to find nothing except two tiny ropes spilling down the rock like spaghetti and disappearing. My minds were overheating with the predicament - the moves, the consequences - everything was haywire. The slab above was short, perhaps two moves, but there wasn't a single crystal for the fingers, nothing; I had to totally rely on my feet. I knew the cam, 30ft below, wouldn't hold a fall and the bull's nose was another 30ft below that. If I slipped, I was going to slide straight off the planet. I had one remaining trick up my sleeve; I closed my eyes and tried to fool my subconscious mind into believing that I was soloing. So, when I reopened them and saw the safety of the ropes, my predicament didn't seem so bad after all. I smeared up into the termination scoop, where the top of the slab met a vertical wall. An RP slot was just out of reach. It felt ridiculous being attached to ropes, and I might as well be soloing now. Trembling with panic, I climbed the wall, secured the RP and reached some holds, before moving left and up onto another slab. I was so absorbed in my own world of fear that I hadn't noticed the clouds swirling in until I had realised that specks of rain were making dots in the chalk on the back of my hands. I hadn't a piece of gear below me for 100ft that might be worthy of holding even a brace of pheasants, so I switched off and rushed carefully at the final slab in the drizzle. I pulled onto the belay and sat on my throne, regal, lost in a world of chaos and aspirations - the *Icon of Lust* set in stone forever.

Dreamtime

It was five in the morning. I sat restlessly beside a 150ft cliff that I could not see. My impatience was driving my mind into unfurling yet another lunatic idea. As my eyes adjusted to the dark, I got up and began searching blindly for the chalk-stained starting holds of *Muldoon*. It wasn't a difficult route by any means, and because it was popular, I knew there would be plenty of chalk on it. After a few minutes, I located a heavily chalked line fizzling out into the night sky.

I was eager to climb, but something was holding me back; common sense perhaps. It was like a dare at school. But here my own conscious was daring my subconscious into a nocturnal game of Russian roulette. Risk assessments were being critically analysed. Eventually I decided that if I got stuck, I could either down climb, or hang on for an hour until dawn broke.

I pulled onto the chalked holds and continued, not knowing what size or shape they were until I touched them. *Muldoon* was steep, overhanging even. The holds were big though. I wasn't that concerned because I had no point of reference. Whether I was 5ft or 500ft above the ground, it really made no difference. I had inadvertently found a new dimension of fun. When I reached the summit of the cliff, I felt as though I had created a masterpiece, to be eternally stored in my cranial gallery of experience.

I sat down on a flat stone in the half lotus position and stared into the night sky, gazing at the constellations. Slowly, darkness disappeared; black to inky blue, blue to an apricot hue. The earth spun from its dormancy; silhouettes appeared along with the call of the magpie that drifted out of the trees, hundreds of feet below. The plain beneath me swept away for miles. Washed out colours began to intensify. Then, as the sun bobbed onto the horizon, some lethargic shrouds of fog began to vaporise from around the scattered copses of eucalyptus, and some kangaroos hopped across my screen. My life was blissful as I sat there, absorbing the sense of freedom, the landscape, the sky, the lifestyle and the newfound warmth of the sun in the tranquil morning scene, like a Dalai Lama without destiny . . .

The nightclub was all push and shove, choked with people – chaos ensued as waves of people rippled to and from the bar. I don't like nightclubs, and I never really understood why I frequently ended up in them until the early hours, explicable perhaps in part by the fact that I had a flat by the Somerset tube station, essentially party-central. This time was no different, but I was out on the town with Don Cattanach. Don was a couple of years younger than me, and a party animal. He loved it, and once he started he just didn't stop. We arrived at ten. I was buzzing at the thought of all the Singaporean girls in petite dresses. I had fallen 'in love' with one such girl once. I hadn't known her long, and it was the eve of Valentine's Day. During the middle of the night, I had climbed five stories up her tower block with a bunch of roses in my teeth and left them on her windowsill. The conversation that followed didn't go to plan. First of all, she was concerned that I had climbed the building; it was directly opposite the police station. If I had been caught by the police, then I would have been given a prison sentence and the cane - law and order was tough in Singapore. Moreover, she was upset at the gift of roses, and said that if I really loved her then a Louis Vuitton handbag would have been more appropriate. I always seemed to attract my polar opposites - story of my life. That was the last conversation I ever had with her.

By two in the morning, I was tired and just wanted to go back to the flat and get some sleep before getting up at six for another gruelling twelve-hour shift in the shipyard. I tried to drag Don out, but inevitably he had put on that impish grin of his and told me not to be boring. I realised then that I was in for the duration. Don bought more drinks and began to cause havoc on the dance floor, before persuading the DJ that he should take over playing the tunes. He was a loveable rogue who got away with everything. Sadly, I heard on the grapevine over a decade later that Don had died of a heart attack.

We emerged into Orchard Road at five in the morning. Singapore's busiest street was deserted apart from a few taxis, early morning cleaners, and the odd girl looking for business. The streets were clean, polished even, the wealth so apparent in the buildings and hotels, and crime non-existent. Singapore is a superficially sustained Utopia – a comfortable and safe city, but painfully unaware of its own artifice. We found the truck and headed west towards Jurong – the industrial side of town. I felt awful because I hadn't had any sleep and was facing the prospect of another twelve-hour shift. Don nodded off blissfully in the passenger seat.

We pulled into the shipyard, parked up, and wandered down the jetty past a line of super tankers whose bows loomed out of the darkness. A number of rats scurried along in between the crane rails, foraging for food. The shipyard workers started to turn up in their droves, jumping off the back of trucks, holding their bags of sweet tea in their hands. The workers were of all nationalities, from South East Asia and beyond, and some hadn't seen home for two years.

Finally, we arrived at the gangplank to our rig. Welding cables were everywhere, like spilled spaghetti; the deck plate was cut out in places as though shredded by a bomb. It was chaos. We reached the drill floor and then started to climb the 150ft of ladders to the crown atop the derrick where we were working, fixing cable trays and electric cables that ran up the derrick legs. When we arrived, Don climbed onto the crown and fell asleep.

The sun emerged on the horizon and light spilled over the densely industrial setting in one fluid swoop. The mercury was rising, the shipyard cranes began to yodel and the skyline tasted of sweat and hard graft. I both loved and hated it.

I sniffed at the heaviness of the humidity that stuck to my throat and lungs. I sighed *... another day, another dollar*. Working on the equator was like living in a time warp. The sun rose and set at a similar time every day. There were no seasons – no winter, no summer. One day blended into another, one month into another, one year into another. You didn't want to blink for fear your life would have disappeared in the haze of those meaningless days.

I put my harness on and set off abseiling down the ropes with a bagful of nuts, bolts, spanners and tie wraps. At least to the drill crew looking up from the drill floor it would look as though we were working. No one came up to bother us – being at the top of the derrick, we were in the safest place in the whole shipyard. Safe was a good place to be! In recent history, one worker had been impaled through the shoulder by a falling scaffold tube, another had been crushed by an eight ton electric panel in the dry dock, and yet another had lost a limb in the machine workshop. Life was cheap in an oriental shipyard.

Hours passed by; I felt delusional, sleepy and dehydrated; no different from any other day. By the position of the sun in the sky, I knew it was time for lunch. I woke Don up, and we headed down to the shipyard hawker centre for our daily bowl of rice, be it Chinese, Indian or Malay. When I had finished eating, my head fell into my lap and I was sound asleep within a few seconds.

Back on the crown, Don was livelier, but I was worn out and began to ask myself the usual questions: *What am I doing here?* Then there was a sudden jolt and a humming of steel. We both looked down and we could see the shipyard's tower crane had nudged into the derrick. It was a few feet below us. Don turned to me with his impish smile and said:

'Jules, you do all this solo climbing; I dare you to jump onto the crane boom.' He read the instantaneous reaction of horror in my face and countered with: 'Chicken!'

That was it; I had woken from my stupor. The dare had been waged, and I immediately countered with: 'OK'. Adrenalin exploded from inside me; I climbed over the handrail with nothing but 200ft of fresh air to the base of the dry dock. I hated jumping, I wasn't good at it, but the boom was close. I stretched out a tentative hand towards it, summing up courage, gauging the distance, trying not to look down to see where I would end up if it all went wrong. I just couldn't do it. I looked at Don, and instead of a face etched with fear, he still wore his grin and repeated the word 'Chicken.' He was driving me nuts, I had to jump . . .

Come on . . . jump, you gutless piece of . . . The crane boom edged further away, and my chance had gone; I was never going to live the humiliation down. I climbed back over the handrail, and we started to put our harnesses on, Don still jibing at me. He was worse than a cloud of midges, so in a last-ditch effort to regain some pride, I pulled some slack in one of my ropes and tied into my harness. I climbed onto the handrail and leapt out towards the boom. I was airborne, sandwiched in parallel worlds of fear and mischief. I caught the boom cord with both hands, slipping from it, grasping, slipping again . . . going . . . then in the last moment I threw a heel over to stabilise myself. Don was laughing: the Indian crane operator was horrified to see me hanging upside down on the end of his crane a hundred or so feet away, and his gut instinct was to pull the boom away from the derrick. I simultaneously cursed and let go, cutting a pendulum across the skyline, narrowly missing a collision with the derrick leg. Don just stood there with his big smile before we dissolved into hysterics. Just another day in the shipyard – but it was a good indicator that I needed to get out of there and go and travel.

Ahead: rows of vineyards flashed by on the straight, empty road. Behind: nothing but dust, emptiness and a vast open sky. I could have been passing the vineyards of Bordeaux, but I wasn't; I was ten thousand miles away in Western Australia. From the Singapore shipyards, I had flown to Perth, and my friends Marc and Diana Mills had loaned me their four-wheel-drive sports car. Australia was vast, endless miles of eucalyptus-clad plains and semi-arid desert without a soul in sight, so different from the densely populated bustle of Singapore. Travelling through Australia's outback is a journey through vastness, and measured in driving hours in the way that reaching outer space is measured in light years.

I was heading south from Perth towards Albany and a climbing area called Mount

Frankland - a granite plug that pushes out of an indefinite, eucalyptus-rich plain. Another hour or two perhaps - I was getting impatient. I wanted to climb, so my foot pushed harder on the accelerator. Finally, I arrived at the car park. I was a little undecided about the wisdom of getting out of the car, for this was Australia, where all the dangerous beasties live. My friend, Andy Corbe, had warned me that tiger snakes were common down here, and their venom was fatal. He had also said that they were offensive, unlike other snakes. I wasn't sure if he had been joking or just trying to scare the crap out of me.

The granite slabs were over 100ft high, and after referring to the guidebook, I located the bolted line of *Hannibal*, a tongue of granite hanging down on itself in the form of an elephant's trunk. What surprised me, however, was the vast amount of unclimbed rock. *Hannibal* enticed, but the unclimbed rock to the left appealed more, and the idea of getting off the ground away from any tiger snakes appealed most of all.

I pulled onto a flake-line, and it disappeared some way up into a crystalline surface. I wasn't sure what to do – part of me wanted to go down, part of me wanted to continue. I committed to the crystals, picking my way towards some bigger holds, and then I thought of tiger snakes . . . slipping, falling and crawling in the undergrowth back to the car, amongst all those tiger snakes. Above were some smooth scoops in the rock. Shaking lightly, I took a few minutes standing in a toe-scoop with no handholds, calming myself. Then I hurried on up through a perplexing overhang at 70ft and onto the bald top of the dome. I was happy to have soloed a new route straight off, using a mixture of faith, guts and judgement – a third millennium ethic.

The view from the summit was lacklustre - a half-burnt eucalyptus forest radiated to the horizon, where it met with a bruised ceiling of greyness. It began to make me think how wonderful the Scottish landscape is – the lochs, the hills and the golden tinge of the autumnal birch. I felt somewhat trapped in the eucalyptus forest.

The Albany coastline was lush, and the sea was a deep, organic turquoise. I had never seen the sea looking so fresh and virginal before, but these waves had pushed up unchallenged from Antarctica. The rocks were gneiss: banded with colour, scoured smooth, ancient - perhaps some of the oldest rocks in the world - two billion years old, half the age of the planet at least, older than any species or single-celled organism, and there they were, sitting proud against the wash of the southern oceans. I was glad to be on the south coast of Australia, just travelling through, taking in the vast simplicities of sea and stone. Beside me stood the egg-shaped dome of Peak Head. I had just climbed *Baylac Direct* – one of the most fluent pieces of climbing in existence – 300ft of flakes and slabs, each move dovetailing into the next like a well-rehearsed dance. The only downside was the forty-minute walk back through the bush, armed with a long Y headed stick in each hand, in case I stumbled upon any snakes.

The following day I went to fly my paraglider on a small hill above the silvery white strip of beach at Shelley's Beach where I was camped. The wind was slight, meaning that I had to tuck in tight to the contours of the hill in order to gain the maximum lift. I was hoping to catch a strong thermal and to be corkscrewed up to 5,000ft, but alas I was barely reaching 1,000ft. After half an hour and growing bored with catching thermals, I made the decision to turn out from the hill and fly over the ocean.

The ocean is an insulator and gives no lift, meaning that the paraglider will gradually descend out of the sky on a specified glide ratio. So the idea was to fly out over the sea and turn back to the beach at the moment when I had just enough height to reach it. I flew over the beach and then the ocean, staring at its deep, hypnotic colour, quite relaxed in my comfy little seat. A fair distance out and a few hundred feet up, I could see small, moving shadows highlighted against the turquoise. I looked up, but there were no clouds in the sky that could produce these shadows. Suddenly, I recalled my conversation with Andy the previous day when, whilst we were bodyboarding in the surf, a seal swam amongst us. When we had exited the water, Andy had said: 'Do you know what it means when seals come close into the surf.' I shrugged my shoulders and said: 'No'. 'Well, mate, it means there is something big and white out there chasing them'.

With this thought, I pulled my left toggle down hard on the reflex. I cut a sharp curve through the sky towards the beach, staring fixedly upwards at the very thin lines holding me, willing them not to snap. Everything suddenly looked very fragile, and I trembled until I was safely back on the beach.

I rolled out of bed in the dark, groped around for my boiler suit, slipped it on and wandered out of my cabin. I hated being a slave to the clock. I couldn't feel free, and I began to kick myself for only booking a two-week holiday in Western Australia. *Next time will be longer*, I promised myself.

I was on a rig called the Marine 202, anchored about two miles out to sea from the shipyards at Jurong. There was less noise and it was cooler and less busy than the shipyard. It was a jack-up, which meant it had three legs like stilts that turned on cogs to adjust the height or depth of the rig to the required level. The legs were large steel tubes with holes in them in which the teeth of the cogs sat. Our job was to inspect the stiffeners on the inside of these legs.

From deck level, we climbed through a cog hole into the inside of the leg. It was an 80ft tube with an 8ft internal diameter and a stiffener ledge every 10ft. The thought of work went out of the window as a mischievous plan started to take shape. Soon, I had summoned up the courage to climb down to the lowest stiffener, take my clothes off and jump down the centre of the tube into the water. It was like a dare; I was scared of being caught; I would be sacked on the spot, but my colleague Marc stood guard and blocked the cog hole 50ft above, whilst Andy and Ronald gave encouragement. We all took turns and then started jumping from the 20ft stiffener. Then at 30ft it became a mixture of frustration and temptation; the optical illusion made the wall of the tube look tight and more dangerous. At 40ft, the linear perspective of the enclosed walls made it terrifying but hypnotic. To think I was supposed to be the team's rope access safety supervisor. There I was, thousands of miles from home, inside a flooded steel tube, in my underpants, quivering with excitement, like a teenager going tombstoning at the end of a pier.

As my eyes opened from a deep slumber, a multitude of sounds wafted in; birds singing, voices and faint background noises. Around me there were leaves on the trees, colourful flowers, and neatly cut, green grass. *Where was I? Eden?* Then my senses returned and it all fitted into place. I had been sleeping in the Botanic gardens in Brisbane, using my travel bag as a pillow, sleeping off my jet lag.

I had travelled to Brisbane after a working stint in Singapore, but I had become bored with the city – eating Subway sandwiches, playing golf, night climbing at Kangaroo point and doing the tourist thing. I hired a car and travelled to the Glasshouse Mountains, the columnar joints of Frog Buttress, and to the Sunshine coast for some surf. Being nomadic by nature, I wanted to keep moving; I just wasn't sure to where. Then one day I found a copy of a climbing guide in a bookshop and that same day I began a two day journey on buses, trains and hitched lifts - to Arapiles.

Midway between Adelaide and Melbourne is the Wimmera plain. Prairie-like fields and the odd salt pan radiate to every horizon. Incongruously in its centre is a lengthy spine of rock known as Arapiles, protruding 800ft above the plain like debris from an interplanetary collision. It is a mystifying sentinel in the desert. For thousands of years, it was home to the Aborigines who lived in the shelter of the caves and gullies that the rock provided. They made weapons and tools from its hardened sandstone – a smooth, hard, tangerine-streaked stone that also happens to be one of the finest climbing mediums to have been cemented by nature. Arapiles has it all - slabs, overhangs, walls, all sizes of cracks from fingers to fists, safe routes, run-out routes, easy routes, hard routes, sport routes, and not least . . . *Muldoon* and *Punks in the Gym* . . .

I arrived mid morning, not knowing what to expect. Little did I know that my intended five day stay was going to run until my three month visa expired, such was the addictive lifestyle of The Pines campsite. It was the central hub of Arapiles, where international climbers and travellers alike gathered to camp. It was basic – a forest floor under the canopy of pine trees, with a borehole tap, a sink and a toilet. It was cheap, but it had status and a certain ambience of peacefulness. Rumours had it that the record duration of a stay there was two years, although it had also been rumoured that there had been one of five. A Kiwi laid claim to this longevity prize; he also claimed another prize every week from the Natimuk Post Office in the form of the dole. In an imaginary way, The Pines might be Australia's answer to 'Hotel California' . . . *you can check out, but you can never leave . . .*

As soon as my tent was up, I was itching to climb. The campsite was empty, but I could hear voices somewhere in the distance, so I went to familiarise myself with the many facets of the cliff and the climbs and to see if I could find anyone with whom to tag along. That evening, after climbing the famous roof climb of *Kachoong*, I went to bed in good spirits – the weather was brilliant, and the quality of the rock was even better. I had some routes lined up to solo in the morning, but I couldn't sleep in my new surroundings with all the excitement, so I left my tent in the dark and headed off in search of *Muldoon*. Later that morning, I arrived back in camp having soloed eleven routes. I crawled into my hammock and fell fast asleep.

The climbers there were lazy and no one really stirred until mid morning. I chatted to a climber camping nearby as he made his breakfast. Bob Scheier was similar to me in many respects – quiet, down to earth, keen on skydiving, base-jumping and solo climbing. He came from Kansas. Places like this brought together similar minded people like us, and before long we agreed to twin-solo *The Bard* the following morning. We soloed one behind the other, winding our way up the buttress like a pair of squirrels foraging for nuts. Twin-soloing was strange, and it unnerved me when I was directly above Bob, 200ft up, for if I fell we would both be free-falling, swimming through the air to the desert floor together. This was soloing with responsibility. *The Bard* dished out sickening exposure on the largest holds imaginable, remarkable for a relatively straightforward climb. Afterwards, Bob invited me to a breakfast of scrambled eggs and my eyes lit up at the thought of hot food - my usual breakfast consisted of muesli and water.

I soon worked out that when climbers departed camp there was a gathering, and all the left over food and furniture was plundered. I didn't travel with much gear, so I hitched a lift into town to buy all sorts of clothes, rugs, pans and cutlery from the local charity shop. Once a week, most climbers would have a rest day and wander the two kilometres down to the local, organic farm. This was owned by Reg and Hazel, friendly and kind folk who were willing to allocate jobs to climbers in return for some fresh, organic produce that would sustain them through the week. Stories of backbreaking weeding work were common, but one climber managed to turn up at the right time and ended up elbow deep in a cow, on midwife duties. Everybody hoped for a job that might be a little more exciting than just weeding the vegetables.

Most evenings, I would return to camp with an armful of bush timber which I burned on the fire to heat my large pan of organic soup. The pan was never cleaned, just topped up every day with fresh, organic vegetables and borehole water and then re-boiled. After dinner, I would curl up close to the flames in my purple beanbag, which I had acquired from someone. God knows how old it was. I didn't care - it was comfortable. I had also acquired a sofa which had a resident mouse that ran around its inners. The favoured pastime was to punch the mouse when it rustled about. Then one night, I punched it and heard no more. I was wracked with guilt – I presumed that I had killed it. Thankfully the rustling resumed the following day – I punched no more.

Every night after the others had turned in, I sat by the fire, alone apart from the possums in the trees waiting earnestly to scavenge for food. Although I'm a morning person, I do like nights by the fire, alone, reflecting on the day, my life, the soloing – there are so many answers to be discovered to so many questions. I watched the flames trace their forever-changing shapes, wisping into the stillness of the night. This was perhaps the time when I might unearth exactly who I was, or what I was doing. After an hour or so, the fire turned frigid, the embers dimmed, and it was time for me to turn in.

Arapiles is home to a few thousand climbs; some seek passage in dark clefts that have been forgotten over the course of time, whilst others are white with chalk, their every move naked for all to see. One climb without exception was *Quo Vadis*, on the bluffs; its name resonated through the pine trees most evenings and snippets of information could be gleaned if one so wished . . . polished . . . tricky . . . hard for its grade . . .

The line of *Quo Vadis* follows a compelling sickle-shaped feature on a vertical wall, 300ft above camp. Its neighbour, *Scorpion Crack*, was even more obvious: a fracture that split the top of the bluff in two. It was probably the most striking line at Arapiles. The endless, epic stories were the reason that I became so nervous about soloing on the bluffs. But having soloed over three hundred routes, I was running out of feasible climbs at realistic grades. Rumour had it that Peter Croft (the Canadian soloist) had visited a few years before and had soloed 110 routes in a day, carrying around with him nothing more than a bunch of carrots.

One morning, I decided to put my ghosts to rest and headed in the direction of the bluff in the darkness with a head full of endorphins. *Eurydice* was climbed in twenty minutes. At the top, I sat on a ledge below the final bluff and watched the sky ripen with colour and warmth. 200ft below, no one so much as stirred in The Pines and I began to feel relaxed.

The base of *Scorpion Crack* was too wide for my fighting fists; it was all arms and legs, a little ugly and frightening, especially when the safety ledge was only a few feet wide and dropped away vertically for 200ft. I fought my way up the crack with body jamming techniques until I managed to secure a fist, then another, punching away into the empty stone orifice. I levitated smoothly now with a good rhythm as I approached the summit of the bluff. Nerves began to jitter, but solid hold after solid hold kept coming without much commotion, and an easy down climb led me to the base of *Quo Vadis*.

This is it . . . my state of mind began to break down. I needed to gather control of my subconscious so that I could override the superficial fears born from the stories of other climbers.

I sat down on the ledge, tucked my legs in, and glanced over the plain before closing my eyes, tuning in to imaginary Aboriginal spirits, hoping for guidance. When I reopened my eyes, I moved out of *dreamtime* and climbed upwards and outwards along the scythe of *Quo Vadis* in a dream-like trance, with 300ft of air beneath the soles of my feet. On the summit of the bluff, I felt light-headed, humbled and also untouchable, as I gazed down across the vast continental canvas that is Australia.

Days drifted on, one week soon fused into two and so on. Sometimes, I wandered down to the remoter southern end of the rocks, half an hour away. I found a perfect solo in the shape of *High Kicks*, a route hidden behind a canopy of gum trees. A blank wall barred my access to an appealing flake at 25ft. Then a carrot stared me between the eyes. Not the carrot you might think – in Australia, *carrots* are old bolts that need a special hanger to be placed over them before a karabiner can be clipped in. The hangers are kept in one's chalk bag. The rule of thumb: if there is a carrot bolt, there is going to be a hard move. In the next instant, I was flat on my face on the ground. Luckily the landing wasn't too bad, and I hobbled sedately back to camp with a flap of skin hanging from my palm. My friends, Stuart and Guy, suggested cleaning the wound, but I declined until I had slugged down some of Guy's cheap whisky. I lay down on the forest floor and fainted as they used some sharp implements to scrape out the dirt and patch the skin back. For days I wandered round camp with my hand wrapped in a honey coated T-shirt . . . it didn't stop me from soloing hand jamming cracks though. I was becoming feral.

If one stays long enough in The Pines, the seasons become noticeable. The nights draw in, the rain becomes more frequent, and the temperatures drop. The dust-coated floor begins to turn green; the kangaroos become visitors under the pine canopy and in general the place smells fresh and natural. The numbers of climbers slowly ebb away as they depart in search of warmer climes, to Queensland, or even back to their homes in the northern hemisphere.

The cycle of life comes even to paradises like this, and this particular year the rain was really persistent. I had grown disenchanted with the dampness and most of my friends had departed. I wanted to leave too, but as always with the drug-like tendencies of climbing, there was always one more route . . .

It didn't help that the route I had set my eyes on was as hard as anything I could attempt with a rope. It was overhanging and only 60ft! I climbed as far up as I could and, when my arms began to fade, I climbed back down and jumped off. Intent on climbing the route, I built a bonfire of bush wood underneath it to use as a crash pad.

My visa was expiring the following morning; it was the wakeup call for me to move on. I packed up and gave my inherited furniture away, but in the dying hours that remained at The Pines, I found myself heading up to the cliff for one last try.

I climbed the overhanging wall on pockets, some good, some not so; I knew the holds and maintained fluency and confidence to my high point. I climbed higher, reaching an irreversible power move to gain an overhanging flake. Stopping for a fraction of a second, I was caught up in one of those deadly moments of indecisiveness; climbers loathe them, soloists even more so . . . I should have taken the risk and carried on quickly, but I didn't - I pissed around for too long and the lactic acid drilled into my arms. I stared down at the bush wood, closed my eyes as I felt the power and grip draining, fingers uncurling . . . Nomadic or not, it was time to go home, one way or another . . .

Voices from the Abyss

If you must play, decide upon three things at the start: the rules of the game; the stakes and the quitting time – Chinese proverb

Location: ninety nautical miles north east of the Shetland Islands. A number of steel structures litter a stormy plane, holding fast against the monumental force of a volatile North Sea. The *Cormorant Alpha* oil rig is one such structure: a rust-ridden relic of bygone engineering standing on four squat legs, siphoning Brent Crude from under the seabed like an iron mosquito. For a while, on a two-week on, two-week off basis, I had endured the perpetual hum of the diesel generators, the smell of oil and exhaust. I felt I had become yet another minion selling my soul to the lucrative oil industry. It wasn't ideal or totally in tune with my ethic, but I had to work - and the upside of this kind of work was that it was reasonably well paid, and it gave me enough time to travel and climb.

I worked night shifts. My body clock loathed them, but our radiography work required that we work at night. At the start of each shift, I would wander into the locker room – a hive of blue lockers, slatted benches and a green linoleum floor – before reluctantly pulling on my boiler suit. I would make some herbal tea in a polystyrene cup, slump onto a bench, and put the world to rights with my three work colleagues: Davie Reid, Frank Cox and Dave Salta. Davie organised our permits so that we could start work, but this sometimes took as much as an hour; such is the bureaucracy on the rig. Permits were compulsory requirements – one couldn't leave the accommodation without gloves, safety glasses and a hard hat, and we were not able to step off the ground without wearing a harness – in stark contrast to my habitual lifestyle.

Frank was admirably laid back and chatted affably about anything from coal mining as a lad in the 1960s to current affairs and the nature of the economy. The fourth member of our team – Dave, from Australia – was always deep in thought and away with the fairies. He was surfing on an exotic beach in Indonesia, or trying to figure out how he was going to maintain his romances whilst travelling around the south coast of Europe, which he did regularly during his fortnight breaks between stints on the rig.

All three dabbled in online gambling. This was understandable - drinking is prohibited on the rigs and boredom has to be relieved. Apart from the gym or the television, the best form of entertainment is surfing the net, if there is ever a spare computer going. Davie, a keen fly fisherman, bought and sold *Hardy* reels on eBay. During one, two-week trip offshore, he spent £1,800 on reels. It didn't go down well with his (now ex) wife. Thanks to the Internet, oil rig workers have the ability to spend money from the confines of the sea before their partners can lay claim to it.

Young Dave was adamant that gambling on tennis was the way to make money as it appeared to be a weighted fifty-fifty. I had never once gambled in my life, although friends had pointed out that I did exactly that every time I went climbing without a rope.

I thought long and hard about the idea of gambling on tennis, delving into some mathematics and probability. I concluded that I could make better returns at tennis than by leaving money festering at the bank's base rate. I opened up a William Hill online betting account. Setting it up and transferring money was so simple; a couple of presses on the mouse and a telephone call were all that were needed. I mentally noted it as *investment gambling* because it sounded more responsible to my frugal tendencies.

It was nearing midnight during one night shift as I sat at the computer and placed five grand on five matches. My hand was shaking on the mouse – each click meant that a thousand pounds had been placed as a bet. My colleagues watched over my shoulders in stony silence. They were in shock. Once completed, I felt a mixture of anxiety, mischief and guilt as if I had accidentally burnt down a rainforest. The thrill was similar to soloing, and I buzzed away like faulty electrical wiring in a rainstorm.

We were all winning, and our spirits were unusually high for a night shift because we were taking William Hill to the cleaners. My bump down to earth came when the last two of my five matches lost, and my pocket was suddenly twelve hundred pounds lighter.

We were due off the rig in the morning, and the U.S. Open Tournament was due to start the following week. There was still hope. Tomorrow I had my freedom. Once I had disembarked from the helicopter, I went in search of my patient French girl, who was waiting for me out in the industrial estate. I called her *Mrs. L.* She looked shabby, but she was reliable and didn't drink too much either. My friends laughed at her and wondered why I hadn't binned her for a younger model; I was sentimental and would not part with her. She had been having problems recently; only her passenger door would open, so I had to swing in and out through the window, and the horn had been replaced and was wired to a doorbell taped to the steering wheel. With over 160,000 miles on the clock, my trusty Peugeot 205 had purred effortlessly up and down the country to the furthest climbing destinations imaginable.

Once again I was entombed in my comfortable seat. The monotony of tarmac and cat's-eyes flying under the bonnet hypnotised me as I headed south towards Pembroke. It was late summer, the preferred time for deep water soloing as the sea is at its warmest.

Long after midnight, I arrived at *Mother Carey's Kitchen*, one of Pembroke's most popular and atmospheric sea cliffs. There was a locked gate across the car park entrance. I parked beside it, threw my sleeping bag into the grass, crawled in and curled up, hoping that it wasn't going to rain.

I had a sleepless night, and at 5.30am the ranger arrived to unlock the gate. He was not pleased at the sight of a large, red maggot sprawled in the verge.

My explanation fell on deaf ears. I drove off into Tenby to get breakfast, but it was too early, so I went for a wander around the streets in the hope of finding an Internet café where I could place bets.

Tenby is a lovely castle-walled town, popular with tourists. At 6am, it was quiet apart from a few gulls squabbling over the previous night's chip shop litter. I approached a man who was cleaning windows and asked him where the Internet café was. He muttered a couple of words I didn't understand. I continued on down the street, somewhat perplexed, before I finally realised that he had spoken in Welsh. Like some Welsh people, he probably disliked the English, so he had done it to annoy me. In actual fact, I could not be considered wholly English; I was born near Belfast, raised in Yorkshire, educated in Scotland and have English, Welsh, Armenian and Italian blood in me - I am what can only be described as a thoroughbred mongrel.

I returned to the cliffs. The fog gradually dispersed to produce a bright day. I was exhausted, and my mind-body coordination was very disjointed. Despite this, I wanted to climb something, anything . . . and within an hour I was 70ft above the sea, scrabbling up vertical grass and loose stones, having succeeded on a new deep water solo . . .

I needed to sleep, and my best option was to find an official campsite because my preference for camping free and illegally on National Trust land would inevitably lead to another sleepless night. I found a place and the farmer charged me ten pounds for a pitch. My astonishment didn't go unnoticed. The prospect of a hot shower made it worth it though.

In the morning, I woke early and took the opportunity to go into Tenby and place some bets. On the way to the Internet café, I bought *The Times* newspaper to check the weather forecast and the tide tables for Swansea. The café was bustling with clientele of all ages, stuffing themselves, as the British do, with full English breakfasts, gateaux, doughnuts and flapjacks, washed down with tea and coffee. The aroma of freshly ground coffee was homely, and the waitresses were all young and appealing. I caught the attention of one of them:

'Err . . . do you have the Internet please?'

She took me upstairs, and I ordered herbal tea and checked my Hotmail account before clicking on the William Hill online betting website. I sat on my stool, studying all the games and the odds in both the men's and women's tournaments. I topped up my balance with a further five grand, money I had been saving towards a deposit for a house.

A message flashed up on the screen:

Hi Julian, your balance is 8,805 GBP.

The *Hi Julian* was a nice personal touch by William Hill; he obviously wanted me to feel at ease before he robbed me a little more. I selected ten matches and then pressed: *Place Bet Now*. Within minutes, my balance had whittled down to zero. I hopped off the stool with a buzzing head, went downstairs, paid for my tea and left the café. It was time to go back to the cliffs and some fresh air.

I wanted to try out my new dry-bag; it was allegedly 'the bees-knees'. I put in a towel, some shorts, my boots and chalk bag, closed the special seal with my teeth and threw it into the sea. Naked, I jumped after it and swam into an atmospheric sea cave close to *Mother Carey's Kitchen*, known to climbers as *Blind Bay*. The further I swam, the deeper and spookier the shadows became. I climbed out onto a smooth, black ledge, dripping with water and tingling with excitement. I gazed upwards, neck back and mouth agape like an art-lover inspecting the Sistine chapel. This ominous roof didn't have the same aesthetics - it was menacing - and here gravity resided as king. Cutting through the roof I saw a vague line of weakness that was above deep water if I should fail. Motivated by the thought that there was at least one possibility, I put on my gear and climbed easily to an impasse where the roofs were welded together at incomprehensible angles.

I utilised a sequence of body locks and upper-cut hand jams to attack the roof's weak axis, which finally succumbed to less effort than I had expected. I was spat out

Sharpening my Kitten Claws in Pembroke © Mike Robertson Photography

On the summit of Half Dome, Yosemite © JL collection

Dreamy summer haze over the Loch Quoich Munros © JL collection

Foot treads approaching the summit of Ben Nevis (opposite) © JL collection

Paul Ewing and I on Bheinn Bheoil, Ben Alder behind © JL collection (John Forbes)

Joe Hayes (aged 16) on the Cuillin Ridge in winter © JL collection

The infamous 'easy' ridge of the Inaccessible Pinnacle © JL collection

Backpacking south of Torridon © JL collection

Me, Jim and Joe at the Muir of Knock woodshed © David Hayes

Fred Harper guiding on the Aiguille de la Vanoise © JL collection

Liathach from Beinn Eighe © JL collection

Looking for a landing site after flying off Rois Bheinn © JL collection

March Hare's Gully, Beinn Bhan © JL collection

Reawakening my Guardian Angel, Northumberland © JL collection (Daniel Laing)

Northumberland flutes
© JL collection

Millstone grit
© JL collection

Desperate measures on Clipperty Clop... (opposite) © JL collection (Paul Higginson)

Early morning light stroking the Dubh Loch © JL collection

Kev outside the howff under the Dubh Loch © JL collection

Shere Khan, The Red Tower (opposite) © Cubby Images

A lone heartbeat on Diuru © Cubby Images

Cracks in Reality, South Cove © Cubby Images

One toe pocket leads the dance, Sardinia © Cubby Images

David Balfour Bay, Erraid © JL collection (Gary Latter)

Shelterstone Crag the morning Athene was born (opposite) © JL collection

Traversing The Needles, Isle of Wight © Mike Robertson Photography

Derrick dismantling in Jurong shipyard, Singapore © JL collection

Beneath the Statue of Christ, Rio de Janeiro (opposite) © JL collection (Alcino Falcao)

The North Face of Ben Nevis, Mega Route X in sun on the right © JL collection

With BASE rig, Riglos, Spain © Mike Francis

Approaching the base of Emerald Gully, 1986 (opposite) © JL collection

Sunrise across the Gulf of Aqaba © JL collection

Relaxing the mind, The Burren, Ireland © JL collection

Abduction in the Alien Cave, Pembroke (opposite) © Mike Robertson Photography

A view over Rocklands, South Africa © Mike Robertson Photography

Salt Pan, Namibia © JL collection

Mike Robertson bouldering in 40C Cederberg (opposite) © Mike Robertson Photography

Desert Storm, Namibia © Mike Robertson Photography

Namibian Granite © JL collection

Mega Tsunami © JL collection (Jo George)

Lewisian Gneiss, Made in Scotland © JL collection

The road ahead, (or is it behind?) © JL collection

Buttermilks, California © JL collection

Nevada Desert from the Lunar Crater © JL collection

onto a ledge beneath a further roof on the right edge of the cave mouth. I pulled through this and traversed across the lip of *Alien Direct*. I was 50ft above the sea, but I might just as well have been fifty miles up. I didn't care – I was in a dreamlike state.

Topping out, I lay in the grass under a warm sun for a while before returning to the cave to retrieve my towel and dry bag. I continued my swim to the other side of the cave and out onto a small, square-cut ledge incarcerated by overhanging walls. Shivering lightly, I pulled onto *Aristocrat*: an 85 degree wall of bitterly sharp limestone that stung my soggy fingers like swarms of angry wasps. Blood started to trickle from my fingertips. I was ready to let go, but bigger holds appeared. I clung on and reached the foot ledge on the mid-height break. I took stock of the impressive upper wall and set to it, finishing with a wobble at 60ft when a couple of holds began to creak a little.

On top of *Mother Carey's Kitchen*, I met a climber who had been watching me. He tried to scare me with a tale of his friend's jump into the sea from 60ft, describing, in vivid detail, how he had punctured a lung. This wasn't the best of thoughts to dwell on, so I decided to relax for the remainder of the day. Once darkness had fallen, I slept out on the cliff top under the stars because I couldn't be bothered to pitch my tent. I lay on my back in warmth, staring for ages into the depths of the polished, ebony sky. The stars were ablaze, and I tried to identify a couple of constellations before I became distracted by a shooting star that tore through the Earth's atmosphere and burst into a ball of flame, gone in an instant. I propped myself onto my elbows and stared into the distance towards the dim, shimmering flash of the lighthouse on Lundy and then on towards Cornwall.

A wave of sadness washed over me. I knew that my ex girlfriend, Karen, was on holiday with her two children, Holly and Sophie, in St Ives. Karen was as calm as they come – an all-encompassing angel. I hoped that she was happy. It always made me smile to think of the time that she had accompanied me to the Nth Cloud on the Staffordshire moors, where I was attempting the project that I later named

The latest project finally coming to fruition:
Hold Fast-Hold True, a world class solo © Cubby Images

Judge Jules. Karen had always supported and understood my climbing lifestyle, but on this occasion, I needed her to belay, holding my ropes and running to take in enough slack to prevent me from hitting the ground if I came off. This is, of course, exactly what I did - I fell from the crux at 30ft. She stood rooted to the spot in shock. I hit the ground. She was visibly trembling – I laughed, gave her a hug, and said I was going to have another go. I came off again, and this time she tore off down the slope, bringing me to a halt as I clipped the ground on the rope stretch whilst she ended up face down in the bracken, still clutching the rope. It was certainly an example of extreme belaying for someone who had never so much as put a harness on before.

My body was congested with aches and pains when the sun rose, so I took a swim to wake me up before driving to Tenby to check my bets. I walked through town, picking up the paper on my way to the Internet café, my heartbeat quickening with every step. I ordered a strawberry milkshake at the desk, climbed the stairs to the computer, and logged on to William Hill. I was trembling as my username and password were typed in seemingly involuntarily. I was in a world of my own; a bomb could have gone off outside and I would still have been transfixed to that screen. My betting slip popped up on the screen and my eyes were drawn directly to the balance, anxiety drowning me in the millisecond it took for my neurons to relay the message from my eyes to my brain:

Hi Julian, your balance is 9,944 GBP.

I slumped in disbelief.

I had won back eleven hundred pounds overnight. I felt invincible, and when my milkshake arrived, I slurped it through a straw, reduced my bets drastically, and went out into the street, lost amongst a surging crowd of holidaymakers. I vanished down to the coast.

The sea sparkled, the rock was dry and I felt at peace, miles away from the vexations of gambling. I climbed down to a small ledge just above the high tide mark on the eastern edge of the cave; it was hidden from above, and that meant I could sunbathe naked in privacy. The tide was out, so I relaxed with my book. I read a few chapters, did a *Killer Sudoku*, and ate a bunch of grapes before lying down, waiting for the high tide. Life, it seemed, was idyllic . . .

A climber swings away from the sunlight into the shadows of a sea cave, water lolling beneath him. The path ahead is a maze for his imagination to follow, as the overhanging rock-architecture above juts out at bizarrely obtuse angles. I am watching him with a pang of jealousy as he searches for possible avenues. An arête lures him into a niche with no exit, and he becomes exasperated with both the dark shadows and the lack of holds.

'Swing right . . . swing right above water!' I scream, knowing that a fall to the left will probably break his bones before he drowns. He lacks power and this is frustrating him, although his tenacity is commendable.

'You're pathetic . . .' I mock, hoping to drive him on, but this doesn't help. All I can hear are my own echoes bellowing from the cave. Shafts of light distort my view momentarily as he hangs upside down from a niche by his left toe, his right hand now punching into shadows.

'Lucky . . . !' I scream as he blindly locks in a hand and swings away on it before jamming in a knee. Further horizontal moves lead to a resting perch below the final 15ft roof which bows to the lip. A salivating sea swills 50ft below him, its invisible surface tension ready to fracture his anatomy. His inverted body swings out towards the lip slowly and tentatively; he is growing tired with every move. I want to look away, but I am glued to the action; is he going to make it?

'Go on . . . Go on!' I shout, but my words are muted by the coastline waves. His body is expanding with oxygen-depleted blood and lactic acid; I wait for his body to drop like a stone. But wait . . . what the hell is he doing? He shuffles both his legs up into the roof, thigh deep. His head and arms hang plum vertical downwards towards the sea, perfectly tracing the invisible axis of gravity.

'What an outrageous position!' I mutter under my breath, somewhat envious

of the capacity to rest like a bat in such an inverted environment. He rests long enough to gain composure before turning the lip on reasonable holds. I can see the disbelief clearly etched on his face. Above him, a friendly, vertical groove provides neat mechanics and balance, leading him to the top. He sits down, relieved, and closes his eyes.

Minutes drift by . . .

My view was different; I was sitting on the cliff top, realising my own *Abduction.*

The morning wind was refreshing but didn't appeal. The air was humid, and the sea spat like a green-brown broth in a boiling cauldron. The sight unnerved me, but the spring tide lured me on to gamble with the eloquently named *Anti Matterhorn.* I traversed into the cave and followed its devious twisting path. The climbing was far from eloquent; it was cramped and corrupted my body into inelegant positions. I scrabbled into the roof, exhausted and relieved that there was a vague rest. The route now inclined past the horizontal, and it was blank apart from a 3ft stalactite shaped like a rhino horn. It looked impossible to pass, but the heartening thought that Crispin Waddy and Andy Long had passed this way, with ropes and adventurous spirits, spurred me on. From the back of the cave, I performed the splits onto the horn, cementing myself into the apex of the roof. My groin ached, but I had no option but to endure it as my hands were waving about frantically, searching for holds. Then I stole a glance down into the cauldron 45ft below. The sea cajoled me with a wink, wanting me to play, proposing an enema - my sphincter twitched and my body started to tremble. I had little option other than to pounce across onto the horn and cling to it. Indecisions swirled in my head. I looked down at the sea, then to the horn . . . then to the sea, then to the horn. The idea of leaping sideways onto an inverted horn and holding on with a bear-hug, 45ft above the sea without a rope, was definitely a crazy gamble - *place bet now . . .*

On the way back to the car, I weaved past the bracken and talked to the three resident black cows that I spoke to every morning. There wasn't much other conversation to be had. I sat in the car eating muesli and water out of a plastic mug and caught a glance of a rugged stranger's face staring back at me in the rear view mirror. My heart leapt:

What the . . .

The stubble-ridden face had given me a fright - it was mine. I searched under the seat, found an empty yoghurt carton and filled it with water before crouching by the wing mirror and tearing at my stubble with a blunt razor. I later drove into town to check on my bets. I was about evens with the bookies; I left it at that . . .

The following morning was damp, and it rained continuously . . . so I rested.

The next day, somewhat remarkably given the amount of rain that had fallen, I found that the inside of the cave was dry. I had managed to climb along the west wall and into the cave with absolutely nothing to spare. A bizarre, sixty-degree, overhanging off-width that cut through the middle of the cave roof appeared to be the easiest way out. Lime and cream coloured rock hung over my head like the palette of a fossilised dinosaur. I trembled in disgust, realising that this was what adventurous deep water soloing was all about: finding paths that defied sense. I had nothing to lose. If I hit an impasse, I would simply fall in the water and swim out.

I kicked at the crack and it swallowed my leg, followed by both fists. Unperturbed, I moved out along the fissure and then my fists started to hit fresh air, and my body started to disappear as the crack widened. Somehow I stuck in to the end, utilising a psychotic hip-jam before moving up into a body-bending niche. My arms and legs were a mess of spent tendons and muscle fibres. The rock was damp, and my neck-jam was dangerously insecure and painful. I twisted and my flailing hands groped blindly for the rock above, but there was nothing . . . I kept persevering. On the edge of despair, ready for the inevitable, I felt a small pocket out to the left. This was my chance: a chink of light. I contorted into a different position, poked in a finger, and swung wildly out of my tortuous body-jam and onto better holds. I grappled before total fatigue overtook me and I slipped away, spinning face first into the sea.

Searing flames of brine ripped through my face. Dazed and confused, floating limp, the heaving swell sucked and splashed at me for an unknown period of time before I shot back into reality. I clawed through the water and onto a rocky shelf. Dripping with water, I started to scramble out: both feet slipped simultaneously, leaving me hanging from a hold above a chasm of serrated limestone that would have sliced me up, had I fallen.

It was time for breakfast and the inevitable trip to check my bets and pick up the paper. I walked through the narrow streets, like a clockwork robot now, straight to the Internet café. I ordered a hot chocolate this time and went upstairs to log on to my Hotmail account. I had e-mails from friends who were telling me that I had embarked on the slippery slope with my foray into gambling. They were right of course, but I found slippery slopes far more exciting than non-slippery ones, and I hated being patronised more than anything. It spurred me on all the more. I logged into my William Hill account. My betting slip popped up . . .

Hi Julian, your balance is 10,722 GBP.

Seven hundred pounds up!

Winning was such a good feeling! A waitress arrived and placed my hot chocolate beside me as I typed. I glanced up at her with a smile and a greeting of thanks. Her eyes were full of horror as they looked towards the keyboard. I looked too. Slumped on the keys were my shredded and blood stained hands that looked as though they had been fed to a tundra wolf.

For the remainder of the afternoon, I whittled away time and went for a walk along the beach, waiting for the tide to forge in so that I could make another attempt at the cave. This time I climbed along the traverse; each hold was now coated in chalk, indicating the sequence of moves that led to a rest on a smooth slab of rock below the roof crack. I launched up the crack, only to find myself once again out of breath and constricted in the body-jam. I shook out the lactic acid from my arms and swung up to my previous high point and secured a skin-tearing fist jam. With a mixture of hope and stupidity, I launched outwards along the cave roof, taken aback at my positivity. My hands fell upon big holds, one after another, and I hauled up into a perfectly formed, human sized tube of rock in the roof, and disappeared . . .

This is unbelievable!

I chuckled to myself as I lay gawping out of the hole in front of me onto the sea, 45ft below. Although my recumbent pose felt safe and comfortable, my body was exhausted.

After ten minutes of thinking about the tantalising possibility of success, I dropped out of the hole in the roof of the cave like poo from a stone sphincter, and climbed out towards daylight and the lip, 20ft away. I looked around, but all the undercut holds were out of reach, and gaining them looked difficult. I climbed within reach of one and lunged for it . . . my hand slapped the hold, but it sloped, and my body's inertia tore my fingers from the rock, and I fell backwards into the abyss, my arms pedalling through the air before I plunged once again into the dark waters below.

After a glossy, clear night under the stars, the morning had attracted a wafer-thin morning mist, but no mist was going to deter me from beating the cave. Within twenty minutes, I was once again embedded in the tube in the roof. Blood trickled from a cut on my finger where the sharp pocket had worn through the skin - there was nothing I could do except to powder it with chalk and continue . . .

I slapped again . . .

The brine acted like an acid and burnt deep into the cut as I resurfaced from under the waves. Enough was enough.

I checked my bets. The screen popped up: *Hi Julian, your balance is 11,440 GBP.*

I left the café feeling good and went to the chemist to pick up some plasters to protect my finger from any further abrasions. During the afternoon, the mist cleared and the wind dropped. The surface of the sea turned to glass, and the tide returned unnoticed. It was a fantastic opportunity to climb, but I was bushed. I lay in the grass on the cliff top, losing my thoughts in the pages of my book. I woke up the following morning with a multitude of pulled muscles, but this didn't stop me from taking two further 45ft falls. I was becoming accustomed to them, although starting to doubt the possibility of ever succeeding.

By 11am I had checked my bets; my winnings had increased further:

Hi Julian, your balance is 11,732 GBP.

I had won three grand in one week. Tax-free solo climbing! I left the café without putting on any further bets. I wanted to have a break from the stress. Halfway down the street, I turned round and started back to the café to place something else on, but decided against it and went instead to shop. Coming out of the supermarket, I felt irresistibly drawn to the Internet café where I gambled again.

As the mist was down again in the morning and the wind had now picked up, I threw my tent in the car and drove off towards the Isle of Wight for a brief family visit and some much needed rest. Halfway down the M4, between Swansea and Cardiff, the news on the radio made me go limp - my bets had crashed.

I sneaked into the Internet café in Newport and rallied my position. I won, and with my total winnings at just over a grand, it was a good time to quit and I withdrew my money.

On the return journey to Pembroke, a constant spray of water splashed across the windscreen; the tarmac and cars alike were invisible behind curtains of water, and by the time I reached Tenby, the thought of either camping or sleeping in the car gave way to the urge to book into a B&B. It was a first. Walking into a stranger's home was weird and quite unnatural. The smell was unfamiliar and the air stale, but the room was clean and carpeted and the proprietors were welcoming enough, although I did not feel at all at ease. The landlord asked if I wanted either tea or coffee with some homemade scones; my reply of just some hot water and a slice of lemon brought a raised brow.

Ensconced in my overly large room, I stared at the double bed and its cleanly pressed white sheets, thinking that it was too luxurious. The thought of sleeping on the floor crossed my mind, but I had paid for some comfort, so I tore back the sheets and bounced into the softness, grinning like a kid who had found a hidden stash of chocolate. Lying in the big bed had a sensation similar to being spread-eagled on a blank rock face and not being able to reach any of the holds. I found it difficult to sleep with all the unfamiliar noises around me.

In the morning I refused a cooked breakfast, surprising my hosts further, and I then explained to them that I climbed upside down in sea caves with no ropes. They must have thought I was either crazy or a liar. As I left the house, the mist had begun to disappear, and the sun started to warm the air. I wandered back down to the cave and started to climb; my body felt rested and my finger had almost repaired itself. I found myself in the knee-bar rest below the final moves but, rather than snatching upwards, I traversed on a lower set of undercuts. I slapped leftwards into the first undercut, my body bunched, muscles writhing with power and pain . . . moments later I jammed my knee into the next undercut, upside down, on the lip of all things. The position was fantastic and inspired me to fight my way up into the comfy confines of the hanging chimney, ultimately leading me away from *The Abyss* towards my freedom, 80ft above the tinsel-lit sea.

I was contented; my ordeal was over, and my limbs sagged with tiredness. I lay in the sun all day to compensate. I bivvi'd close to the cave at *Mother Carey's* for the night, watching a multitude of black specks randomly flitter and dissolve into the darkness. I felt eddies of air whispering across my face as silken wings sliced by with only millimetres to spare – it amazed me how precise the ultrasonic navigation system of bats could be. The moon was a deep, dusty yellow and perfectly hemispherical in shape, like a salad bowl balanced on the horizon. It travelled very low in the night sky before it vanished altogether. I had never before seen the moon sink. Did I believe in omens?

Enduring the long, dark winters above an inhospitable North Sea on the *Eider Alpha* oil rig inevitably drew me back to gambling. It was something to kill time and gave me a much-needed buzz. Like soloing, it becomes addictive and knowing when to stop is the hardest part. Instead of sticking to tennis, I branched into rugby. It was France versus South Africa. I made a tentative decision on France to win, and then, after studying the odds, I changed my mind and decided to go with South Africa to win.

I had come in from work early to watch the final minutes, and to my horror France was leading 26-20. I stood immobile, and then South Africa had a penalty in front of the posts in the dying seconds. I could barely watch: South Africa needed to score a try. Tense moments. They failed; it was over and I had lost a grand.

I was at rock bottom and couldn't bring myself to eat dinner. I sat and stewed in my own self pity and silence before logging on to my account to assess the damage and take out the remainder of my money. Gambling was over for me. Astonishingly, when I went into my account, I had nearly two thousand pounds more than I thought. Further checking revealed that I hadn't properly cleared my first bet on France to win, so it overrode my other bet. I had won by default.

Was it an omen for me to stop? Davie and Frank thought so. But no, the next year I bet on the Scotland versus France match in the Six Nations. Although played at Murrayfield, France were the odds-on favourite. I thought it was a safe bet to put money on France. At half-time, Scotland were winning 13-3, and I was part trembling and part numb, as though someone had just syringed me with a curious mixture of caffeine and general anaesthetic. I thought about placing money on Scotland to win to even up the bet, but for some reason I couldn't and I didn't.

It was like soloing; once I had decided to commit to a route, I wasn't going to change my mind halfway through, unless, of course, I was going to die; but this was only money and that was the way my mind worked. I had the feeling that Scotland would hang on for a win, so I decided to go out and work and save myself the trouble of a nervous breakdown. When I saw Frank and Dave later, they were silent. I knew the answer. Scotland had won 20-16. I tried to feign a smile and shrug my shoulders to show strength of character on the outside, but in reality I was thoroughly depleted on the inside.

The following morning, I went outside and leant on the handrail underneath the flare boom, staring down at the lucid troughs of waves and the boiling white horses hoofing it towards the Arctic. I mulled over my loss. It was only money - in the greater scheme of things, it was irrelevant compared to the loss of a loved one's life – Jim - who only a few months previously had been cast from his yacht off the coast of Greenland during the night.

I stared into the inhospitable sea, and I thought of Jim.

Vanishing Point

Serenity spreads over the Gulf of Aqaba and the warm desert sand. I am sitting barefoot on a rock - content, relaxed. The moon, still bright, arcs above the jagged mountain profile to the west, while the sun rises and begins to ignite the horizon to the east, its flames flooding out across the skies and the mountains of Arabia. I begin my apnea exercises; breathing deeply - long inhales and even longer exhales. After ten minutes, I am prepared. I take a long inhale . . . time passes . . . one minute . . . two minutes . . . my lungs start to burn, but I continue to hold . . . strange contractions start to occur . . . I ignore them and continue to hold up to my absolute limit. I check the time: five minutes and six seconds . . .

The light intensifies, and a golden hue seems to drizzle over the mountainside behind me as if the hand of Midas has just stroked the Earth. It is making me feel that I may have discovered another spiritual home. The silence is broken by the grinding of rock on rock somewhere on the slopes above me. I scan them, and into view scurries a nimble desert fox, following his path, a path with no prescribed destination; he knows that; I know that . . . and nature dictates that.

Lochranza gradually edged into sharper focus. Unlike the village, the mountains behind did not - they were fused within the haze and held no physical presence. It was their anticipated existence that was attracting me to them. Gasps of sunshine filtered through an expressionless, grey sky. My mood, along with that of the day, was rather sad.

A piercing screech punched me out of my lousy thoughts as the steel of the small Caledonian MacBrayne car ferry pushed its way up onto the concrete jetty. I swung my light rucksack onto my back, descended onto the pier, and reluctantly wandered off in the general direction of the mountains. The discreet footpath left the road a few hundred metres past the Isle of Arran distillery. In a few moments, the scene turned strangely quiet, remote even, as though I might have just stepped through some fantastical wardrobe into the Highlands of Narnia . . .

Three hours had passed by the time I approached the summit of Caisteal Abhail, Arran's second highest peak. The grassy, summit plateau was narrow, flat and randomly scattered with crusty, granite tors and boulders, spooking me as they emerged through the mist and darkness. Spits of rain tickled my face playfully. I cursed them as I searched for my jacket, but I cursed even more when I realised that I had forgotten it. I carried on towards Cir Mhor, hoping that it wasn't going to rain too heavily. The cone shaped peak imposed itself out of the mist like a Sumatran volcano smouldering in its own sulphurous smoke and ash. I traversed round its flank and into a distant corrie in the hope of finding a suitable place to pitch the tent. I found one; well it wasn't really that suitable, but it had to do.

Within seconds, the sharp nip and the high-pitched whine of the midges had started. I put up my tent by means of an uncoordinated tribal dance as millions of them homed in. Once it was up, I dived into its tiny, nylon space, cursing at the zip because it was burst in the corner. I had come prepared though, and sealed the hole with some sticky tape before lying back with a huge sigh of relief . . .

I was hungry, so I fumbled through my food in the dark. I opened a tin of tuna, drank the brine and ate the chunks with my fingers – the drawbacks of lightweight travelling: no torch, no cutlery and no jacket . . . I located the entrance to my sleeping bag and shuffled in.

Daylight intensified on my flysheet, and I poked my head out with little optimism - the lack of visibility left me with none. There was nothing but a choking fog. Annoyed with the fickle Scottish weather, I carried on ethnically cleansing any remaining midges from the inside of my tent with my fingertip. I have a Buddhist type attitude towards killing creatures, but I draw the line at ticks, clegs, mosquitoes and the dreaded midge. Forget the English; these miniscule, silvery, winged mutants are the Scots' number one enemy. Satisfied that there were now no midges remaining, I curled up again, waiting for the weather to improve.

In time, the mists slowly rolled back to reveal Cir Mhor's pristine sweep of granite slabs, whilst the midges began to recongregate by the door of the tent. I made a dash from the tent towards the slab, with a jute bag stuffed with the usual suspects - boots, chalk bag, oatcakes, water and a fleece.

I had wanted to climb on Arran's granite slabs for the past fifteen years, and now I didn't quite believe that I was here, standing beneath such historical and compulsive rock climbs: *Sou'wester Slabs* and *South Ridge Direct* are special, a must-do for any rock climber visiting Arran. Both routes were first climbed during the Second World War when pioneering was only accessible to the favoured few. Hob-nailed boots, tweeds and a hemp rope round the waist were the usual attire. However, deep in the back of my mind I knew that these were not the routes I had come to climb. I was looking for a harder, solo challenge to push me to my own limits. I didn't want to enhance my ego, nor did I want money from sponsorship or publicity – no, my reasons were personal, and innate, of the sort that I didn't quite fully understand myself.

I found soloing in the mountains stimulating and humbling, clearing my conscience in a modern world that doesn't seem to have one. It is unlike all other dangerous sports, bar free-diving on one's own, because there are no mechanical safety mechanisms involved such as parachutes, hydraulic brakes, ropes, oxygen, and so on . . . it's just raw tendons, muscles, sinews and psyche. It does have its limitations though, because pushing your limits whilst soloing, to be honest, isn't that enjoyable; in fact it's downright terrifying. And it can all go horrifically wrong in an instant.

Vanishing Point is technically the hardest route on the Cir Mhor slabs and had been an objective of mine for many years. Somehow, the idea of soloing the route had begun to grow; another of my unrealistic obsessions that had become a real possibility as I found myself standing beneath the 300ft slab. Firstly I had to become accustomed to the Arran granite - to understand its frictional properties and the way it determined my movement - before I could allow any mind games to ensue.

The rock was still damp after the previous night's drizzle, and a number of streaks seeped down the face like cold tears. I had to wait for the sun, and that meant patience, and patience was a commodity that I had in short supply. So I resigned myself to reading the guidebook and figuring out which routes went where.

I traced the line of *West Point*. Its first ascent was in 1986, by Kev Howett and Mark Charlton, and I wasn't sure if it had been climbed since. However, it looked like the driest route, so I scrambled to the start, looking forward to being tested by the subtleties of the Arran granite at last. At 40ft, I encountered a thin traverse; I read it easily, but the rock was gritty and damp in parts. I finally fell into a rhythm, surrounded by a sea of rock that swept away beneath me in a smooth, graceful way. I wanted to enjoy the climbing more, but it was my first route here, and understandably I was a little on edge. Presently, I was on the finishing ledge, 300ft up, wondering which might be the easiest way down.

I found some perfect holds and followed them down the slab, weaving a trail and reaching the base of the cliff in five minutes. Later, when I checked the guidebook, I discovered that I had just descended *Sou'wester Slabs*. I felt certain guilt, knowing that the mountain gods would be annoyed at my lack of respect towards one of Scotland's finest climbs: a route created by them so that everyone could enjoy it and experience the basic fundamentals of rock climbing in the Scottish mountains. In the flow of it now, I set about *West Flank Route*; definitely a climb of different characters, which always makes for a good experience. I enjoyed using my repertoire of techniques in those initial, damp, man-eating chimney grooves that seemed keen to chew my fists and devour my body; but I was equal to the challenge, utilising some three-dimensional bridging manoeuvres. Once out of the clutches of the chimney, the route opened up into slabs, and the final few hundred feet were taken at a more sedate pace.

Back at the base of the cliff, I sat amongst some grass, munching an oatcake, still wondering about an ascent of *Vanishing Point*. From the little information I had gleaned, I knew that the route had a thin crux section at 90ft where the crack in the slab vanished – the 'vanishing point' – and then possibly a second crux over 200ft up. It was so tempting, and that temptation made my conscious and subconscious minds go to war . . .

'I'm going to solo it. . . '

You're in no state of mind yet!

'I can do it!'

Be patient, you need to acclimatise first . . .

The decision hung in the balance, and since the sun wasn't shining, I wandered away and turned my attention to another slab route: *Insertion Direct*. A small, stubborn seep in the upper scoop dribbled down. I had no option but to wait for the sun to emerge and burn it away, but it still sulked rather forlornly behind a thin wafer of white cloud.

The initial, 150ft pitch was smooth and passed by without much incident, but above that the climb changed its character. Wet, slimy hand-jams mauled my knuckles as I fought the damp cracks with a variety of unusual moves before I could exit onto a platform of rock and enjoy a welcome breather. I sat a while to appreciate the view down heathered Glen Rosa to Brodick and the sea behind. Beyond that was the Ayrshire coast, and somewhere out there on the canvas of the ocean was the infamous, bird-infested dumpling that was Ailsa Craig. But, more importantly, behind me reared a blank granite wall, which fortunately wasn't that blank as a couple of hidden pockets materialised and led the way.

The sun appeared against a pale blue sky; the rocks started to warm and the appearance of those few gentle shafts of light lifted my mood. I decided to climb *South Ridge Direct* because the idea of soloing such a powerfully historic route in the evening light would make for a uniquely memorable experience. I traversed round the flank of the rock buttress to take a better look at this 1,000ft ridge, thrusting its presence down the glen like an indeterminate, ragged spine. It is one of Scotland's finest mountain features and its main obstacles are serpent-like: the scales of the S crack; the forked tongue of the Y crack . . . the route flowed by with raw, emotional power, depositing me on the summit with a contented high.

Daylight began to flicker out, but I had just enough time to solo *Hammer*. In the mood now, it felt to me like a pleasant evening stroll, a bit of light exercise, like taking the dog out for its evening walk - a stress-free time in which to reflect at the end of the day. On my descent, I saw a fine arête that tingled with exposure up on the skyline. I made a mental note and retreated to the tent to psyche up for this new line that I had just discovered, which would involve climbing the smooth slab left of *Insertion Direct* and finishing up at the skyline arête. Yet again I was restless, but I must have nodded off between bouts of nervous tension . . .

Twenty-four degrees; the sea is warm, but not overly so. I'm floating on my back; eyes closed, inhaling air, oxygenating my body, relaxing. I'm immersed in gently lapping water; I would prefer flat calm for better relaxation. As I make a long exhale of air, my body begins to lose a little buoyancy, and my arms paddle lightly to compensate – not ideal. I have to find that zone of total calm, shivering and over-using my muscles isn't good, so I continue the process for a few more minutes, blanking my mind, trying not to think of what I am about to do.

In the morning, I awoke bleary-eyed with a few sore muscles. I checked outside the tent, and the mist hung low on the rocky apron of Cir Mhor, but, like the day before, the curtain of mist rolled back at a similar hour. It was time . . .

It is time. One last inhale, clench my nose, blow once to equalise, turn onto my belly and duck-dive vertically down into the colourful world beneath the sea. I feel free. I pull one stroke and equalise . . . 10ft, another stroke and equalise . . . 20ft. I am concentrating hard; I shouldn't be though, I should be completely relaxed. The coral wall drifts past; there are thousands of small, colourful fish, keeping close to the sanctuary it offers. It is indeed a very fragile ecosystem; I feel fragile down there too, going deeper. Equalize; another stroke, deeper still . . . 50ft . . . 60ft, all is good.

. . . It was time. I sat down at the base of the slab where it slid under a carpet of vegetation. Relax! I couldn't. I pulled into a lonely groove and, near its top when it decided to blank, I sidled rightwards onto another slab. It was fair, and I was finally waking up and easing into a rhythm . . . 100ft . . . the angle eased slightly, relax, gather confidence . . . 130ft; all is good. . . 160ft; concentrate . . . 180ft; confident . . .

. . . all is good . . . 70ft . . . I am well past negative buoyancy and sinking like a stone. I can start to make out the sandy bottom, but distance is hard to gauge in the water. Another 30ft, another atmosphere of pressure, squeezing my body like plastic shrivelling in a fire – I am slowly being vacuum-packed by the weight of the sea. How long have I been going down? Do I have enough air to get back up? The bottom - it is getting close. I equalise again. I can feel myself panicking; I know that fear uses up oxygen . . .

Don't panic!

I smeared up to 200ft; the rock reared up into a dramatic wave. The smears became steeper - I began to panic. The penalty of losing adhesion here - certain death . . .

Don't panic!

. . . Whatever distance I have gone down, I have to go back up; it is a frightening concept. Free diving on one's own breaks the golden rule. To me, it is like soloing - it is

exciting – it is about knowing my own limits and having the choice to test them if I desire. It is pure freedom. How much time do I have before the possibility of a shallow water blackout? One minute. A shallow water blackout is okay if there are people there to retrieve you from the water, they are a safety net as a rope is in climbing if you fall, but soloing deep in the water means the same as soloing on the rock face – another game of Russian roulette. Nearly there, sinking, arm outstretched for the seabed, a little bubble of panic . . .

  No, don't panic!

. . . I started on the wave with fingers and toes, scratching, sticking, being brave, naively believing that a pocket would appear. I was gambling with the laws of probability, and when I realised there wasn't one in sight, a whirlwind of panic blew the confidence right out of me. The stakes had instantly been raised. My game of Russian roulette had not one, but all but one bullet in the chamber. Both minds were smouldering in the fires of irrational thought.

I didn't relax, and I didn't look down; my destiny was down there – a clutch of shattered bones spilling down the mountainside. I was no longer breathing. I was drowning in my own fear. I knew that panic meant death, so what could I do?

  Freeze!
  'I've got to move.'
  DO NOT MOVE!
  'I'm going to die if I don't move . . .'
  Reverse then.
  'Reverse?! I can't. Impossible.'
  REVERSE!

Reverse is harder than forwards on a slab, and when I started to engage, I started to shake as a new dimension of fear took over me. Every black fleck of mica, every shard of feldspar and every crystal of quartz had become my token lifeline. Nothing else existed. I felt as if I were on trial in front of an invisible jury. Each downward smear was excruciatingly tense . . . palms sweating, blood seeping . . . please stick!

I grab a handful of sand and turn. Relax; don't look up! I never look up when I know I'm over 100ft deep; I know how I would react and panic means blackout. I have no fins to propel me to the surface, nor any buoyancy from a wetsuit. I tuck in my chin in order to maintain maximum relaxation. I begin to swim. I can feel myself inflating, inching closer to the surface . . . keep holding breath; stay calm . . . another stroke . . . glide. Then it happens . . .

. . . With a wave of relief, my left foot met an easier angled smear; the jury had found me *not guilty* as I traversed leftwards to the comfort of some holds on the companion route, *Hammer*. When the fires had cooled, I continued up *Hammer* for a while before aiming for the shelf below the soaring skyline arête. The wind had increased, and strands of mist seemed to blow right through me and on without end. A slot at the base of the arête lured me onwards and upwards . . .

. . . The contractions start and I begin to gag for air . . . I react by looking up, and I am surrounded by a vast volume of water. I feel that I am levitating through deep space without air or gravity. What a feeling. I stick my neck down tight, close my eyes and count what might be the final seconds . . .

. . . The thin, exposed upper arête became less generous with holds, making me dash upwards in a rush of panic, snatching greedily into the unknown, hoping that all those millions of years of erosion had created enough pockets to save me. My heart punched away in tune to the *Hammer* and the *Anvil*. My eyes were sore with fear; my thoughts had all but evaporated, a fall incomprehensible, but there proved to be just enough holds and *The Forge* was born . . .

I am in a race. I need to reach the surface of the sea before a shallow water blackout reaches me. I break the surface tension like a suppressed cork and make a rapid exhale before a long, relaxing inhale. I glance around - the sky is pure azure and the distant coasts of Arabia converge towards their Vanishing Point.

Brazilian Learning Curve

The dormant, uniform hills were stencilled to the monochrome of the sky. The day was lacklustre, the air neither humid nor dry. My mood was transparent as my gaze shifted away from the shadow-doomed hills and focussed on the black, inert, overhanging rock that punched into the invisible ozone above. My movement felt fluent and weightless as I climbed upwards on positive holds, and the ground beneath blurred into obscurity. The cliff tilted and a hostile gravity was increasing with every stretch. My momentum receded and my forearms burned as my fingers strained to hold on.

Unwittingly, I had broken the solo climber's Golden Rule – it was no longer possible to reverse to safety. My strength was ebbing away, and the inevitability of falling made me hold on harder and tighter, white knuckled. In the moments that remained, I willed my spirit to depart my body before having to endure the mortal pain of broken bones and a shattered corpse amongst the talus slope far below. Each agonising second slowed to a lifetime. My last fingers uncurled, a knuckle popped, and with that my final, conscious touch with the planet was gone forever. Words bubbled out, but they were stolen, meaningless now, as they vanished into an infinite black hole.

Suddenly, my torso sprang bolt upright as though being raped by rigor mortis. My eyes opened, and sweat drizzled from me. My brain re-engaged and tried to sort out the mayhem. The three-foot fan on the ceiling was humming away in tune to its rotation, and I was shrouded in damp linen. I had endured another one of my nightmares in which fantasy and reality had entwined to produce another intangible soloing exploit.

Drained, I lay on the bed, hypnotised by the fan. I could hear all of the normal late afternoon noises going on in the street five stories below - they were alien to me. There was a television in one corner - it was on, with the volume turned down and Portuguese subtitles on the screen. I felt as though I were in a cell in a foreign country, imprisoned in a foreign language, with no one to talk to. My colleagues were away and working. As I came to properly, the lethargy of boredom overtook me.

I loathed boredom. I picked up my paper knife, brain idling, bringing the blade to my chest, slicing through my skin in a neat line, thinking perhaps to see my heart beating. Crimson tears trickled down my chest. I became queasy and stopped before I went too far. Boredom drove me to the verge of insanity sometimes. I needed to get out and find some adventure.

I ambled into my company's office after a six-hour flight from Qatar in the Middle East. I was glad to have finished my few months of work in those strict, sand-swept, soulless countries. I had barely stepped through the door when I heard a voice pipe up out the blue:

'Jules! Do you fancy going to Brazil next week?'

I stopped dead in my tracks. What I actually needed was a holiday, and I had only ventured into the office to sort out my wages. Working offshore did, however, require that you learned to take the opportunities as they arose, and another stint in a far-away corner of the globe was not to be sniffed at.

Working abroad is never as romantic or as glamorous as it may sound, and Rio de Janeiro was no exception. Arriving with my work colleagues, we found ourselves denied visits to the famous landmarks of the Sugar Loaf, Copacabana beach and the Statue of Christ. Instead, we were driven for four hours to the oil town of Macae and flown out to the oil rig on the next available helicopter. Our six-man team was hired to replace the flare tips, a job that required rigging and welding skills along with a good head for heights. I could never understand why we were flown all around the world to do such menial tasks. I wasn't complaining though; it was a good mix of sunshine, travel and rig work. When we arrived on the rig, we all sat through a half-hour safety induction spoken in Portuguese. No one understood a word, it was a total waste of time.

It was hard, physical work hauling the heavy tips to the top of the flare boom via our cableways pulled taught with our Tirfor ratchet device. It was oddly peaceful, working in suspended space between the sky and the sea on the end of a 300ft flare boom. We started at six and even at that time of the morning our rigging container was like an oven; the flare boom was cooler in the breeze though. We looked forward to lunch when we could sunbathe on the helideck. The locals thought we were 'loco' going out in the midday sun. After supper it was the same - either the gym or the helideck - as the cabins were small, dirty and hot, and none of the television channels were in English.

We completed the work in ten days, and then we were required to do alterations on a drill-ship's derrick in Salvador's naval shipyard, a thousand miles further north – Brazil is a vast country. Alterations required steel to be burnt through with a 'gas axe' (an oxyacetylene torch). This job, whilst dangling from ropes, was the most exciting abseiling work available, especially cutting through rusty steel, because hot rust spat violently, burning holes in boiler suits, flesh and the sheaths of ropes. One slip with the flame could cut through a rope instantly, and it had happened, which was why we used two ropes and sometimes a steel safety link. It was adrenalin-filled work, and I loved it.

The culture of Brazil, even viewed from offshore, never failed to amaze. Whilst I was working on one drill-ship, 80 miles from the coast, a few small, painted, wooden fishing boats appeared. Twenty men stood shoulder to shoulder down the side of a boat, each holding a bamboo pole. A bucket of fish-bits was thrown in the sea and the motor churned the water. In a matter of minutes, the water began to boil frenziedly; blue fin tuna and Dorado were being hooked non-stop. Some of the bamboo poles snapped and floated away. It was fascinating to watch - here I was, working for a 21st century Global Corporation, sucking out black gold in 8,000ft of water, using complex engineering, and there they were, just a few feet away, locked in the 17th century hunter-gatherer lifestyle.

During the helicopter flight back from the drill-ship, I looked out across the vast interior of Brazil, towards a mountain that had a unique index finger of rock piercing through a deep green canopy of jungle. The finger intrigued me, and I wanted to investigate, but thoughts of bushwhacking through miles of jungle in strength-sapping heat, to reach a plinth of rock that was perhaps impossible, put to bed any more ideas. I was far keener to go down to the beach and relax. When we landed, there was a mad rush to grab our bags, check into the hotel, and get to the beach-bar. After a few beers, one of my colleagues waved me over to the back of the bar and into the men's toilet – a small, fetid cubicle.

'What is it?' I remarked in surprise. I couldn't understand what he had to tell me here that he couldn't discuss in the bar. He pulled a small bag out of his pocket and held it up.

'This stuff is pure; have you got a one Real note?' He opened the bag and poured a little of the powder onto the back of his hand before edging it neatly into a line with the edge of his bankcard.

'Right, this is yours!'

'No way, I can't take that!'

'Come on, where's your sense of adventure?'

Sense of adventure! Those words were a red rag to a bull; it wasn't in my nature to be boring. I hunted out a crumpled, green note from my pocket. I flattened the note out on the wall and saw a picture of a bust with evil, opaque eyes. It didn't fill me with confidence in what I was about to do, so I turned the note over, finding a hummingbird printed on the other side. I carefully rolled it up and inserted it into my nose. I pushed one nostril shut and inhaled; the feeling was strange as the powder burned and tickled simultaneously. I walked out of the toilet, propped myself on a stool, and felt rather deflated at what I had just done. I sat there swivelling my bottle of beer on the bar before my mind began to fill with strange, uncontrollable energies.

My trips offshore were random: four days, five weeks, eighteen days, etc. I didn't have a work schedule, which meant I was on standby and couldn't travel away for more than a day or two. I also found it difficult to get motivated for climbing because of the heat, and I didn't know who to ask about the index finger of rock that I had noticed in the jungle. I simply got bored and did mad things, like cutting myself open, because there was nothing better to do. Sometimes my work colleagues were around, sometimes not. On one memorable occasion, there were four of us together and we took a taxi to the bar. The police stopped us for what we thought was a routine check. Some 'gear' was found during the police inspection – I was adamant that they had planted it. They demanded twenty five thousand US dollars. Obscenities burst out, but after half an hour of poor communicative negotiation, we were looking at a fine of two thousand Reai (£700) each. We were given two days to pay. I went for them, furious at their corruption. They began to draw their guns from their holsters. I didn't care that I might be shot; I was having none of it. The others restrained me and calmed me down, before informing me that one of us had actually bought some gear from the taxi driver. We had been set up, and I was told plainly to pay up or we risked the very real possibility of being thrown into prison. I was learning about Brazil the hard way.

I never went out after that. Instead, I studied Portuguese and tried to glean information on the index finger in the jungle. In the meantime, I was given the job of training the local Brazilians in our industrial abseiling techniques, in an indoor football gym. It was hard to teach people who didn't speak my language, but I was lucky to have Alcino, a talkative and excitable character, who was warm, friendly, and spoke good English. When it came to aid-climbing, my students were slow to learn. I wanted them to climb a vertical, steel box-frame up the side wall of the gym, and then to aid climb along the roof to the apex, using ropes, etriers (rope ladders) and cows-tails (short, arm-length links of rope attached to their harnesses). They trained in pairs and it took them up to an hour each. When they were lowered down from the apex on the ropes, they were sweating and tired. By the time they had all eventually finished their aid climb, I was bored, so it was time to liven things up. I gathered them round, and with an impish grin asked them to watch. Barefooted and dangling only from my arms, I climbed up to the roof of the gym, along it and down the far wall in under a minute.

'Now that', I motioned, 'is how you do it.'

That didn't need to be translated; they all stared at me, shaking their heads. We then played football and they ran rings round me, of course, looking at me as though to say: 'Now that is how you do that!'

Some of the guys were climbers and were keen to take me out to some of their local crags. After the first week of training, I organised a churasco (barbecue), where I discovered to my disbelief how much meat and beer Brazilians can consume in one evening. The next morning, nursing a hangover, I was picked up and driven out of the town towards the interior with Fred, Daniel and Peachy. Fred was obviously the person in charge - he spoke a little broken English and was very warm and friendly. Daniel was short and muscular, and I couldn't understand him at all. They were the two active climbers. And Peachy, whose proper name was Herald, was the wheels, the logistics - he was a little more laid-back than the other two in regard to climbing.

There was a lot of animated discussion between them in the car as I tried to catnap. Occasionally, I would bounce up when my arm or neck was burned on the car's hot upholstery. I wasn't sure how I was going to climb in that heat. After half an hour's drive, I suddenly lurched forwards as the car screeched to an unprovoked halt. Daniel opened the door and ran across the road, dodging the traffic, before bending over in the verge and picking up what I thought to be litter. He strolled back to the car with two Coke cans. I wanted to ask what was going on, but trying to decipher what Daniel was saying would only serve to aggravate my hangover. We continued a few miles down the road and the car stopped, and we got out into the potent heat. Above us, poking through the trees, was a white cliff - this was obviously our destination and I became apprehensive about the poisonous creatures that might lurk up there in the jungle.

The cliff was only a fifteen-minute walk away, but as soon as we were under the leafy canopy, the abnormally large mosquitoes latched onto us and were siphoning blood at an immeasurable rate. Fred then slowed, turned, and proclaimed in his best English: 'Julian . . . house of bees!'

Within a few seconds, my foot crunched on a hollow stump. I didn't have time to utter obscenities as the humming intensified rapidly. Overtaken by fear, I turned and tore through the undergrowth with a speed and agility that I didn't know I possessed. All the while I felt sharp, burning sensations in my scalp - how many? I wasn't sure - I just kept running until I heard no more humming and felt no more stinging. My senses soon became overly alert to the dangers of the jungle, as I proceeded to pull the bee stings out of my head before locating and taking an alternative route to the base of the cliff. I crumpled in a heap, glazed in sweat, with a head throbbing from the stings and alcohol poisoning. Things weren't going well at all. Peachy had set the undergrowth on fire to make smoke that would hopefully clear the fog of mosquitoes which had now become unbearable.

The vertical wall above me was about 130ft high and still in the shade. I was hoping the sun would come round quickly, then it would be far too hot to climb, and I could go to the beach and erase my hangover without being bothered by insects and the overheated stress of climbing.

I could see two lines of bolts up the cliff and I was expecting to see some shiny, silver hangers on the bolts for clipping the karabiners, but there only appeared to be iron bars sticking out of the rock, some with eyelets and some without. Fred told me that one of the climbers had welded the eyelets onto the bars in a welder's fabrication shop on an oil rig. The Brazilian bolts, which they called grimpos, were basic but looked sturdy enough. What the hell, I thought . . .

Elhaio - 'Lightning' - was the name of the left hand route that sported a forked crack. Even with a thumping headache, I was thankful for the sharp-end of the rope that had been passed to me – I wanted to vacate the mosquito-infested jungle floor as soon as possible. The steep start was intense on the fingers and quickly turned my forearms into useless lumps of aching lead, and for the remainder of the route I clung on with tenacity rather than finesse, not wanting to fail in front of my new climbing partners. Words rose from the jungle floor; English words in Fred's accent:

'Julian . . . house of bird . . . house of bird!'

I saw a peregrine nest ten feet to my right, but the birds didn't seem to be bothered about me climbing so close to them. Taking precaution though, I climbed to the next bolt and lowered to the jungle floor, withered with dehydration. Once on the ground, Fred, Daniel and Peachy all wanted me to complete the right hand line which still required to be fully bolted.

'Julian, you must complete the way!' Fred insisted, handing me a heavy, green canvas bag and a drill.

'I don't place bolts! There is a crack up there that will take gear', I replied as I pointed to a crack about 30ft above the last bolt. They didn't understand what I was saying, so I pulled out my dictionary to look up the Portuguese word for 'crack'.

'Fenda . . . fenda!' I shouted, motioning with a camming device that I had pulled out of the rucksack. They stared at me in surprise, and spoke hurriedly between themselves before Daniel seized the vacant, sharp end of the rope, tied in and climbed up to the last bolt. Above that, he started drilling a new hole for a bolt, pulled a coke can out of the bag, cut it into slithers, and wrapped the can-foil around the bolt before hammering it home. The 'litter stop' on the road now made sense: they were using Coke cans as expansion devices for the bolts. The strip of aluminium would crush and concertina inside the drilled hold, securing the bolt in place. I laughed and shook my head appreciatively at their inventiveness. Daniel placed two further bolts in the impending headwall before lowering off, exhausted. The sun by this time had come round onto the wall. They turned to me and cajoled me to complete the route. Reluctantly, I tied in and climbed to the last bolt, above which I placed some cams in the crack. Then, out of the blue, the peregrines became angered at my presence, and they dropped out of the sky, dive-bombing me at ungodly speeds. Their margin for error was minimal because they had managed to knock the cap off my head. I managed to cling on to reach the finishing holds and a dilemma: either take a 40ft fall onto the cams or hug a giant cactus to finish. I moved up slowly and pushed my chest towards the cactus and began to wrap my arms around it, as though I were slow dancing with someone I didn't find at all attractive. I managed to raise my centre of gravity and finally release myself from the prickly embrace, continuing to some large tree roots for a belay. I was quivering with fear, checking for holes and snakes, unsure if it was safer to tie in to the roots or just sit untied so that I could leap down the cliff if a snake appeared and became aggressive. I tied in to the belay, alert and shaking, hoping that the boys would climb as quickly as possible.

I was glad to leave the jungle behind. When I returned to Macae, I wandered down to the beach. It was unusually fresh and stormy. I went into the surf with my body board in an attempt to wash away the toils of climbing in the jungle. When I got into the waves, they tumbled me and my board was lost. I was spun round and round. I couldn't escape the powerful motion, and when I popped up, I had a split second of air before the next wave crashed in on me. I was spun again - there was nothing I could do. I knew that I was drowning, and then, miraculously, I popped up again. Grabbing air, I waited for the next killer wave - it never came. I was way behind the line of the breaking waves. I had been saved by a rip tide. A lifeguard had seen me and aided me back to shore. He was pretty angry - he spoke only Portuguese and pointed out the 'no swim' red flags. I sheepishly handed him 50 reai; it made him happy and we parted company.

Fred had managed to organise a trip to the Index Finger in the jungle that I had now found out was known to the locals as The Frade. The north face of The Frade had not been climbed, although Fred had managed to climb three-quarters of the 2,000ft dome, and now he wanted to return to complete the route with Jonathan (a friend of Fred) and me. It was a total bonus that Jonathan was an American and fluent in Portuguese. We left Macae in the depths of the night and drove inland towards the mountains, the roads becoming narrower, steeper and bumpier, and the potholes more erratic. The track coiled round the back of the mountain into another valley full of banana plantations and tussock-grass fields before we reached a rickety, wooden shack. As I got out of the car, I was met by a flock of partially feathered chickens, scratching their feet and pecking in the dirt. An old man came out of the shack, smiling with a toothless grin. His clothes were falling from his bony limbs and his face was like creased leather, withered by the many years of exposure to the sun. Fred spoke to him, pointing up towards the mountain; the only word I managed to decipher was *escalade*, which meant 'climb'. The old boy looked suitably impressed.

Fred had organised everything and our rucksacks were heavy with bottled water. After the one and a half hour approach up steep fields and through a small section of jungle, we eventually arrived at the base of the huge expanse of concave slabs. I was handed the ends of the ropes to lead the first pitch: a shallow-angled slab. When the ropes had been run out 150ft, I sat down on a small ledge and called them on to climb. What I didn't realise was that they both began to jumar up the ropes; I braced and shouted for them to stop, but they couldn't hear me. I was being pulled from the cliff - then, miraculously, I saw a bolt two feet away from me. I clipped into it just in time - otherwise I would have ended up skinned in the jungle.

When they arrived at the stance, I asked who was leading next; they looked at me and Fred queried: 'Julian, you're guiding. Why you not clip grimpos?'

'I didn't see any,' I replied.

We continued up the slabs – they gradually became steeper and more tenuous over the next four pitches. I found about five bolts per pitch, and I began to feel that the Brazilians were braver than I had given them credit for. Pitch six was a loose and wet traverse, but it gained the base of a gully that provided a feature with which to climb higher. There was a small ledge and a weird natural spring at the base of this gully feature: a good place to top up our water supplies. After a brief spell of relaxation, I began to climb a pillar of shattered rock up the left edge of the gully. I couldn't find any bolts, and I had taken no protection. I went into solo mode and tried to stay calm and not think about the consequences of breaking a hold and falling. When Fred and Jonathan reached the belay, I realised how dark it had become; Fred assured me that there was only one more pitch to the bivouac site and that the pitch wasn't too difficult. With that information, I swung off the belay and climbed round the corner . . .

'Crikey!'

I was stunned at the sight of the grossly overhung chimney system cloaked in mud and bushes that towered above me. I was finding it impossible to start until I reasoned the only way to climb it was to swing and pull up through the tree roots like a primate. It worked, and I continued into a more solid, rocky groove above. However, the rock soon mutated again - into a shattered groove, full of mud and vegetation. After 100ft of humbling climbing, I saw Fred's previous bolt out on the right; a little beacon of security. The terrain was appallingly loose, and the bolt was out of reach, so I decided to climb up towards a slender tree. Then my foothold crumbled, and I started to slip, retching internally at the prospect of an 80ft fall through cactus, and down through the shattered groove . . . I managed to grab a clump of grass and leap for the tree in desperation, choking it and throwing a sling round it before stretching across to the bolt. I'd had enough of this ludicrous climb; my body was beaten, my mind frazzled and I just wanted to go down, survive, eat and sleep. I clipped into the solitary bolt and hung there in silence, whilst Jonathan and Fred jumared up the ropes behind me. I tried not to dwell on the fact that we were all hanging from one home made Brazilian bolt secured by the skin of a coke can. As Fred arrived at the stance, I muttered, mutinously:

'That is the worst pitch I have ever climbed in my life!'

Fred looked somewhat perplexed. I think he thought it was actually quite good, but then he mentioned that a large chunk of the gully had collapsed since the last time he had been there. I think I rolled my eyes . . .

Only when the three of us were all hanging side by side in the dark, 1,500ft above the jungle floor, like triplets on ropey placentas attached to one tiny metal womb, did the heated discussion begin:

'Let's go down to the base of the gully to bivouac, because it's too dark to climb'! I said.

'We are nearly there!' Fred replied as he fumbled in his rucksack to find his head torch.

'Well I'm certainly not leading anymore, I'm knackered!'

Jonathan, amicably taciturn for an American, didn't speak a word. I knew he felt out of his depth and worried. Fred was having none of it; he turned and tried to ascend the crumbling gully above us, but to no avail, spilling head torch batteries on us in his efforts. There was no option now - we had to go down, but Fred had different ideas as he lunged up and leftwards into an overhanging cornice of tree roots, branches and anything else he could grab in the failing light.

'You crazy Brazilian!' I shouted, amused and bewildered at Fred's ignorant audacity. Then, a distant cheer tumbled down through the night as he gained the relative security of the bivouac ledge. I followed behind Jonathan in the dark, pulling on the rope and branches and roots. Beneath all my tiredness and anger, I was chuckling away at the madness of it all. Our belay ledge was a small, soil slope strewn with a number of saplings. We shook them, finding them mercifully sturdy enough to support our hammocks. I craved food and water to replenish the energy that had long since vanished in the twilight, hundreds of feet below. I hoped that Fred had brought some food as I heard him rummaging for an age in his rucksack. Eventually, he produced some biscuits, tinned fish and water.

'Thank god,' I sighed.

After a snack, I crawled uneasily into my hammock, feeling incarcerated – bonded as I was to the Index Finger in a veil of mesh. As I lay back, the hammock enclosed itself around me like a Venus flytrap. An hour passed before I decided to sit recumbent in the middle of the hammock and hang my legs over the side. This position felt more relaxing, more human. Fred and Jonathan hung one above the other in their hammocks, like rotund pupae in a weird bunk bed formation. My hammock was on its own. It seemed to be taking the brunt of the wind, or so I thought. The mesh was utterly useless as protection against the elements, especially the impertinent gusts that rifled through my T-shirt every few minutes. Awake and agitated, I stared into the hollowness of the night, dreaming of my lost warm fleece.

In the bar, time began to dissolve; noises became chaotic, shapes morphing, the whole scene effervescing and sparking like nuggets of sodium in water. My mind grew intoxicated, misfiring like a scratched movie starting and stopping, hallucinating between short phases of reality as images appeared and disappeared randomly. The noise and heat of the bar dematerialised, and in the next instant I felt a warm wind caressing my face, and then silence, apart from the tap, tap, tap of footsteps and a dark, cobbled street pulsing with shadows – I must have been on my way home. With whom though? Darkness rolled in again, and all was at peace. Then a chink of light spilled through the darkness and a naked, copper-hued, feminine form appeared in the light.

'Who are you?'

She was laughing and jumped onto the bed beside me on all fours, begging for coition. My head was spinning, and my normal inhibitions – a mixture of coyness and civility - were thrown to the wind as bare carnal desires overwhelmed me. Then utter frustration overrode everything as one hand tried to attain tumescence, whilst the other tried to satisfy her needs. My head was slumped over the curve of her back with a roll of currency hanging out of my nose. Suddenly, two gremlins appeared inside my head, caricatures with lascivious expressions of lust and sin, escalating into frenzy, shredding imaginary pillows with silvery daggers, grinning with intent. White feathers burst everywhere like a ferocious avalanche, smothering me into the deepest oblivion.

Some time later, I re-emerged from my self-inflicted tomb as a shaft of sunlight probed across my eyelids, awakening me. Millions of atoms spun wildly in my skull cavity, and I could do nothing other than lie there in a pain-ridden vacuum. Then the reality of the images replayed; I winced in denial, but it must have been true - my money and my fleece were gone.

Another gust blasted through my hammock. I tossed one way and then the other, and I whinged in despair:

'Is anyone else awake?'

'Me . . . ' Fred's voice rallied from out of the darkness. There was no reply from

Jonathan - he had a wind-proof hammock and was far away from our cold and windy insomnia.

'You want some joint?' Fred asked. I have been known to draw on a joint or cigarette on the odd occasion, to be sociable, but I have never been able to inhale without coughing my lungs up.

'Yeah, I'll come over and join you,' I replied, hoping that the company and the conversation might speed the night along and stop me from going insane. I unclipped from my hammock and swung across to Fred's, where we hung out until dawn. All the while, Jonathan lay blissfully asleep in his cosy pupa above our heads.

The sun slowly emerged, casting shadows down in the valley - we were thankful that the long night was over. Then, rather incongruously, Jonathan's mobile phone rang. He talked for a while, and we knew that the news wasn't going to be good news. He had to go back to work. Fred and I were annoyed at having to retreat so close to reaching our target. Most of the morning was spent abseiling down the wall and back into the jungle. On the abseil, clouds swirled in and engulfed the cliff and, later when we emerged from the jungle, a fascinating electric storm broke out, illuminating the grey sky with jagged lines of yellow light. Water fell in torrents, and the roads turned into rivers. Thunder bellowed around the valleys, with pitched echoes. It was like being in a feature film, except that it was starkly real. We looked at each other, speechless, realising that Jonathan's chance phone call had probably saved us from exceptional misery and the possibility of a lightning strike.

After Christmas, I went to Rio to visit Alcino and his family. They never let me go out alone except to cross the road to the Internet café. Alcino had an optimistic slant on life and always had something to say. He wanted to guide me around his city - he was so proud of it. However, crime was rife in Rio, due to the huge divide between the rich and poor. Cardboard-box homes and the stench of the *Favelas* (slums) sit side by side with fragrant multi-million dollar homes and marinas. It left me feeling humbled, dismayed and lost for words. Our first port of call was the Sugar Loaf, the world famous dome of rock. We climbed the classic *Italian Route* (up the centre of the dome) via two spiritually absorbing pitches. Later, we caught a bus through the city, hopped off, and then climbed some smooth, chocolate-domed slabs rising straight out of the storm drains. 100ft up one of these slabs, I turned to view the city and I peered straight through the window of a hospital ward, its elderly patients peering back, expressionless. They had seen it all before no doubt. I spent the New Year at a party on Copacabana beach, amidst fireworks and partygoers. The following morning, Alcino took me up Copovado Hill to climb a 400ft route that had the most enlightening views over the expanse of Rio. Just below the summit, we rested and shared a joint before scrambling over the balustrades under the statue of Christ, much to the amazement of the tourists.

When I returned to Macae, Fred wanted me to help him to complete a route that he had started some years before. The route was known as *The Pillar* - a 500ft wall of granite, of which the first 300ft was a detached pillar sitting against the main face. The pillar top was the size of a kitchen table and an ambient seat on which to relax and enjoy the view of the baking countryside. Behind me, the face reared up, steep and clean. There was a line of six bolts, which suddenly stopped in the middle of the face.

'Julian, you need to finish the way,' Fred announced, handing me a bag of tools. I pulled out a small lump hammer, a homemade chisel, which had some foam glued to a big washer to protect the hand, and two bolts. He also handed me a white piece of pipe.

'Err . . . what's this for Fred?'

Fred demonstrated by blowing into it.

'Ah . . . is it to clear the rock dust out of the bolt-holes?'

I smiled and took the pipe, placing it round my neck. I thought to myself that I wouldn't need any of it and I would just climb with no protection until I reached an alcove where I could place a belay bolt, and then afterwards Fred could fill the bolts in between to his requirements. Or so I reasoned. I was about to step across the void between the pillar top and the parent face when Daniel shouted: 'Julian . . . !'

That was about the only word that Daniel had spoken that I had understood. I looked down at him lying on the flat pillar top, holding out his stretched arm, offering me the joint that he held between his fingertips.

'Nao obrigado,' I replied.

I turned, clipped the first bolt, and started the climb up the blank wall. Soon I had clipped all the bolts and was on my own. Tension began to mount because the moves were far more precarious than I had thought they would be. My only security now was the bolts, which were hanging from my harness. I had never placed one before and I wasn't sure if I could place them, or even find a place to stop. Eventually, I found myself over 30ft above the last bolt, on a small foothold. It would have to do . . .

I delved into the bag for the hammer and chisel. My eyes glanced downwards onto the pillar top 80ft below, catching sight of three tanned, expectant faces: stoned expressions of angst and of relief when they realised I was going to put in a bolt. They had a great view. I didn't know if they realised that if I fell off now, I would pendulum down upon them and knock them off their little perch, like skittles blasting into eternity.

Ping! The chisel just bounced off the surface of the hard, flawless granite.

Bloody hell, I'm never going to make a two-inch deep hole with this!

Eventually, I managed to smash my way through the skin of the rock. Once the hole was started, the rest became easier, although time-consuming. The day was heating up, and the sun emerged from around the shoulder of the adjacent hill. My feet started to sweat and ache in tight boots, and my legs became cramped from the strain. Intermittently, I blew rock dust from the hole with my pipe; it coated my face and mingled with sweat to produce a clay paste. The remainder went down my parched throat and into my lungs, making me cough. After forty minutes of toil, the hole was deep enough; I pulled the bolt out of the bag and hammered my lifeline into its home. I clipped in, felt secure, and climbed on to place a further bolt another 30ft above. The sun made me squirm as I tunnelled, yet again, into the rock. The alcove was still another 20ft above me; I had no more bolts - a good excuse for retreat. I had put two bolts in 60ft of climbing, to their six bolts in 60ft: they weren't happy, so we returned to complete the route and place yet more bolts. I was learning to drill the Brazilian way . . .

I had done very little work as I was waiting for a rig-building job. George, my boss, would leave me the keys to the company car whenever he went away. It was fantastic to have that freedom, and I started to explore the wilderness on my own. I passed one crag that I thought might be good, and I set off in the abhorrent midday heat to check it out. The cliff was hemmed in by jungle and far bigger than I had originally thought when I had seen it from the road. I caught sight of a beautiful line that followed a tiny flake feature, merging with some pockets, above which hung a big slab. With the urge to climb overtaking any common sense, I pulled onto the flake with fingertip-sized holds. My fingers sweated in the excruciating heat, but I climbed on. The flake ended and I found the pockets to be useless. I looked down to the jungle floor, and to my horror realised that it was already 40ft away. I started to panic, calming down when I realised that I could jump into the foliage of the tree behind me and that it might somehow slow me down and cushion my fall. It was a marginal option, so I continued, scratching fiendishly at the shallow pockets, pulling out onto the slab above. The fear of falling disappeared and was replaced by the fear of whatever poisonous creatures I might encounter: giant ants, bees, snakes . . . I charged my way down through the untrodden jungle, scared as hell, brushing off all the imaginary spider webs. When I had exited the trees, I looked back at the climb I had done; it looked quite blank and was undoubtedly the hardest climb in the region. I didn't name it or tell anyone because the locals would want me to go back and bolt it, name it and grade it - such is the nature of human beings and their ideals of colonisation. I preferred to let it rest in peace.

My next job was failing to materialise, so I decided to fly back to the Far East. On the morning of the flight, I bought myself a new pair of trousers with plenty of pockets - I needed to stash a backlog of wages on me in cash. The major drawback was that I had to catch a taxi into Rio and pick up thirteen thousand US dollars from the company's head office before going to the airport. I stuffed wads of notes into my trousers and walked out into the street, feeling vulnerable and highly electrified; it was a well-known fact that some inhabitants of Rio would shoot you dead for ten dollars, let alone thirteen thousand! I was wary - someone in the office could easily have tipped off a friend. I was certainly getting an unorthodox fix of adrenalin. Later, a customs official found the money on me, but his boss waved me through; my company had already paid him off. It was all corruption and backhanders in Brazil.

I had been in Singapore for a fortnight before I was recalled for the job. My journey - from Singapore to Tokyo, to Seattle, to Miami, and then to Rio - took another three days. I arrived in Rio with chronic jet lag. Initially Brazilian customs weren't going to let me in because of discrepancies with my work visas. I didn't really care, they could send me back if they so desired, I just wanted to sleep. It was one of the few luxuries in life that couldn't be denied and anywhere would do. When I finally arrived at the company house, known as the 'casa de gringos', I found a bed in a hot, mosquito-infested room with torn mesh around the windows and dried blood splats on the walls, and slept for seventeen hours in someone else's rumpled sheets.

I was on the helicopter in a few days to start what became my most harrowing month's work. The company had priced half a day to take down a windwall and four days to install a new one. A windwall is the galvanised sheeting, about 20ft high and 40ft long, on each of the four sides that circled the fingerboard (a framework of steel fingers that holds the drill pipe in position). It is situated halfway (80ft) up the drilling derrick to protect the derrickman from the elements. I was given a team of three Brazilians and an ex-pat (Ben Stagg). We were supposed to do the work on nightshift, hot-bedding some of the time too (this is where the same bed is shared between dayshift and nightshift personnel). As soon as the job started, I found out that all the walkways were attached to the outside of the windwall; this meant when we took it down there would be nowhere to walk safely.

It took five days to take the windwall down, and the new one did not fit. Also, the rig cranes could not reach up high enough to lift the replacement one into position. The Brazilian welder was slow, didn't understand English, and was terribly scared - he was a fatality waiting to happen. In fact they all were, so I made them run the winches and kept them on the drill floor. Ben and I cut steel, welded, fabricated, ran up and down the ladders and across the fingerboards in the dark, very rarely attached to a rope. We were behind time, but we grafted, sometimes for 16 hours a day. I had never known anyone to work so hard - we were pushing each other to utter exhaustion. It was really fun in a mad way. We were twenty days behind schedule when the last piece of windwall was ready to be put into place. The rig crane was going to pick it up, and Ben and I were going to hook it up to the derrick winch and unhook the crane. The crane picked up the sheet off the helideck; the wind caught it and it began to spin crazily, like a demonised kite. The deck crew tried to hold onto the tag lines to maintain control, but they were having difficulty, and one of them was lifted off his feet and flew off the end of the rig, hanging on the end of the tag line 100ft above the sea. I stared down, frozen in astonishment. Finally, everyone on deck was holding on and managed to get it under control.

Once winched up, we bolted and welded it into place during the middle of the night. I slept on the helideck the next day, so relieved was I that it was over and that no one in my team had been killed. Never again, I thought; this work was more dangerous than soloing.

When I returned onshore, I felt that I needed a week's recuperation at the beach: balancing on the slack-line, swimming in the surf, trying to forget the physical and mental stress of the rigs. Fred wanted to go back to the Frade. However, I had made it clear that on no account was I going back to climb that loose, overhanging gully. Instead, I preferred to climb straight up the centre of the 2,000ft face. It looked clean, and clean, aesthetic routes appealed more to someone like me with mild OCD inclinations. I had decided to take a rack of traditional gear to supplement the 12 bolts Fred had. As the first four pitches were already bolted, I reckoned that there would be a further eight pitches or so to the summit. Each pitch would need a belay bolt and the remaining four bolts could be used as and when necessary. In retrospect, my idea turned out to be a ludicrous misjudgement. Halfway up the face, the rock became seamless and featureless apart from some weird shrubs whose roots dangled down, clinging to the bare rock. It made me pause and think about 'natural selection' on the extremities of life. The plants were striving and thriving where nothing else could, whilst I was clinging there for an experience - I had a choice.

Nerves started to fray when I was 70ft out from the belay on the seventh pitch, with the rope dangling uselessly from my waist, the drill dangling awkwardly from my neck, and Fred shouting persistently from below:

'Place grimpos . . . place grimpos!'

I realised the gravity of the situation – a 140ft fall onto a slim, metal rod, only half in, from which all three of us were suspended. I felt kind of reckless and free, but Fred had two children and a wife, and Jonathan's wife was expecting a baby. I had no responsibilities, but knew I had a duty. I shakily pulled the drill round and pushed the bit into the rock . . . bolt in, and up I continued. The heat was abhorrent, and my thoughts centred back on the beach and the surf . . .

I walked along the beach - golden sand, blue sky and warm surf - it was what most people would consider a paradise. Life seemed idyllic. I had work, loads of sunshine, and massive rock climbs in the jungle to attempt. My mind started to analyse life though, and I began to realise that although Brazil was beautiful, it simply wasn't 'home'. I missed the fresh air, the chill, the green fields, even the snow and the storms - the harsh, ever-changing charisma of the Scottish landscape and its coastline. As I stared out into the blue distance, a cloud of sadness floated over me. The learning curves of my Brazilian experiences flooded back in, good and bad, but I knew then that I had to be resilient and leave for home - before home, wherever that might be, disappeared without a trace.

Howff Dwellers

Debates: love them or loathe them, they are an integral part of our society. Everyone has an opinion. If you ask a random climber in Britain where the best mountain cliff in the country is, they will probably point you in the direction of North Wales and Clogwyn Du'r Arddu, affectionately known as 'Cloggy'. It has its very own guidebook; sagas spill forth from every page, and tales of first ascents are loaded with recollections of bravery, rivalry, skulduggery and out-and-out passion. Cloggy is made up of a random assembly of geometric walls, grooves and slabs scoured into the north west bow of Snowdon. The infamous routes of *White Slab, Great Wall* and *The Indian Face* all abide there, and, because of these routes, Cloggy has gained a Hollywood stage presence amongst climbers. Others may point you in the hallowed direction of Scafell, England's second highest mountain. Its summit is dripping with volcanic precipices that have lofty views over Lakeland and brilliant, unfathomable climbs that have undergone pioneering persistence for well over a century. *Botterill's Slab* and *Central Buttress* are prime examples. However, a few climbers might point you in the direction of the Dubh Loch. Many might raise a brow and say 'where?' Creagan Dubh Loch is named after the loch beneath it - it means, quite simply, 'the cliff of the black loch'. It bathes in its own secrecy like a recumbent, sleeping giant in the remote, rolling plateau of the eastern Cairngorms, a shoulder away from its more famous neighbour, Lochnagar. It certainly doesn't have the infamy of Cloggy, or perhaps Scafell. This may be due to the low profile nature it has in the corresponding guidebooks, or perhaps it is due to the taciturn nature of the local climbers, but it has meant that some of the best mountain climbs in the British Isles have remained moody, esoteric and secluded.

The 1985 guidebook to the Cairngorms was a workhorse with no pictures other than those on the cover. It did what a guidebook should do, and 'pointed the way' rather than inspired. Paradoxically, the front cover picture of Pete Whillance, surrounded by a deep menace of exposure whilst clinging tenaciously to the beautiful slab of *Naked Ape*, had drawn me in to a deep feeling of wanting to be there, to experience the bold and technical climbs the Dubh Loch had on offer.

My first trip to the Dubh Loch was such a wonderful experience that it sparked a long-lasting romance that endures to this day. It was April 1990, and my climbing partner was Wilson Moir, the Dubh Loch's most favoured son for many years. As we cycled in, Loch Muick was a giant mirror, without a ripple; adders basked and the heather-clothed, granite hills baked in temperatures more akin to North Africa. As we approached along the gently elevating, worming footpath, waterfalls hissed and then, up ahead, this sumptuous, naked rock revealed its textural audacity. Blessed with the whole cliff to ourselves, we were spoilt for choice. We decided on *Voyage of the Beagle*; six pitches that foil their way through a maze of inhospitable, granite architecture, embracing the true, quirky nature of climbing. I soon found out that I was unused to the discreet style of climbing that is required there, when I fell from a thin seam in an otherwise blank plane of rock. I found myself nearly 30ft lower than I had been a few seconds ago, staring Wilson in the face on the belay. I was greeted with a stone-cold stare, and since Wilson was uncannily frugal with words, not a word was spoken. He swiped his prized bandolier (consisting of old hemp rope coated in a plastic tube) from my shoulders and led the remainder of the route with supreme confidence. Two days later we departed. The cloud billowed in, the temperature plummeted, and whilst cycling down the shores of Loch Muick, Wilson disappeared ahead into an oncoming blizzard as I pedalled vigorously to keep up on his Mum's fold-up bike. It inspired many return visits.

Over the next few years, Wilson and I climbed many of the most prestigious routes on the Central Gully Wall. They weaved their deceptive brilliance through flaunting overlaps and devious slabs. Wilson was a PE teacher and immensely fit, and the usual script was that whenever I failed, he succeeded. It was pretty humiliating to be tugged up routes by a human winch. On *Perilous Journey*, I had severed the sheath of his brand new rope when it had caught on an edge after I had fallen. On *Cannibal,* my arms had burnt out on the steep, first pitch. He took control on the three remaining punishing pitches above whilst I sat uselessly on the belays, paying out rope, watching in awe at the sheer determination, commitment and will to succeed of the quiet Shetlander. It was a great privilege for me to share the same rope as him on that day.

In those early years at University, I used to occasionally swerve the library and sneak into the Dubh Loch on warm, spring days, to solo a big slab route such as *Black Mamba* or *Cyclops.* The freedom of escaping and losing myself in the hills was like a drug to me at that time. Mostly I had the cliffs to myself. However, on one occasion I found myself accompanied into the Dubh Loch by Danny Laing and Welsh guidebook writer and climbing fanatic, Paul Williams. Danny is a close friend of mine. I had met him when visiting his climbing shop in Aberdeen. He and his wife, Lorna, treat me like family and in later years I have climbed a lot with their son, Daniel. Danny is a very down to earth and sociable type, and the only time I have ever silenced him was when we were abseiling off *A Likely Story* on Eagle's Rocks with Daniel. After they had abseiled, I decided that I did not want to leave the gear behind, so I took it out and abseiled from a juniper root instead. Danny and Paul were going to climb *Goliath,* and I was going soloing. On the path up the glen, the morning sun streamed down and the cliff lit up in the distance. Danny and I were persistently but jovially trying to make

Paul admit that the Dubh Loch was in actual fact a better cliff than his beloved Cloggy.

On our arrival at the beach at the head of the Dubh Loch, Paul and Danny headed off straightaway to go up Central Gully. I remained there, listening to their progress as the stones rumbled underfoot, until there was silence as they were out of earshot. I had a swim and then slept in the heat of the day. When I woke, the sun had gone, leaving behind only long shadows down the far side of the glen. I listened intently for voices up in the gully, but there was nothing audible. I had no idea what time it might be. I picked myself up and hastened to the base of the 1,000ft Central Slabs and the start of *Dinosaur/Pink Elephant*. Soon I was 200ft up, beneath a large, fearsome overlap that extended for the full length of the slab. The traverse left looked deceiving and difficult in parts. I felt that I had climbed too high and decided to try a downward traverse. I hated downward traverses whilst soloing, and I lost my nerve. I became stuck, but I scoped out a tiny ledge to my right, climbed over to it, and from my small seat of reprieve, contemplated fate and a possible solution. I thought the best one would come in the form of a rope, so I waited for Danny and Paul to appear out of the base of Central Gully, having completed *Goliath*. But time passed by, and there were no human voices and no crunching of rocks. They had simply vanished. I began to fear that they might have wandered straight back to Loch Muick along the summits. With that thought, I began to shiver, realising that nightfall was imminent. The prospect of benightment became a reality, and with that realisation my mind switched into survival mode. I untied my 4mm chalk bag cord and I tied a small knot in one end that I jammed into a flared crack. In the other end I made a loop and tied it round my wrist. I felt a little more secure in the knowledge that I had handcuffed myself to the cliff; if I were to fall asleep and roll off the ledge, the cord should guarantee my security. Soft, velvety shadows rolled down the distant hillsides, and my mind spun out all kinds of combinations and permutations. Time was slowly ticking away, the sky was becoming darker and the cold was increasing. I began to reconsider my choices.

The idea of waiting and shivering all night, handcuffed to the cliff, was not an option to someone who had zero patience. I could not bear to sit for another ten minutes, let alone through a whole night.

Get up and climb! I kept telling myself.

I untied my cord, reattached my chalk bag, and tried to get moving, all cramped and sluggish. I juddered my way across and into *Dinosaur Gully*, following it to the upper terrace. I thought about sitting it out until daybreak once again, but instead I continued. At 900ft, I could barely make out the loch beneath me, nor the mountain tops against the lighter grain of the night sky. The cliff then became near vertical. The holds were bigger and more functional. Each move, each pull, was another foot closer to safety until my vertical world gave way to a vast, horizontal plateau. In a strange sort of way, I enjoyed my nocturnal adventure. I ran along the plateau, barking with relief at nobody and nothing in particular.

I spoke to Danny the following morning - from what I had gleaned, they had climbed *Goliath* quite quickly and had probably vacated the crag whilst I was still sleeping amongst the boulders. Notably, on the way back out and with the Dubh Loch in their wake, Paul had finally admitted to Danny that it was indeed a very fine cliff, perhaps finer than Cloggy, but he had made him swear to maintain the secrecy of his admission. Tragically, Paul died soloing a few years later after falling 30ft from *Brown's Eliminate* at Froggat Edge in the Derbyshire Peak District, the sad loss of one of climbing's most insatiable characters.

After a few years of absence, I desperately wanted to return to the well-remembered smells and sounds of the Dubh Loch and to touch the granite once more. That I did, with Kevin Smith. Known to his friends as 'The Fruit Bat,' Kev was a plumber to trade. He had a wiry frame and immense strength, and he spoke a language all of his own. He lacked common sense when it came to climbing - he had no idea of racking gear, reading guidebooks or following a line. Many times he would shout down in his best Aberdonian twang:

'Pher do I go now?'

I would shake my head in despair and shout back: 'up the crack!' or 'into the corner!' or just mumble under my breath: 'Follow the bloody holds!'

Late one summer's evening, when we were bivouacking in the howff underneath the central slabs, Kev was keen to try a new line following an arching corner. Darkness fell, but this didn't deter him - he was stoned! He nearly made it, but had to retreat in the dark. He smoked weed long into the night, eventually forcing me to move out of the howff. I slept on the flat, snooker table-sized tablet of granite that formed the roof. Having space, fresh air and watery moonshine was far more pleasurable than suffocating inside the cramped, rocky hole beneath me, 'spooning' with Kev.

I awakened to the warm tickle of the morning light across my eyelids. It was a beautiful dawn, and the rock gleamed with an ancient purity in the sun's low glow. I wandered down to the loch for a swim. Kev emerged from the howff late and couldn't remember much about climbing the night before. This showed when he made a right pig's ear of trying to complete the route he had so dreamily climbed the night before - it was amusing to watch. He finally succeeded and named the route *Howff Dweller*. I didn't see Kev much after that, but I heard later that year that he had burned down his flat in Aberdeen, and the police were keen to point out his huge lump of hash concealed in cellophane, melted on the living room floor.

I tried thereafter to make annual visits to the Dubh Loch, but during the late nineties I did not manage due to work commitments abroad - 1997 was no exception. This was the year that Stork and Gary Latter were to attempt an audacious, new line up the unblemished right arête of the *Naked Ape*. Gary was on the belay at the top of the first pitch, 60ft above Central Gully. Stork was in the lead, 20ft above Gary, when he pulled a block off and fell with it. The block hit Gary on the head and knocked him unconscious. There was nothing now to stop Stork from falling the 80ft into the gully, where miraculously he had managed to hit the only soft patch of ground amongst multitudinous boulders. Stork, in shock, shook himself down, and getting no response from Gary, untied his ropes and soloed the 60ft to the belay where Gary hung limp with a head wound. Stork then performed a rescue. Undeterred, they returned to complete *The Origin of Species* within a fortnight. Such is the addictive lure of securing a first ascent of one of the best mountain rock climbs in Scotland. Four years later, I returned and made the second ascent with the enthusiastic Tim Rankin - 'The Portlethen Terrier' - known for his strength, voracious consumption of snack food, and his bouldering prowess.

A few years later, I was more in tune with soloing and had almost discarded ropes for good. At that time, I was staying in a small cottage in upper Deeside with Joanne Apps and Dari Roberts. Jo, an IT consultant, commuted to London for three days a week, and Dari was nocturnal, so I rarely used to see them. The Dubh Loch was now so close at hand that it became my local crag. It wasn't the most appropriate place to be soloing, but that didn't deter me.

One clear day, I decided to go and camp by the loch to experience the magical, incandescent light that sparks across the cliff at dawn. This light never lasts long and by mid-morning it has all but dissolved into hazy air. I cycled in with no particular sense of urgency – it was time to enjoy soaking up the atmosphere, the scent of the heather, and to listen to the refreshing din of icy spray from distant waterfalls. At the end of Loch Muick, I passed by Queen Victoria's summerhouse, through the pine forest, and out onto the open hillside. I ambled on, and when I reached the far end of the loch, I pitched my tent on a flat patch of turf by a sandy beach, at the point where the river issues into the loch. Having got my campsite organised, I lay back and gazed up at the granite bulk of the Dubh Loch - it made me feel vulnerable and insignificant. Climbing on it was a commitment in itself, but to solo such long mountain routes required something altogether different. I was in no mood to solo on it for now – instead, I hastened to the south-facing slabs of Eagle's Rocks on the friendlier, sunnier side of the glen. A strip of lush, stalky grass lay beneath the slabs, like a comfy hammock; a place to sleep, to ponder, to meditate, or even to look across to the Dubh Loch whilst revelling in sunshine. After an hour of resting here, I became bored and wanted to do something. An idea had taken shape: I put on my boots and chalk bag, sheepishly looked up and down the heather-clad glen to make sure no one was around, and then climbed the 250ft slab of *A Likely Story*, naked. I pulled my chalk bag round to cover my front because, ironically, I felt self-conscious. The light breeze tickled my bare skin, unnerving me and making me visualise a fall and the outcome: a strip of raw flesh, blood, and a friction burnt, naked body - quite perverse really. Within twenty minutes, I had soloed up and climbed back down. I continued to sunbathe, somewhat nonplussed. After a few hours, the sun dropped below the hills, shadows sprang up and accentuated the surroundings, and the air began to chill. It was time to descend to the tent.

My dinner consisted of a lump of cheese, two hard-boiled eggs and a few carrots. I had taken minimal food because I believed that a toxin-free diet would lead to a clear mind for soloing. Was I losing it? My stomach pined for more, but that was all I had allocated. I considered a three mile walk, four mile cycle and ten mile drive to Ballater, simply to buy some chocolate or something luxurious, but Ballater had no 24 hour shop, so the effort would have been in vain. As darkness rolled in over the mountain, a dust-yellow moon emerged at the far end of the loch. It was twice its normal size and hung there, untouchable in its allure. I decided that this was a good omen for successful soloing in the morning. After a restless night, a diluted sun appeared over the horizon, exactly where the moon had been the night before. The ever-strengthening rays began to splash the Dubh Loch with a divine veneer of gold. The sight of the cliff made me glow, but I wasn't really in a positive enough mood to solo *Blue Max*. It seemed to me that it was a day to enjoy life, rather than to lose it. I rummaged for breakfast and found only an apple, a banana and a kiwi - that was it, sum total.

The approach to *Blue Max* was only a five-minute walk over heather-choked boulders. I stopped to go to the toilet, crouching down like a furtive, wild animal - out here I was exactly that, feral. I didn't care. I never carried paper in the mountains, so I did my usual, making use of heather, grass and sphagnum moss. Unfortunately, there was little of the latter around and I ended up tearing my rectum with heather twigs.

I had mixed emotions – the sun–glazed folds of granite were inspiring me, but embarking on a 1,000ft solo was at the same time intimidating me. I ate half of my banana, and as a seal to my commitment to survive, I told the other half that I would eat it on my return. I scrambled to the base of the climb and started my well-worn ritual – carefully adjusting my chalk bag and attempting to find relaxation with the compulsive therapy of crushing chalk between my fingers. I made sure that the handwritten description of the route was in my pocket, wiped my boots on my trouser legs, and had one last gaze down the glen. The initial overlap at 30ft is tough. This I had found out a couple of weeks before, when I had retreated from it with frozen fingertips, thanks in no small part to a howling gale. Above the overlap, friendly holds followed for a further 200ft to a small ledge. I stood here for a while, relaxing into the zone. Above loomed a large overlap, and out of the corner of my eye I saw the ledge I had been stuck on eleven years earlier. I smiled because absolutely nothing had changed: I was still feeding the same old rat.

Beads of water dribbled from the overlap and down the slab like baby asps – thin, unassuming and lethal. I smeared between them, tense and cat-like, before I made the final pounce to gain a comfortable hold. The overlap itself was easier than I had expected. My trail bent back into a groove and here there were more lethal dribbles. I soon reached ladder-like holds of runnelled granite that led to the terrace. Soloing on the upper slabs had an almost humorous air about it, and I felt untouchable, floating in space and time, with a free spirit and a cleansed soul.

I pulled dreamily onto the plateau. I had come to understand that, paradoxically, it was these brief spells of derring-do that gave me the space I needed to remain sane in this world. I descended into the huge, inclined fan-delta that carves the Dubh Loch in two - Central Gully. The gully is choked with chunks of rock that resemble a turbulent, granite river. The smell of cordite lingers to remind us of the explosive forces at play, and it feels humbling to be dwarfed in the gully. At the base of *Blue Max*, I ate the other half of my banana and then wandered down to the beach at the head of the loch, intent on a siesta. Mentally I was in the eye of a storm. Next up was *King Rat*, and for energy I had the choice of an apple or a kiwi fruit. I opted for the kiwi and kept the apple for the seven mile journey home. With the amount of food I was eating, I might well have just stepped out of James Clavell's novel, 'King Rat'.

I looked up to the hovering roof of *King Rat*. It looked rather insignificant, although I was well aware that the cliff is deceiving and grossly foreshortened. I gathered my boots and my thoughts. They were exploding . . .

Why do you have to do it?
'Because I want to . . . '
Is it worth it?

It didn't matter what my subconscious was telling me, my inner drive was too strong, and there was nothing that could be done to remedy that. Without much further thought about what I was doing, I found myself 120ft up, beneath the roof that flew out over my head. I gulped. I had always been frightened of climbing roofs; they were my Achilles heel, unless, of course, they were above deep water. So for me to solo a roof 120ft above boulders the size of cookers was unthinkable. I continued, nonetheless, as though I were under the influence of some Medici force. I stretched out for some holds in the roof, tentatively playing with their textures and grip, trying to get an idea of what was needed to overcome the obstacle. My first attempt halted when my feet cut loose; my heart punctured my chest cavity with fright. I swung back down and sulked in the back of the niche, reviewing things and gathering more commitment. Finally, I crept back out, pulled on, and kicked my left leg out across the void, watching intently as my foot cut a curve through the air, locking onto a tiny foothold . . . precise and edged. I prayed that it would hold against the jitters that were vibrating through my legs. I wanted to close my eyes and escape from the diabolical situation. I let go with my right hand and swung outwards over a realm of exposure. Realising that the flake from which I was hanging was loose, any remaining rationality that I may have had was obliterated. I couldn't breathe or think. In cranial meltdown, I pulled and torqued without recognition onto the blissful sanctuary of a ledge. The final 500ft were functional and simple.

On reaching the plateau, although slightly joyous, I found that I also felt empty and completely raped by my own adrenalin. It was time to descend and to take a swim in the loch to wash away all the angst. The glacial meltwater did just that. I shot out quicker than I had gone in, and lay outstretched on the beach, pondering the great geological cycle: magma to granite, granite to sand, sand to beach, beach to sediment, sediment to sandstone and sandstone through metamorphism to magma . . . primary processes driven by temperature, tectonics and time. After a few hours of revelling in the contemplation of what was important to me in my life, seeking direction, I became acutely aware that I was starving. I hoped that my last apple would be enough fuel for me to make it to Ballater - and the thought of a white, Magnum ice cream spurred me on my way.

Déjà Vu

Dartmoor – subliminal, abstract, elegantly simple to the eye - disappeared into the horizon like an infinite fairway. The colours that bounced back embraced the spectrum; purples, greens, browns and yellows, all blended affectionately. The mottled grey tors seemed out of keeping, protruding from the moor like dinosaur coprolites. The edge of the moor tapered away into quaint and mysterious valleys clothed in bracken and oak. It was here that Conan Doyle's Hound of the Baskervilles bounded through his imagination. The absence of wind instilled lethargy and the scent of the gorse brought back teenage memories. I spent many an hour searching for my wayward golf balls amongst these bushes with their spirited thorns. I lay there for some time absorbing the mid-September warmth, pondering, until the hound appeared, floating across the moor with silent paws and supernatural stealth. Was it a trick of the imagination, or just the inert shadow of a cumulus cloud, teasing and tickling its harmless trace across rural England? The hound within me awakened, wanting to feed on a diet of exercise, adrenalin and excitement, rather than dreams, myths and bygone literature.

I was lying against the largest tor on Dartmoor, Hay Tor. Standing 100ft tall, its slowly-cooled skin is coarsely crystalline and tough, a perfect medium for soloing and on which to harmonise both faith and fear. Today wasn't a day to flex muscles and sweat testosterone; it was one on which to pass over the rock in humility and silence. Within ten minutes, my rubber soles were whispering to the warm-blooded rock of *Aviation*, a varied test of granite craftsmanship - grooves, delicate shuffles, overlaps and slabs - leaving it lightly dusted in chalk. In pursuit of more of them I turned, leaving peace in my wake, pressing on to a new destination in a whirlwind of dust and diesel fumes, searching out the sweetest granite kiss that the moor could provide. The back end of Vixen Tor provided the setting. The slab portended an exercise in delicacy; gentle yet dangerous. The holds were like diamonds; tiny, glittering and crucially precious. Amongst stunted oak and bird song, my boots licked crystal teeth and breezed by the *Docker's Dilemma*.

Without indulging in the local delicacy of clotted cream teas, I dumped Devon for Cornwall - on and on to a no-man's land tapering into the sea. My chalk-wizened paws had never before clawed at the Cornish granite and greenstone rocks, but now my tendons were taught and twitching. After a hundred-mile dash from Dartmoor, the seaside town of St Ives passed by in a sunny haze, and excitement welled in me at the idea of one whole week's worth of clear, autumnal skies. The West Country was going to be inspiring. I parked up close to a farm and ran down the narrow-worn coastal track towards Gurnard's Head – a formidable, 200ft precipice of greenstone dropping vertically from gentle heathland into the ravages of the Atlantic swells.

Sea air filled my nostrils, and the open aspect of the coastline gave me energy enough to overshoot the descent path, finding myself negotiating a sea of thorns in my flip-flops. Amending my approach, I was soon sandwiched between the ebony-lustre rock of the greenstone and a glittering sea, strolling sideways in a trance. The odd pre-chalked hold comforted, leading the way, never too far above shimmering water until a friendly groove seduced me upwards and away from the prancing white horses, the *Astral Stroll* complete. Drugged with delight, and needing another fix, I locked onto *Behemoth* and traced a path up its seemingly impossible flank on hidden, positive edges, lost in the intricacy, the spell broken only by the horizontal world 200ft above the splashing waves. With the greenstone experience behind me, I carved down blind, twisting, country lanes in need of a fix of Cornish granite before daylight dissolved into dusk. My canvas was pitched at the sleepy hamlet of Treen before I ran through surreal fields of giant corn, fields without views where only a blue sky and a dusty trail hinted at the existence of an outside world. On to Cribba Head, a squat buttress of alluring, dangerous arêtes, some of the finest in the land. The best of all, *Pre Marital Tension*, cut through the air like Saladin's sabre. It became an instant aspiration beyond reach, but perhaps one day I would return and make it happen, with a rope, a fistful of skyhooks, power and technical sorcery. The consolation prize was the clean, cracked groove to the left: *Boysen's Groove* – good, but not quite the main event.

An eerie noise perplexed me throughout the night, an amalgam of intermittent whirling and whistling that could have been the wind brushing with the coastline or the warning horn of a distant skerry. The morning dawned fine and I latched onto the wriggling coastal path, following a line past secluded coves, through tight-knit bushes, up steep slopes, winding lazily through fields of hay bales, past churches, an open-air theatre, sleepy villages and springy grass cliff tops, eventually arriving at Barra Head. The structural features of the granite were neat and clean. Wave-washed boulders at the bottom were inspiringly huge. The aura of the sea, the sand and the intricacies of the granite meant that one climb was enough. I trotted back down the coast to the next port of call: Chair Ladder. Having located a descent, I was confronted with a number of friendlier, sunny, granite walls. The tide was going out and I relaxed on a sea-washed ledge, relishing the peace of the day and the lazy ocean. *Terrier's Tooth*, a slender pillar starting with a stretch mark of a vein, glinted, enticing me to follow the simplicity of its large holds, concluding one of the best climbs on these islands. *Diocese* followed - a beautiful line and an immaculate concept of granite ergonomics between shadow and light. Could climbs be any better designed? The rumours I had heard were true – Chair Ladder granite was superb to climb. I felt confident here, trusting - my soloing began to flow.

Days passed and rolled into one, the granite wore down my hands, strength dwindled, and climbing became sporadic. Then the scummy sea mists rolled in, trying to steal my fun as I fumbled a descent into the sheltered Sennen Cove, only a stone's throw from the final gasp of land - Land's End. The damp rock didn't deter me. The feisty, overhanging wall of *Gillian* led me on with long reaches on positive edges, but before I could think about reversal, I was too high, slipping, fingers straining, feet slipping, mind racing . . . back there again - déjà vu . . .

The mist lasted no more than a day. I turned north towards St Just and on into the celebrated tin-mining country. Here, I parked at the ruins of the Carn Galver mine and made my way down through fields to the main cliff at Bosigran, perhaps the most historically famous cliff in the Cornish, granite arsenal. Its steep, clean-featured rock was imposing but had large holds, and this was the reason why it had attracted many a pioneer over the year. It was a pleasant, Cornish, coastal setting. I warmed up on *Anvil Chorus* – a fine layback corner - before psyching up and waiting patiently for the route I had really come to climb to dry out. Then, my solitude shattered as thirty climbers arrived: it's hard to compose a soloist's mind on a cliff busy with ropes, climbers' calls and prying eyes:

Excited voices and the clicking of Karabiners whip away the morning silence, and then two climbers uncoil their ropes at my feet. I watch the ropes snake into coils on the ground, slowly running out. Anxiety wells within me. In a moment of unfound bravery, with a half- swallowed tongue, I ask to go first. The answer is yes . . . The initial, damp-coated wall makes me grip far too hard and I try not to think of all those eyes staring into the back of my head. I hate the predicament and the dilemma I have put myself in by soloing above people that I don't know, but needs must. Am I showing off? No, everything but, though from a roped climber's point of view my actions are probably unjustifiable. Whatever the feelings of those below, I am on my own up here, and all I can do is endeavour not to fall. The wall is leaning at an unfriendly angle; my forearms throb and fear rifles through me. At 120ft, I thrust a trembling fist into a deep-looking crack; the jammed fist is stubborn enough to reduce both fear and the aching of forearms. Deep breaths . . . air rushes through into my stomach, expanding and subsiding, my eyes close . . . I feel safe in the dark. On reopening, I can see glacier-white eyes staring back in disbelief, mouths open with taught lips like eagle chicks waiting for the kill to be dropped from their mother's beak. My head swivels back into the crux of Bow Wall. Desperate positions under the roof smell of betrayal, so I quickly assume a more elegant sequence a little lower, a sequence to which I owe my life. Simmering with commitment, I tease my passage across a delicate wall that is demanding a cool head for freedom. I slump on the summit, absorbing the colours, the flora, and the smell of the Cornish coast, content with the fact that fresh air can truly smell sweet sometimes.

On arrival at the base of the cliff, it is role reversal . . . I look up and watch the roped team on Bow Wall which now stoops ferociously in the autumnal sun. The lead climber moves into the crux - like me before him, he is too high, but he struggles on unaware before plummeting off into the soft comfort of his ropes. It makes me thoughtful, but only for a moment . . .

I disappeared in search of Bosigran's Great Zawn, a hidden cleft that shears straight into the ocean, a few minutes' walk round the coast from the main cliff. The routes in the zawn are definitively more atmospheric. In the 1970s, the freeing of old aid-routes by modern-day rock athletes such as Ron Fawcett and Pete Livesey was much in vogue. And the Great Zawn was no exception. Cornwall - with its delightful rock, turquoise seas and deluxe ice cream - was the epicentre of climbing activity. Not many climbers went abroad to clip bolts in those days; it was too expensive. So the tip of the mother empire was as good as it got, and routes such as *Dream Liberator*, *Déja Vu* and *The West Face* were the most prized climbs.

I peered across at the golden-brown face. The water beneath slopped with a silvery surface, twinkling to gain attention. I watched two climbers jump across a short, bottomless trench to access the start of *Dream Liberator*. I was offered a rope-end for the journey too, but declined as I didn't want to trade freedom for a rope. I watched for a while and then turned away.

I drove on to St Loy, a large, granite slab with bold slab test pieces such as the fittingly named *The Baldest*, first climbed by the West Country's most prolific adventurist, Pat Littlejohn. It was one of the few cliffs along the south coast that wasn't affected by the tide. Instead, it ran amok amongst stands of bramble and foxglove, patches of sea ivory covering the rough granite surface. The lines looked honest enough, and the skull and crossbones doodles depicted in the guidebook encouraged rather than deterred. I chose *Finesse* and set to, cold and lazy, but within minutes I had picked up speed, accelerating across the uncertainty. *Finesse*, along with the routes *The Baldest*, *The Damned* and *Chlorophyl Cluster*, were all completed in a two-hour flux of self-possessed belief and reality. I was 'in the zone'.

Sunday, the Sabbath, the proverbial day of rest, wasn't to be. I managed to make contact with my nomadic, Welsh friend, Stuart Hughes. Stuart was, as usual, penniless and in desperation he had turned to the Internet to scrounge a job. Miraculously, he had conned his way into some animal feed silo job. It sounded like hard work and long hours. I thought this was unlike him, until he told me it was for a trip to Canada to visit his long-lost love. Stuart was in North Cornwall and pointed me eagerly towards the north-facing wall of Pentire Head – *Darkinbad the Brightdayler* the objective, yet another superb Pat Littlejohn climb. Stuart provided the rope and gear; I provided the commitment. The single rope whipped across the face like the mark of Zorro: rope drag, burning arms, belay, and happiness. Stuart took the sharp ends, tussled in the overhanging groove above, and then pulled cleanly into the horizontal world. Together we sat on top - astounded. A random, boozy night and tales of long-ago adventures followed, in a run down caravan in some random field, somewhere . . .

On Tuesday I was both excited and nervous. I wondered if I was mentally and physically ready for the hardship that was going to follow. I cycled rapidly down the steep hill to Sennen Cove, the rush of sea air purifying and exhilarating. On the sea front, no one stirred apart from the opportunist gulls. I walked over and dropped down into an insulated world of granite. As I moved, the granite came alive; the giant, feldspar crystals reflected light from a multitude of angles, a natural kaleidoscope. The slab of *Demolition* was the route in mind, its seriousness only enhancing its appeal to someone so enamoured of danger. I stood at the bottom, took measure of the slab, calculated the risk, and tweaked my way to the halfway break. With my pulse racing, I dabbed chalk into the foot smears, stepping onto them in a momentous rush of confidence – a three-year objective demolished in a little over three minutes.

My next objectives were a long way above the water. I had to be patient because the tide was out. The morning was spent lying in the sun, failing miserably at 'The Times' crossword. This frustrated me and so I sought out the classic slab of *Rock Dancer*, a 150ft sweep of greenstone. I climbed lethargically, strolled back to the car, and in great excitement filled in two further clues.

Down at the Great Zawn all I found were a low tide and a rough sea crushing against granite walls. I tried to sunbathe and relax, but I was distinctly unsettled, so I jumped up and climbed out via the jagged spine of *Commando Ridge* which provided me with much needed and light-hearted entertainment along its sheer, knife-edged flakes, releasing bundles of tension.

Impatient now, I drove down high-walled, twisting lanes back to Gurnard's Head. I lay on my belly at the top of the cliff in order to view the chalk line of holds up this imposing-looking black-barrelled wall - but last week's chalk trace had vanished, rendering the route invisible. Now it looked simply impossible; still I needed to find out for myself . . . I scrambled down to the tidal zone and immediately felt lost in my surroundings, dwarfed by 200ft cliffs and an inhospitable, noisy ocean. I pondered over the strength of the Atlantic currents, but not for too long. Falling wasn't an option, just a last resort. I traversed in along the splash zone where the sea spray varnished the smooth greenstone with lethal intent. In high spirits, I rose out of the ocean's grasp, carefree. The rock was deceptive, concealing all its positive holds from below, but I warmed to the game and the first pitch passed dreamily. The ocean felt distant; the sun felt lovingly energising, and I felt my way through the awkward bulge 100ft above the sea. Focused only on the next hold, a smooth rhythm built up, enabling me to gibber in style to a small haven just below the top. The overhanging crack snarled, and I coiled away up the easy exit. I wanted to relax and enjoy the experience of soloing *Mastadon*, one of the classic extremes of Gurnard's Head, but there was another appointment awaiting me in the Great Zawn.

Back in the zawn, the sea had risen and calmed, and the sun had illuminated the smooth, granite folds. I shook with anxiety – I knew there just weren't any more excuses. I flicked through the guidebook for one last time to check the path of *Déjà Vu*. A few days ago, I would never have dreamt of soloing this route, but somehow the wicked parasite of desire had laid larvae in my mind. *Déjà Vu* was a brave undertaking when first climbed (in 1974) by the legendary American climber, 'Hot' Henry Barber - all brawn, self-confidence, white flares and a flat cap. He travelled the globe and left behind a trail of climbs that were both audacious and punishingly difficult.

From the viewing platform, I descended to a spacious ledge at the edge of the zawn. There, I was faced with reality: a small ledge known as the Green Cormorant Ledge, requiring a 5ft jump across a gulch. The penalty of a mistake was a 30ft fall into the ocean. The jump was a point of no return and would seal my commitment to the route. The slope on the other side could just as easily tip me into the ocean. A standing jump was the answer, but twice I tried, and twice fear glued me to the spot. I built up courage . . . then I was airborne . . . thud . . . committed . . .

Pathetic now, hemmed in by warm, radiating granite walls, a mischievous ocean beneath my feet, and without a soul around to help if things went wrong. My pulse quickened.

50ft up, my rhythm faltered because I had taken the wrong line; shadows started to be cast and the blue waters vanished to black. I was shaking and started to lose focus as I regained the line. The odds began to stack up; everything felt wrong and fatalistic doubts crept in. It was my destiny to drown in the crushing swell, now 80ft below. The zawn baked like a kiln as I moved out onto a smooth wall with tiny holds. I started to wobble uncontrollably, froze, and then reversed back onto a guano-stained ledge to take stock of my limited options: either climb on and risk it all or jump off with similar consequences.

I was 'safe' on the ledge. I took off my sweaty climbing boots and lay down, using my boots as a pillow. I wiggled my toes in the warm air, closed my eyes, déjà vu again – juggling the dilemmas of being alone, crucial decisions to be made, trying to stay cool. I was in need of a hug, touch, or just someone to talk to more than anything.

After twenty minutes, the situation had not changed in the least. The abhorrent heat had made my mouth dry, and I could feel pain on my salt-cracked lips and see only demons dancing on the swell far below. I tied my bootlaces and once more began climbing towards those miniscule holds. Seeing it as the glass half full rather than half empty, I was only fifty vertical feet away from skin-tearing brambles and a clotted cream tea; life could not be simpler.

Feeding the Hens

The aromas were foreign, the air still, and the temperature now plummeted well below zero. We sat under the concrete camber of a bridge like a pair of trolls, chatting idly in hushed tones. I was trembling lightly, with either the cold or the thought of what lay ahead. Once it was dark enough, we scrambled up the slope, climbed the barrier onto the road, and began to run along the storm-drain. A vehicle's headlights appeared in the distance, approaching rapidly, the hard-worked petrol engine breaking the silence. Automatically, we threw ourselves down flat in the drain, below the line of sight. My numbness was only broken by the sensation of my heart pecking like a hungry hen feeding. The vehicle came closer, louder; tense moments until it had passed. We picked ourselves up and recommenced our run until another vehicle approached from behind us. Again we lay flat out in the drain - it too passed by. We continued, getting closer, closer . . . eddies of doubt arose, risk assessments were all haphazard . . . Finally we stopped, breathing heavily, focused and alert; we had reached it - the point of no return . . .

Large flakes of snow swirled round in hypnotising vortexes before they disintegrated on the windscreen and were brushed aside by over-worked wiper blades. The driving conditions were treacherous, but this didn't seem to bother the driver - my long-time friend, Mike Francis. I sat in the passenger seat, shrugging my shoulders and huddling inside my down jacket, shivering. Mike told me that we were nearly there. I peered through the window, but I couldn't see anything but low cloud and snow.

We were approaching Riglos, a village on the fringe of the Pyrenees in Northern Spain. The houses were shrouded in snow, windows were shuttered up, and no one stirred - not even a dog's bark. Cars had been abandoned in the iced up streets. The place was deserted. A couple of hours had passed before we saw the first villagers emerging from their extended siestas. I wanted to find somewhere cosy and warm so that I could have a drink and hibernate from the cold, but the bar was closed and Mike had designs on a far more adventurous afternoon. We headed for the mountains, still unable to actually see them. I didn't share Mike's inspiration or optimism, but I set after him like a dog following at his master's heels. After an hour's walk up the mountain, the sun sank below the clouds, and the snow started to sparkle with a delightful, salmon-pink hue. It felt wonderful and invigorating; it was the first sunshine we had seen all day. However, mist started to billow in around us - the mountainside turned inhospitably alpine. As the sun sank below the horizon, the temperatures dropped, and the slope steepened. A slip would have been fatal, but we finally arrived at a pole in the ground with a ribbon tied to it – a type of tattered Himalayan summit flag.

Mike descended to the edge of an abrupt drop, and in the next instant I saw his spread-eagled body superimposed against a canvas of mist. Then he was gone. My heart jumped at the realism of it all. I tried to count the seconds, but I couldn't . . . then I heard a boom and its resultant echo bounce around the mountainside like a miniature thunderclap, followed by the baying of dogs in the distance and darkness. Alone now, I turned to the Alpine snows and retraced my footsteps into the darkness.

After a lifetime of being generally in control of the risky situations I put myself in, I realised that it could easily end with a simple slip off this snowy peak in a pair of shoes that I had worn to a wedding. When the slow and crucial icy sections had been negotiated, my confidence reappeared, and I descended at a more leisurely pace. Within the hour, I was down. Mike had already found a place to stay and booked us in. It had hot water and a log fire, and at last I felt warm.

The morning revelled in icy serenity, and the purity of the air felt sublime, warm breath crystallising and sparkling as it funnelled out of my mouth and vanished.

The sun rose and began to regain control of an empty, blue sky, warming the air to above zero. The snow started to melt from the beige, ceramic roof tiles, the drips of melt-water splashing into the ground, producing a weird chorus of tunes. Towering in the background were the spires of Riglos – phallic, orange precipices of cemented, organic rubble towering 1,000ft above the village. Below me were a number of orchards – sorry trees planted in lines, covered in fresh snow. A footpath wound its way up the mountainside behind the spires. Its snowy skin twisted and recoiled through stunted bushes and between short rock faces. Mixed aromas of juniper, thyme and rosemary scented the mountainside. These familiar herb fragrances brought back memories of Sal's homely kitchen: the herbs, the warm AGA, the smell of freshly brewed coffee, the pine, wood carvings, sea shells, coral, Sal's homemade bread and raspberry jam, and the usual mess of paper that gave the kitchen that comforting lived-in feeling. The treacherous, icy trail that we had followed the night before had turned to slush and water in the warmth of the sun. Now the trail was far less dangerous, and we made quick progress to reach the pole – the exit-point. After half an hour of preparation, I was ready, nervous, relying solely on Mike's judgement and expertise for my first BASE jump. BASE jumping is illegal in some countries - it is usually done at night on clandestine stealth missions, although thankfully not at Riglos.

As a rule of thumb, most skydivers do a minimum of 150 skydives before going BASE jumping. I had done nine! My first, accelerated, free fall skydive - at Empuira Brava in Spain - went drastically wrong. I jumped out of the plane too early, surprising my instructors; I tumbled with them for 3,000ft before gaining stability. I forgot to do my practice pulls, so when the time came to 'pull', I couldn't find my release toggle. My instructor pulled for me, but not really knowing what was going on, I seemingly carried on searching and pulled something, anything - it just so happened to be my main parachute cut-away toggle. My main parachute flew away, and my reserve opened with such startling ferocity that it thrust me into a reverse somersault, my legs close to tangling with the parachute's lines. It all passed so quickly that I had no idea what had happened. I suffered whiplash to my neck, but still hadn't been deterred from trying BASE jumping.

One thousand feet below me, the snow-coated landscape radiated outwards towards frosty horizons. I was feeling strangely electrified, tottering on the edge of nature's dais, asking myself the usual question . . . *What am I doing here?* I wondered why I couldn't be normal, or at least partially normal: a wife perhaps, kids, going out for a Sunday lunch, a nine-to-five, an all inclusive holiday, watching football, drinking coffee in a city street . . . I began to muse on the idea of the big city for a while, living for materialism. I shuddered at the thought of the rat race and realised that the grass was not greener on the other side. Anyway, I wore a suit to work every day, albeit a boiler suit. At least I didn't have any ironing to do. I stared into the deep blue sky and shed my thoughts, hearing only sinister whispers like the sound of frosted leaves tingling in a light winter's breeze. I looked down into the void and witnessed an eagle soaring 30ft beneath me. I gazed at the size of its wings as they sliced ever so softly through the air. The bird tilted its head in an inquisitive manner, to see what I was up to. We seemed to decipher each other in that locked glance; I saw a lifetime of effortless flight - I wondered what he had seen? A few moments later he was gone, and there was nothing apart from my heartbeat and the force of gravity, both seeming to grow stronger as I wavered on the edge.

I took one last breath, reasoning that it might be my last, and jumped . . .

The calm, frosty air became ferocious, tearing at my skin and face like a big, invisible bear, powerful and hungry. My lungs choked at the onslaught of air that rushed in unchallenged and my eyes weren't making sense, as if I were looking into a smashed mirror. Then they shut tight and my subconscious began to ask questions in the incoherence . . . *Is the chute ever going to open? Has it been packed correctly?*

The feeling of free fall was one I couldn't get to grips with that easily – as a free solo climber, the belief was that free fall could only have two outcomes: broken bones or death. I had enough faith in Mike's pack-job to believe that neither of those would happen.

When I felt that my free fall had ceased and the canopy had taken my weight, I opened my eyes and checked to make sure I wasn't on a collision course with the cliff or indeed any eagles. I floated away over the melting landscape, landing amongst the brush in a cloud of relief.

Later that night, Mike and I sat in the village's smoke-filled bar. It was full of elderly men with weathered faces and flat caps. We drank tumblers of Cardhu, gradually becoming woozier as we talked about our exploits over the last two decades. I admired Mike for his laid back manner in the face of danger; he hadn't changed in all the years since our first solo climbs together at the Pass of Ballater in Scotland, and later on the grit. We used to climb one behind the other. Falling off never entered our heads; we played a game with no rules, and it was fun. The most dangerous experience we had had back then was when I had misjudged a chicaned humpback bridge at speed. I exited the bend on two wheels, microns from the bridge's parapet. It all happened so quickly; I didn't have time to be scared. I turned and looked at Mike to see what his reaction was . . . he just wore a wide smile and said: 'Oops . . . '

On a further occasion, we were climbing on the Aberdeen coast at Newtonhill. Having climbed *Acapulco*, Mike was keen to jump from the top of the 40ft cliff. It was cold, however, and we didn't have towels. We returned a few days later to jump, only to find low tide and a rocky shelf angling into the sea. We stared at each other knowingly, in a state of shock, and said in unison: 'Oops. . . '

Things hadn't changed that much . . . we had made plans to jump off a 500ft bridge the following night in France. It was illegal and sounded exciting. I sipped at the peaty, yellow malt; it was memorable and timeless, just like old friends and BASE jumps.

Scotland was being subjected to its coldest snap of weather for years, but it still felt tropical in comparison to the temperatures Mike and I had endured in Spain the week before. When I arrived back at Muir of Knock, it was snowy, cold, dark and the house was as empty as the Marie-Celeste. David and Sal had gone on holiday to Saint Lucia. I began to dream of snorkelling in those warm, clear blue, coral seas where the water is abundant with tropical fish: purples, blues, yellows, reds, stripes, dots and all kinds of fantastical shapes.

I had heard that the mountains were drooling with ice, but I couldn't be bothered to go - long gone were my youthful days, when I would spring out to ice climb on Lochnagar at the first hint of a snowflake. Strangely enough, I had climbed on ice before rock – a little unorthodox perhaps, but I was fortunate to have had such keen and accommodating schoolteachers - Tony Gabb and John Hall - to take me out Scottish winter climbing. As a youth, *Emerald Gully* became the benchmark route that honed my drive and spirit – a route that had become significant due to its publication in the iconic book 'Cold Climbs', compiled by Ken Wilson, John Barry and Dave Alcock, a copy of which I had bought when I was fourteen. The pictures and stories of the ice climbs and ice climbers were ones of heroism to my young mind. A black and white photograph of Jimmy Marshall – wedged into the vertical chimney of *Parallel Gully B* in 1958, with a strand of hemp around his waist, bulging calf muscles, and two hands gripping on to an old wooden axe shaft, cutting steps – was utterly fascinating. The thought of cutting steps up sustained sections of vertical ice was mind boggling, and Jimmy's legendary ascents of *Parallel B, Minus Two Gully,* and *Smith's Gully,* to name a few, were truly outstanding tests of nerve, stamina and skill. Thankfully those photographs existed, to demonstrate how tough and enduring ice climbers were in the 1950s, before the advent of two curved axes, front-pointed crampons, wrist leashes, ice screws and other inventions of convenience used in modern ice climbing. However, I was happy enough to use whatever gear I was able to lay my hands on, and the offer from John Hall of the tight end of the rope on *Emerald Gully* was accepted gladly; it meant far more to me than doing school work and passing exams. This rather reclusive gully was found to be in great condition. Catching sight of the first pitch – a 100ft, slightly twisting funnel of near vertical ice

– I was scared and spellbound at the same time; it was so beautiful, yet also cold and ugly, so appealing, yet so terrifying. John led off, and I stood on the belay holding his ropes. He was smooth and accomplished, but it did make me think about the pupil/teacher bond when it comes down to serious climbing. We were sharing the same rope; I was his responsibility, but as the rope wormed out from my belay plate, he had, in fact, become my responsibility – I would be holding his life in my hands if he were to fall. And I began to realise just how truly selfless a notion it had been on his part to drag me up such demanding ice climbs at all. When the rope above tightened, it was my cue. I attacked it with youth and enthusiasm, my technique leaving a lot to be desired. I rattled my axes in as hard as I could . . . foolish, but it had the right effect. However, by the time I reached the final, vertical ice pitch, 400ft up, my forearms were so taught with lactic acid that my axes were just bouncing off the steel-hard ice and my calf muscles burned as if imaginary rats were chewing away at them. I hung on with the help of the tight rope from above, overwhelmed and full of gratitude for my mentor.

Now, twenty years later, my excuses not to climb were bordering on pathetic; I had to feed Sal's hens and keep the birds stocked up on nuts and seeds. I quite enjoyed walking down the drive in the morning, gazing at the soft, fluffy snow that had settled on the ground and built up into thin ridges along the branches of the trees, making them bow submissively. The scenes were delightful, Christmassy, although the hens probably didn't think so. I threw them extra handfuls of corn and brought warm water.

After three days of carefree apathy, I decided to search for my ice tools. I found them where I had left them, stuffed into a shopping bag that hung from a coat peg. I also thumbed through my ice climbing guidebooks in search of inspiration. I was surprised to find that the last ice climb I had done was four years ago! Andy Nisbet and Dave McGimpsey were the oracles I always consulted to find out which routes were in good condition. The thought of walking for hours, only to find that the cliffs were bare of ice, annoyed me. My luck was out – Andy, probably the most prolific winter climber in Scotland's history, had ironically disappeared to Norway to guide, and Dave had finally started mud-logging again in the North Sea to earn some much-needed cash. Dave had been living close to the breadline in 'the bothy' – a basic barn with oodles of character - for the last six years in order to pursue his passion for climbing during the winter months. During the summer, he would turn his hand to footpath erosion work, which paid little but kept him in food and petrol for the year.

After much deliberation, I decided to go to Creag Dubh at Drummochter because of the short walk in and the guaranteed ice in cold conditions. This meant I could feed the hens in the morning and be back for corn sprinkling time in the afternoon – perfect! The crisp morning sparkled with vibrancy as I drove south along the A9 past Meall Chuaich, a pudding-shaped Munro. The hills were gleaming with silky, white snow; it was going to be a lovely day even if I found no ice to climb. I needed the exercise anyway. As usual I left the car park with the minimal equipment and food. I took two wrinkled apples and two dried-out tangerines – old fruit from the fruit bowl, only fit for the compost heap. There was no point in bringing luxuries like a chocolate bar; I would have eaten it before I had left the car. In addition to my axes and crampons, I took a spare pair of gloves and a flask of hot water, to which I added a slice of lemon, a spoon of honey and a cube of root ginger, all stewed together to produce a pleasurably foul brew. That was it - no map, no compass, no helmet - how I hated to wear a helmet!

Heather is a hardy plant that covers a large portion of the Scottish Highlands. Its purple bloom in summer is curiously beautiful, but today a few frosted sprigs gasped through the snow in search of light, the remainder buried and insulated from the outside world. Breaking a trail across the snow-capped heather made me curse at times as the snow collapsed and sapped my energy. A blue hare sprang up in front of me and made effortless haste over the surface of the snow, darting one way and then another, displaying his innate mechanism for evading predators. He stopped and sat on his haunches, his long, slender ears bolt upright, twitching faintly in the cool air. The wind strengthened and raised miniature spindrift storms – wisps of softly curling, snowy smoke that spun gracefully across the icy crust like tiny twisters, smothering my legs and feet.

On top of the ridge, the panorama unfolded into a wonderland of snowy, Scottish mountains. The mass of Ben Alder holds court, its beauty set off against its remote setting and graceful corries. The foreground was split by the long, dead-looking waters of Loch Ericht. The frozen watercourses of Creag Dubh are hard to locate from above, but once down I made a beeline to the thickest and most continuous piece of ice – *Hex Factor* – stumbling over powder-coated boulders to reach it. I had climbed the route ten years ago when there had been a fragile column of ice; today the column was fatter and better formed. The constant changing of the medium interested me; it was like a life form growing and diminishing, colours fluctuating and its mood changing from hour to hour, day to day. Unlike a rock climb, an ice climb will never be the same twice. At the base of the ice, I clipped on my crampons and took a bite out of my apple, but the dried, wrinkly taste made me wretch and I lobbed it away. I swung the rucksack onto my back, armed myself with my axes, and gleefully pounced onto the ice. The feeling of soloing on ice is indescribable – the choices, the freedom, the aesthetics, and no rules apart from one: don't fall off!

I gave up winter climbing with ropes, firstly because I preferred the speed of soloing, and secondly because I had bad circulation in my hands; I attracted 'hot aches' quite readily. They occur when the fingers have gone numb with the cold, due perhaps to sitting on a belay too long. The pain usually kicks in when you start climbing again; the warm blood pulses into frozen fingers and they throb incessantly, then your breathing stops, followed by a grimace and a scream that sounds like a stag in rutting season.

After a bad bout of hot aches, I had vowed never to go winter climbing again with a rope. I couldn't be arsed with the hardship. No more stopping on ledges, fighting with inflexible, frozen ropes that have turned solid; no more heavy rucksacks full of winter climbing gear to be lugged in for hours. I found far more fun in soloing, and soloing is like an old-fashioned marriage, once committed, there is no reverse gear - it's until death do us part.

Thud! My Predator axe sank home, the first placement in ice for four years.

I was a little out of sync, and the first 100ft of easy-flowing, ice steps gave me that much needed tuning in phase to gather some momentum before the ice steepened into the formidable pillar, which had been formed by hundreds of cylindrical, organ pipe type icicles bonding together as they drooled from an ice-glazed corner. The texture of the ice was fascinating, simple yet complex; I vandalised it as my axes struck into the frozen artwork, fracturing its sheen and virginity. Fragments of ice sprinkled downwards onto the ground below, only to splinter into thousands of further pieces. I searched for thin weaknesses in the ice for my axe placements – especially where the two adjacent icicles hadn't bonded together completely, leaving small voids and air bubbles; it was in these voids that I would place my axes gently, to save my arm-strength.

The ice was steep and did not relent. My forearms started to burn, and my axe placements became more untidy and frantic as I began to lose composure; my body was flailing, unused to the rigours of steep ice. Higher up, I started to shudder and wield my axes like tomahawks, thrusting them deep into the ice – the wrong thing to do. I continued, edging up towards a possible rest ledge, but one of my axes had disobediently sunk into the ice, not wanting to move. I began to panic, thumping it from side to side with my fist, knowing all too well what had happened the previous time my axe had stuck . . .

. . . Over 1,000ft up, on the final icefall of South Post Direct on Creag Meagaidh, one of my axes won't come out. In sheer frustration, I pull on it too hard and it flies out, hitting me between the eyes. The humming of bone rings intermittently in my ears. I thread in and out of consciousness, hinging away from the ice, helplessly out of control, and I end up dangling from one axe leash and a crampon point. My survival instinct cuts in, regathering my wits, reattaching myself in an oblivious state of shock. I feel the tickling sensation of warm blood streaming down the bridge of my nose and into my mouth, its taste metallic and salty. My first reaction is to check my head wound, but I can't take my hands from my axes, so I have to endure the silent torture until the wound and seeping blood has frozen into a crust. I have been lucky; it was the ice hammer that had come out and hit me; if it had been the adze which is in my other hand, it might have had different consequences . . .

I reached the rest, thankful that there was a small place to rest tired arms before launching up into the sustained groove above. I soon became absorbed on this vertical highway of ice, and without any wind it was fun; this was where I longed to be - happy, free, and totally responsible for my own destiny. I felt my re-initiation to the magical world of ice climbing had gone smoothly, and feeling a little braver, I went to take a closer look at some pathetically insecure icicles which I had noticed earlier – the possible line of *Olympic Hare*. I stared at the hanging fang for a while, determining a path up icicles and ice-glazed rock to attain this frozen tooth of ice. My mind started to calculate the risks, knowing a good calculation would boost my life, and a bad calculation would end it. I weighed up the risks and shuffled to the base of the imposing ice; it was so steep that it pushed me backwards and I nearly lost my balance. However, once the axes were thrust invisibly in above my head, I pulled on and committed. After 40ft, my forearms were burning as I tried to gain the free hanging fang of ice at full stretch to my right. I whacked it with my axe, and the whole bottom section broke off and shattered to the ground with a boom. The tip of the fang now terminated at chest height. I was going to have to do a couple of footless pulls to get established on it. My chances were about fifty-fifty – not good odds for broken legs or worse. I started looking around for a reasonable alternative, knowing that the one arm pull up method would be my final option. Over to my left were some icicles leading to an ice-glazed wall from where I could cut back right and reach the top of the fang; a better option perhaps?

I climbed onto the steep, fickle ice and reached an overhang that resembled a giant nostril with frozen snot dribbling from it. The overhang drooled with tiny icicles that I duly smashed with the side of my axe. I tried to cower away, but some falling ice daggers hit me, puncturing my face and drawing blood. Utilising the frozen snot, I lurched rightwards onto thicker tongues of ice at the source of the fang. I was up.

I raced merrily up the final 50ft, passing wispy icicles that had been carved by the wind into near perfect circles like a wizard's toenails. I opened my rucksack, starving, but I lost my appetite at the sight of the state of my fruit - I was obviously not hungry enough. With little energy remaining, I went in search of *Flight of the*

Navigator, a recent addition to the cliff. I had come across the description in the Scottish Mountaineering Club journal - it sounded fun, and at grade six, a challenge that I couldn't refuse before my dash home to feed the hens. The route took me longer to locate than to climb. At the top, I was a spent force and I craved food. I wandered back over the ridge and down the glen through the snow, all the time wishing the car would be a little closer.

Temperatures were forecast to remain low for a further week, ideal for winter climbing. After my climb at Creag Dubh, I had gotten a taste for ice climbing again and wanted to climb some more before the season ended. Two days later, I drove out west and towards Creag Meagaidh. After forty minutes, it appeared ahead, glazed in snowy splendour, the clear morning light propelling the mountain into a majestic illusion – it was flirting with me, but I knew better. Those perfect, snowy flanks spelled avalanche, and if I was destined to die on a mountain then I would prefer that I wasn't buried.

I drove on past the mountain and on towards Fort William and Ben Nevis. I had never climbed a winter route on Ben Nevis - a sorry state of affairs for someone who had been a member of the Scottish Mountaineering Club for ten years. Of course, my reasons were straightforward. I hated crowds. I envisaged winter climbing on Ben Nevis to be a busy circus, too many climbers, queues, ropes and echoes. It's all so far removed from my ideals of solitude, extreme focus and peace, and thick, continuous slithers of blue ice in a romantic setting. I rolled up into the car park and counted a total of 34 cars. I decided not to bother with the climb. I turned round and headed back east. I decided, however, to take one last look at The Ben. The north face glinted with a pure crystalline surface, contrasting beautifully against the clear, light blue sky. I couldn't deny myself a day's climbing on it any longer.

On the approach path, I continuously ran my eyes across the complicated north face of the mountain, listening to distant voices and trying to figure out where the climbers were. The popular icefall of *The Curtain* looked like an enormous sweep of white treacle that swarmed with colourful climbers and the lower, icy sections of *Gemini* had plenty of blobs of colour too. The remainder of the mountain looked empty, although it echoed with climbers' voices constantly.

Over the next rise, the CIC hut appeared ahead, sitting sedately under the shadows of the mountain, like a Swiss chalet. I walked into the boot room of the hut to change out of my trainers and into my ice-climbing boots. Sitting on a slatted wooden bench, I began thumping my inner boots into the plastic outer boots. The hut's inner door creaked open and an archetypal SMC member stood there in the doorway, speechless at the sight of me – the intruder – having broken into the SMC's sacred hut. I was lightly amused at his inability to speak; he was speechless at my audacity – to enter the most hallowed mountain hut in the British Isles, uninvited. Whilst he was still trying to find words to express his outrage, I decided to help him out.

'Is there a problem?' I asked in a soft enquiring tone. Before he could stumble over the right words, I decided to be upfront and put him out of his misery. ' . . . oh I am a member of the SMC!'

Those were obviously the 'open sesame' words to him because immediately the frown of disgust disappeared and a wave of friendliness rippled through his face:

'What's your name?' he asked, rather formally.

'Err . . . Julian Lines.' I replied.

'I am Bob Richardson. Come in, come in. Do you want a cup of tea before you go climbing?'

I had turned from foe to friend in the time it took to say three letters – SMC. I had heard we were a difficult bunch, and I could see why we had that reputation.

'That would be fantastic', I replied to Bob's generous offer.

I followed Bob into the inner room of the hut. It was like walking into a command centre: a place steeped in history, where wars had been won and lost. This inner sanctum held a special sort of energy; I stood still for a few moments, absorbing the aura. I thought about the climbing legends that had graced these meagre four walls and had sought its shelter over the years: Haston, Patey, MacInnes, Marshall, Clough and Smith, to name but a few. I tried to imagine the partnerships, the rivalry, the banter, the drunkenness, the passion, the tension and the anxiety on the eve of historic first ascents.

'There is only Earl Grey, will that do?' Bob piped up, breaking the silence and my train of thought.

'Yeah that's fine, thank you', I replied. Bob tended to the hot water as my mind wandered off into sinister undertones . . .

How many climbers had spent their last night in these bunks before being slain by the venomous mountain?

I was rather taken aback by my own reaction - I jumped nervously as a mug of hot Earl Grey was thrust before me.

'Which ice routes are in good condition?' I asked Bob, reining my thoughts back to the present.

'Well, I climbed *Italian Route Right Hand* yesterday. It had good ice, and you can abseil off after the difficult part.' Bob replied. I didn't have a rope to abseil, and I wanted something a little more engaging to climb . . .

'What about *Mega Route X?*' I asked anxiously. At that moment, the door opened and someone stumbled in. The new arrival informed me that *Mega Route X* was extremely thin at the bottom and probably not climbable, and that was the reason why no one was on it. Having gleaned this information, I knew exactly where I was going. I pulled my boots on and left the hut in a rush. In a short while, I was near the base of the route, studying the slinky dagger of ice tapering down from the steep flank of the Central Trident Buttress quite intently. I wasn't entirely sure if the lower section did have enough ice to climb. Closer up, the first 30ft of ice was hollow, patchy and half inch thick at its fattest; it was so thin that it could only be described as resembling a holed shower curtain. I looked below at the snow slope and my fall line and thought . . .

It is soft enough to save broken bones.

I geared up and teetered out onto the impending iced wall, gingerly hooking my axes into the cheese holes, closing my eyes and pulling up, crampon points placed daintily. I was more frightened of my axes popping out and hitting me in my head than I was of taking a fall. I knew I couldn't swing my axes at the ice. If I did, the whole curtain would shatter and disappear down the mountainside, and me with it. I only had one chance, and I felt like a surgeon performing open heart surgery with the wrong implements. With each movement I made, I expected to come hurtling down and be buried like a cod in a fish box. The adrenalin built up with each slow foot of ascent and the excitement intensified at the thought of succeeding on *Mega Route X*! The ice started to thicken into fatter globules, making my axe placements more secure. However, I had been gripping the axes so tightly on the intense lower section that my forearms were on fire - not good, as there were another 200ft of vertical ice to go. At 120ft, there was a discreet rest, perhaps a belay of sorts, over on the left, but I didn't have the luxury of resting. I was soloing, and there was nowhere to relax, no safety net, I was committed for the entirety. I ignored the tiny ledge out left and continued upwards. The ice above me just drooled down in one relentless strip of verticality. There wasn't much variety in technique; I placed my axes above my head and made two small step-ups – crampon points biting into the ice, feet close together, neat. The climbing was monotonous; it was a case of switch off and try to enjoy it as much as possible.

Nearing the top at 200ft, I veered leftwards from the smooth sheet of ice towards an ice formation that snuggled in close to the cliff. I thought a back-and-foot manoeuvre would give some respite to my arms, but instead I lost composure and began to make a real pig's ear of the moves. Cramp was building in my legs, and my body started to shake with the thought of failure so close to success. I pulled back rightwards onto the vertical ice; my breathing was laboured and the axes started to bounce off the hard surface of the ice as my power wilted. There were only ten feet to go, a few more axe placements; I knew which ones. I just had to hang on and use the exact amount of power required on each axe swing . . . not too deep, not too shallow. It was mental now. I didn't look down; there was no point. I secured a good placement with one axe and then dangled my other axe by my knee, shaking some oxygenated blood into my arm, closing my eyes for a moment and breathing slowly. I repeated with the other axe. After a scary few minutes, I could feel the strength and the calm return once more. I slowly climbed my way over the top of the icefall into a snowy mountain arena.

The north face of the Ben is a complex amalgam of coires, ridges and buttresses, and I didn't know the layout of the mountain at all. I had only climbed *Tower Ridge* and *Agrippa* on the Carn Dearg buttress, so I wasn't sure how I was going to find the quickest and safest descent of the north face of the mountain to the CIC hut. A few part snowed-over footprints led away up snow-coated slopes towards the summit ridge. I followed them, twisting a loose zigzag onto the plateau, the surrounding mountains falling away in submission. It is a strange feeling – a powerful one – when you are essentially on the roof of the British Isles. The cold air stung and I felt as though I were standing on a forlorn Cambrian beast, dripping with frost, frozen and preserved from a bygone ice age. I wasn't sure how much daylight remained, so I charged down a gully; I wasn't sure which one. The hens were on my mind; they were my responsibility. I just hoped that I would get home and manage to feed them some corn before they went to roost . . .

Am Fear Liath Mor

Imagine surfing: carving a wake along the axis of a fifteen foot barrel – a translucent tube of perfect proportion; fascinating to watch, exhilarating to experience and vitalising to touch. These waves are perhaps Poseidon's finest creations; beautiful, powerful and self-destructive as they crumble into a frenzy of rabid froth. Only those who have endured years of shredding themselves on the reef and coughing up brine will be permitted to enter the light at the end of those barrels. Soloing in the mountains is similar - only those who have spent many years toying patiently with their mind control will be able to feel comfortable sticking to hundreds of feet of bare rock with only tension in their tendons and the air to breathe.

Life is a wave – a perpetual sequence of highs and lows; the stock market too – bulls and bears and all that hype. After an intense soloing experience, I often sink into a low. It's like the end of a relationship – I lose direction. I have no immediate urge to climb, and I wonder if it is really worth it after all.

I was in the company of a bottle of cheap Chilean Merlot. After downing a glass, my spirits soared, but as the bottle depleted, so did my mood. I awoke in the morning, dehydrated, with a throbbing head, pulsating temples and a fragile body. To make things worse, the sun was bouncing through the windows like a hyperactive puppy wanting to play. I reached the kitchen and started to drink mugs of water, staring out of the window towards Braeriach – the third highest Munro. Its north coire shimmered with a potent clarity in the early morning light, coaxing me with that imaginary, silent voice only the Cairngorms could possess, encouraging me to join them and exist in their warm, elevated bosom for the day . . . so within the hour I was on the plateau, not knowing how my rubbery legs had managed to propel me there so quickly. The odourless mountain air was timeless, but I couldn't appreciate it; my head was spinning and my stomach churned. I reached the top of Hell's Lum and looked down into its void – a savage cleavage of loose rock that ran with water. I shuddered at the thought of a 400ft solo on its adjacent walls. I heard echoes reverberating around the Loch Avon basin, so I walked further along the crest to a point where I could look down towards the glassy sheen of Loch Avon, its idyllic beaches, the huge rambling cliff of Stag Rocks, the plinth of the Shelterstone and the long, concave slabs flanking Hell's Lum. The lower slabs sparkled in the sunlight; their crimson and buff water stains reminded me of streaky bacon – ugh . . . what a thought with a hangover. Dwarfed by the surroundings, I caught sight of a few climbers starting on the 'Classic Rock' route of *Clean Sweep*.

I departed Hell's Lum and walked over the plateau to Coire Sputan Dearg, a remote cliff on the south face of Ben Macdui. I hoped that, by the time I arrived at the Coire, I would be feeling well enough to attempt *Amethyst Pillar*.

High on the shoulder of Ben Macdui, the stillness was deafening. I started to think of 'The Big Grey Man' and the ghost stories that surrounded him.

Myth, mystery or mist? 1891 was when 'Am Fear Liath Mor' was first encountered – when spooky, crunching footsteps chased Norman Collie from the mountain in fright. Ever since then, lone walkers have felt his presence upon them, and heard his laughter oscillate around the windswept plateau. A number of people have had sightings of a hairy beast, ten feet tall, talons and pointy ears – a Yeti that sends the lost and disorientated over the cliff edges in hypnotic terror. Today I waited and looked around for this mythical man, but there was nowhere for him to hide in the purity of the ozone. Maybe he was waiting for the mist to roll in so he could appear, or maybe there wasn't a man at all and it was the Cairngorms that had a supernatural persona of their own . . .

I dropped out of my thoughts and found myself in a regal spot, looking down upon Loch Etchachan and its obsidian glaze. I felt at ease – not often do I encounter the high plateau so warm and still. Beneath me was a tiny pool of glacial melt water. I descended to it, stripped off and waded into its deep, peaty lining. Mud oozed through my toes and soothed the soles of my feet. I stood for a while with numb feet and calves before forcing myself to dive in, hoping that the icy water would drive away my hangover. Instead, the water jump-started most of my organs into an unwanted panic. I warmed up again in the sun, still with an aching head. I was no longer bothered about walking the extra mile to 'Sputan'. Instead, and in a more adventurous mode, I wandered down towards a 200ft high buttress overlooking Loch Etchachan. No one had ever climbed upon its rock because it was almost always sunless and wet.

The Grey Man's lair perhaps?

I trundled down the slope to find a fine, vertical wall, capped by a water-worn slab, in turn bisected by a cracked groove. A dyke of smooth, pink quartz lured me away from safety and up into a blank shield of rock. Here, it dumped me all alone, whispering to me as it disappeared into the parent granite:

'Make your own way'.

My head thumped, and my usual questioning of sanity came to the fore. I hopped into a scoop regardless – a teasing blankness with absolutely no holds. My smears were on the lip of a 60ft drop – a clear head was compulsory, but mine pounded in pain. I traversed the lip leftwards, the smears casual but fair. The scoop ended, making me stretch blindly leftwards with a sense of urgency towards a featureless rib, praying for just one hold, my outstretched fingers inching across the heartless, granite surface, tickling, forever hopeful of feeling some purchase. I gulped, only to feel dehydration in my throat and a metallic taste on my lips, and then I thought I heard the distant laughter of the Grey Man echoing in my head. I stretched further and finally my fingers rolled round onto a smooth edge.

Time was precious and seemed to have stopped. I leaned off the hold and stabbed my foot way out left, pulling sharply into a shallow groove. I stuttered up onto a good hold and regained composure. Above me, water seeped down the rock. Silence rolled across the plateau, and I could sense the Grey Man closer now. I searched for other options, swinging left onto a fresh and dry slab of granite that guided me confidently away from the clutches of the supernatural.

He had to wait patiently for a further three years before I trespassed once more. This time I was free of hangovers, eager, and just as stupid as I leapt along the plateau in a pair of shorts. All the while the distant roar of melt water slapping the thighs of Macdui projected out.

Like a sundial, I cut an axis due south, deep into his country, past boulders, ice pools and the odd, high plateau beach. Finally, the vista opened up as the strong, symmetrical slopes of Derry Cairngorm edged into view. In the distant haze, amongst the rolling hills of the southern Cairngorms, peeked the nipple-shaped summit of Lochnagar, and further to the west Beinn a' Ghlo imposed. This was Tilt and Tarf territory – remote and featureless, heather-draped hills.

The plateau disappeared as crags and debris plunged downwards towards the coire floor of 'Sputan'. South facing, it was light and airy and therefore likely to be beyond the Grey Man's jurisdiction. My feet skidded amongst the chuckling rocks of the steep, scree gully; my elevation and panorama diminished with every step whilst Derry Cairngorm continued to rise in bulk. Soon I was in the hollows of the coire, slipping past the discreet but appealing line of *Grey Slab* and on to the base of *Amethyst Pillar* – this clean buttress had grabbed the attention of the Aberdonian pioneers in the 1950s, but their original route, *Amethyst Wall*, had frustratingly weaved around the cleaner pieces of rock to reach the final overhanging crack. This was climbed with aid but later freed in 1964. The route was then straightened out in 1979 to produce *the* classic, remote, mountain HVS of the Cairngorms that it is today. The first pitch gave me food for thought. The second pitch looked enticing

– a clean, grey pillar engrained with bright lichens. There were two options. I took the right hand one – exposed, clean and positive, but still with anxious moves for someone without a rope to negotiate. A short scramble led to a gritty perch beneath an overhung corner – the crux. A little thrutch, test arm jam, test fist jam, test the loose rock and step down to perch. Summon courage, test it again and step down. Deep breath . . . sweep a glance over the coire to make sure there are no signs of the Grey Man . . . then commit, pull on jams and press into the secure upper corner – great position, airy, easy now but potentially dangerous, 300ft above the coire floor.

I descended the granite wedge of *Crystal Ridge* and wandered across the coire floor in search of something else. Over in the eastern wing of the coire sat a blank shield of rock hemmed by two corners. A vague seam split the centre – it was unclimbed. I went to have a try. It was sequential, and the holds were flared and none too positive. I wobbled and reversed then sat and mulled it over for a while, eating a tin of tuna that I had to break into with a rusty piton I had found in the scree. With a little more conviction, I latched into the seam again, following its devious manoeuvres; this way, that way, toe-poke, twist. Then the seam ran out and I was left clinging to a small finger edge with only blankness above. In desperate measure, I stretched upwards, blind, hoping . . . my fingers kissed an uncertain edge: was it good enough? It was a 60ft fall into the gully if I got it wrong, and I had to make a decision and quick.

I reversed, desperately trying to repeat the right sequence of moves with accuracy and calm. I made it down, but only just. I sat on the rocks all hyped. Deep down I knew that I wasn't going to leave the coire without making another attempt. It was as though the powers of the Grey Man were drawing me in so that he could claim my soul. Addicted, this time the moves flowed easier, familiar now, like reciting the times tables at school. 60ft above the gully, I toe-stubbed a crystal and stretched for the edge . . . Although my fingers felt firm enough, I closed my eyes and I could see the Grey man laughing at me in the darkness. In the next defining moment, my mind struck like the hour hand of the clock, my fingers tensing, my arm pulled hard, feet running, eyes wide open, darting across the rock, this way, that, searching for a hold. My life depended on one hold. The rock appeared to be blank, as it always does from below, but I thought I saw a feature, I couldn't be sure. With no other options, I snatched for it, and my fingers gripped to its tiny, crystalline edge. Fortuitously, more positive flake-edges materialised in the wall, and they propelled me into the easier corners above.

On a high, I wandered around the coire, wanting to find more routes to solo; or was that the Grey Man taking residence in my mind? I noticed a cleanly cut corner low down in the lower tier – a short but fine feature, typical of granite: all fingertips, bridging, balance and body tension. Above, a wide fault choked with black moss slewed an arc. A quick exit left was made via a roof crack. I punched my fists in like pistons in their granite chambers. The coire floor dropped away and its colours became irrelevant . . . all crunched up, my toes popped. I ended up dangling from one arm in space above the coire floor. I regrouped, punched my other fist back in, re-glued my feet and pulled through onto the slab above. A teasingly blank arête awaited, this side, that side, crystals, friction, pinches and smears – at 70ft it was seriously dangerous. I was there for two hours, cleaning holds with the wire brush I carried attached to my chalk bag by some elastic, with aching calf muscles, playing with different sequences of crystals like a child with a jigsaw, trying to make the picture the easiest way, the best way, frustrated that I couldn't commit. I rationalised and managed to escape off. A few weeks later, I returned to complete the route – *Ataraxia*. I had pre-planned and brought a rope to practice the moves, just in case. With the safety of the rope, the Grey Man wasn't happy, but the sequences of moves were just as I had envisaged them . . . if only I had committed the first time . . .

Back on the plateau and on to the summit of Ben Macdui. I stared over towards the lonely, majestic corries of Braeriach and Cairntoul and the infant river Dee bisecting them like a silken thread. I saw cloud rolling in from the west, soon to nudge over the plateau and envelop the summits. The Grey Man was approaching – it was time to leave. I loved being on the Cairngorm Plateau, alone with my senses, the neutral taste of the high ground, the ever-changing sounds and angles of view as I wandered and soloed - a *Remontado* with only apparitions over my shoulders.

Threading the Needles

The Isle of Wight is a sedate, diamond-shaped slice of exfoliation, marooned in the Solent off the south coast of England. Six thousand years ago, a cataclysmic rise in sea level drowned and eroded the geological umbilical cord that made the island part of the mainland. The only remains of that cord are a set of chalky fangs that have now become the island's most famous coastal feature, on show to tourists like Neolithic museum pieces – The Needles.

Occasionally, I would make the six hundred mile journey south from the space of the Scottish Highlands to visit family. I was never that keen, as there weren't any real prospects for adventures on the island. However, it was supposed to be a good destination for paragliding. On one memorable occasion, I went up the hill with my brother in his ex-army ambulance. On top, the wind was not perpendicular to the ridge and it was difficult to take off. My brother helped me to get airborne but didn't let go of me; the paraglider was lifting us both off the ground. He was still hanging onto my legs, shouting at me to go down. I pulled manically on all the risers and then it finally collapsed, us with it, landing in a heap of hysterics . . .

As far as climbing was concerned, the guidebook offered a brief paragraph on the island's rock-climbing possibilities. I'm not sure that the post-cretaceous sediment could be classified as rock at all. According to the book, the island's most revered climb is called *Skeleton Ridge* – a 200ft blade-thin spine that pokes seawards towards the serrated teeth of The Needles.

The guru of esoteric adventure – Mick Fowler – first had the audacity to climb this shapely yet dangerously loose feature. The approach to the base of the climb is either via a long abseil down two knotted ropes, tied end to end, or a 2km long tidal scramble from the beach at Alum Bay. Reading this description, I realised that this was not an adventure for someone without any ropes, so I resigned myself to walking the dog, swimming in the sea, and running across the downs, whilst on my family visits.

I had just succeeded in climbing the *Icon of Lust* on the Shelterstone. Having accomplished that, I had laid my obsession to rest and rid myself of the satanic power of commitment. It was a good time to drive south to the Isle of Wight, to release myself from the mental stress of rock climbing, to relax for a while. I boarded the ferry at Lymington, took a seat and gazed around at people, wondering why they might have decided on the Isle of Wight for a holiday. It was surely far cheaper to travel to the continent nowadays on the many dirt-cheap airlines. Impetuous kids were tearing up and down; it was school holidays, and that meant my half-sister, Karen, would be run ragged with her three wild and unstoppable creations: Amanda, James and Ben. I was glad my sister had three kids. My brother and I didn't have any. I don't think he ever thought about it. Statements like: 'If I can cut hair and cook, then I can live on any beach in the world!' didn't conjure up the elements of a family man. Giles and I were brought up by our father – our outlooks on life were different. It was difficult to be brought up without a mum, but it must have been far harder for mum not having 'her boys' with her and missing our childhood.

I glanced casually around the bustling lounge. Something grabbed my attention in the corner of my eye; I did a double take before fixing a stare on the front cover of the Wight Link magazine. Excitement rose as I studied an aerial photograph of

The Needles – three white, chalky spines towering out of a perfect, azure sea, with a speedboat carving a serene, creamy wake across the centre of the page. My mind drifted away from holidaymakers and all things mundane and became firmly focused on The Needles and the risks involved in traversing one of the most famous coastal features in Britain. I felt pleased to have unearthed such an esoteric idea as I folded the magazine away into my bag, knowing that I had already made up my mind.

As I set foot on the pier in Yarmouth, I gave my mum a hug and announced:

'Mum, I am going to traverse over The Needles.'

There was an uneasy silence for a while and then she replied,

'Well, let me know when you are going; I will inform the coastguard.'

My mother must surely wonder how she ever gave birth to such an eccentric son, obsessed with hardship, adrenalin and danger. These traits certainly didn't run in the family; my sister got her fix of adrenalin fighting over bargains in the January sales whilst my brother loved drinking and womanising. That was until he surprised everyone by getting married to Debbie in his mid thirties and owning a restaurant in the Caribbean. We are all different to each other in every way possible.

During July, the whole of the UK was experiencing a heat wave; the air was hot, even at night, and the sea was a pleasurable temperature. It was warm enough to swim a mile without catching hypothermia! Every morning, my training for The Needles was an hour's swim in the sea with Daisy, my mum's black Labrador. Daisy had a strange personality, quite peculiar for a dog. She hated being stroked and never ate her meals; she was more like a cat. 'Funny old girl', my mum used to say. The mornings were spent swimming with Daisy, and the afternoons and evenings were spent socialising and drinking wine and gin and tonic with the family.

The forecast for the next few days was supposed to be perfect. This was what I needed, but whenever I thought about The Needles, something began to bother me. I realised that soloing The Needles on my own would be a lonely and vulnerable experience, and one I wasn't sure I could cope with, especially with my mum's negativity towards my planned exploit. Sharing the experience and the burden of commitment would make me feel safer. But who was mad enough to listen to my lunatic ideas and go with me? There was only one answer to that.

I rang Mike Robertson, the wacky author of so many hair-raising and gnarly deep water solos along the Dorset and Devon coasts. Mike, infectious as ever, was bubbling over with enthusiasm at the idea. With a head of long, scraggly, brown hair and a honed, bronze body, Mike belied his age of forty plus. Having occasionally worked as a male stripper, he was certainly a ladies man. His trademark cheeky grin could easily secure a date with girls half his age. I was, therefore, shocked when he mentioned to me that he had been married. His vagrant, photo-journalistic lifestyle didn't seem to conjure up the impression of a man who could undertake any marital role seriously. Life, for him, was something worth living to the full, unencumbered. But he is also a man of principle, as demonstrated perfectly when he was arrested 100ft from the top of the 1,000ft Eiffel tower whilst soloing, and again on the Lloyd's building in London, carrying a red flag to raise awareness of the situation in Burma (Myanmar).

Climbing with Mike was always fun, as some kind of shenanigans would always ensue. There was one occasion when we were chilling out for most of the afternoon in lush, green grass on the flat cliff tops at Pembroke, chatting about travels and probably girls – as we always did. We then headed down to the base of Stennis Head where Mike produced a bottle of Rosé and had a few swigs, handed me the bottle, slipped his climbing boots on, and started soloing *Manzoku* – a vertical, 100ft high wall of gleaming limestone above a rocky pavement. I just couldn't watch. I had no problem with myself soloing, but I became surprisingly squeamish when I watched someone else solo above rocks. I wanted to shout . . . 'Don't be stupid and get down at once!' but it would have been gross hypocrisy.

Watching him solo past the halfway point, I began to shake involuntarily; I just couldn't look. I turned round, hid out of sight, sat down and slugged away at his bottle of wine. I knew he wouldn't fall, but I still couldn't bear to watch. When he returned, he was prompting me to solo *Riders on the Storm*. I had soloed it on numerous occasions and was checking out a blank, vertical wall in the shadows on the far side of the zawn. We decided to go for a look. By the time I had my boots on and had located a suitable descent route to start the traverse, the alcohol had gone to my head. I was tipsy, and the dimensions and the distances of the holds pulsed in and out of focus. I felt all giddy and full of mischief. Touching the holds didn't quite feel real, as though someone else's muscles were controlling my movements. I reached a damp ledge at the base of a wide chimney where the cliff changes direction. A vertical, black wall abutted in from the left. It looked impossible and it was inevitable that I was going to fall into the choppy sea. I didn't care – I was drunk; I felt immortal . . .

Mike was climbing behind me, which wasn't a good thing as he climbed decisively and with a certain amount of efficiency on limestone - he was brought up on it. By contrast, I was a slow climber on limestone; I was more suited to the nuances of technical granite, so I climbed quicker than normal into my own self-afflicted cul-de-sac. A vague groove ran up the wall, but the traverse to gain it was devoid of holds. Mike was blabbering away, only a few feet behind. I was laughing at the situation - we were like two kids who had escaped school and disappeared to find something adventurous and naughty to indulge in. I hadn't had this much fun for years, even though I knew exactly where I was going to end up. I hadn't actually worked out where or how I was going to get out of the slopping waves, but I thought the cold water would sober me up, and there was always the thought that Mike would jump in and rescue me. Then there would be two drunks bobbling around in the sea. That idea made me laugh even more. Miraculously, one small finger hold appeared in the middle of the wall. I laughed at its size before pulling on it with fingers and an arm that really wasn't mine. All sorts of shakes were going on as I climbed up the flake. It was sustained and needed stamina, which in turn needed oxygen to the muscles, but my blood didn't seem to be carrying any oxygen, it was carrying alcohol. I felt a strange delight; climbing at my limit with no control over my body whatsoever. We left a neat set of random, white, chalky blobs across the rocky-blackboard and disappeared out of the zawn with our wobbly-boots on. We headed off down to the St Govan's Inn for a well-earned drink – just another random adventure with Mike.

During our telephone conversation, Mike talked about bringing ropes and wondered how to keep equipment dry whilst swimming. I told him I wasn't taking anything. It rendered him speechless for a moment, which I admit was a first. Gradually, he took on the idea of a true solo ascent with optimism. One of the controlling factors of the adventure would be the tides, and after checking the tide tables, I discovered that the high tides were going to be roughly at seven o'clock, morning and night. A high tide would be best because there would be a slightly better chance of surviving a fall, and also the currents between The Needles would be negligible at that time.

Early the next morning, Mike bounced down the ferry ramp at Yarmouth, sporting his usual cheeky grin, before charging into his charismatic and quite uncontrollable chatty mode. Within an hour of being on the island, Mike was in the county press offices in Newport, casually flirting with the demure receptionist, with a sparkle in his eye. He had secured an interview with a reporter and our photos were taken. The weekly paper was going to print that afternoon, and the editor had decided to print our story with our picture before we had even set foot on The Needles: our fate was sealed and there was no turning back. The headlines read:

Daring duo in bid
to thread The Needles.

Mike was soon on the phone to the coastguard, asking about the possibility of a free lift and a watchful eye. The Coastguard were interested and rather disappointed that they couldn't accompany us as it was Cowes Week (the annual sailing regatta on the Isle of Wight). Every boat was busy on patrol. We organized a boat from Yarmouth to take us to The Needles. It was late afternoon. Standing on the jetty, waiting, I grew nervous; the air was thick and hazy, and the unknown started to gnaw at my resolve. A taxi pulled up and a slim woman in a flowery blouse stepped out into the road. She was young and pretty with blonde, wispy hair, her eyes hidden behind sunglasses. Mike and I looked at her and then at each other with a mutual grin of appreciation; just those few seconds reduced the tension, and even more so when we found out that she was Laura, the County Press photographer who was going to accompany us on the adventure. The boat eased out of Yarmouth harbour towards the open sea. It didn't take long for the sinusoidal motion to grip me with nausea. I am no salty sea dog! Mike sat on the other side of the boat next to Laura, oblivious to the motion of the boat. Adding to my distress, Mike pulled on his shortie wetsuit, giving him some protection and confidence; damn, I only had a pair of shorts. As the boat accelerated, the wind-chill escalated. I began to freeze and my knuckles went white as they gripped the hull. I slowly started to lose all belief in this adventure and myself. I kept smiling towards Mike and Laura, trying to conceal my doubts. Deep down of course I knew that Mike would be full of enthusiasm and energy, and that would be enough to pull us through.

The Needles started to grow through a fine coat of humbling fog that seemed to be sucking out all the sun's power. I was uneasy at the sight of the sheer, white fangs rising out of the water like an albino stegosaurus. However, the closer we got, the less intimidating they became. My confidence started to build. We pulled alongside another boat which was moored up by the red and white striped lighthouse, connected to the seaward tip of the outer Needle. Mike and I jumped onto the small, concrete pier. The two men who were doing maintenance work on the lighthouse received us in an unfriendly manner. We were told that we couldn't climb The Needles from the lighthouse because it was private property, and if there were an accident, the landowner could be sued. However, we were permitted to access the Needle from the south, as long as we didn't set foot on the lighthouse or its pier.

We jumped back in the boat and asked to be taken round to the south side. The boat nudged close into the rocks, and then I heard the boatman's voice, partially drowned out by the reverse thrust of the boat's engine.

'I can't get in any closer; you'll have to go from here.'

The swell lopped the boat to and fro, but that was my cue, I couldn't contain myself any longer. With my disposable, underwater camera wrapped around my wrist, I dived from the front of the boat without hesitation. The water was refreshing, although I could feel the uncanny currents swirl around me like invisible monsters, tearing my limbs in a multitude of directions. I grabbed at some rock and scrabbled out against the sucking force of the sea. Both the cold water and excitement had jump-started my kidneys, and I started to pee uncontrollably down my legs in full view of the tourist boat that had just rounded the tip of the Needle. I gave a friendly smile and a wave. It was a strange feeling to be pissing in front of a boat full of tourists. Mike passed me and was busy finding the best line up bulbous features of chalk, reaching the crest in little time. The climbing was easy on loosely cemented rubble, but tricky in supersaturated rock boots. The view east is one of a severely precipitous and dangerous white crest that looks faultless for over half a mile to the mainland cliff top, quite unique for this country. It was a sight more appropriately found on a virginal, snow-corniced ridge of the Alps or Himalayas. It felt almost surreal to be climbing along a diabolically crumbling, alpine ridge made of rock that resembled Wensleydale cheese, all only a mere 70ft above the sea, in a pair of swimming trunks . . .

In sections the ridge could be walked with faith and balance, but for longer stretches it was a case of crawling along guano-infested, chert-noduled chalk. As we moved along the crest, the cormorants vacated their perches, their fetid stench of digested fish making my head shake in involuntary spasms. We came upon a large, chalky block, wrapped with a few ancient lengths of climbing cord, obviously the scene of a previous abseil. We were aware that the two seaward Needles had been climbed before, but no one had done the whole traverse of The Needles including the swims between them. We regularly sent rocks clattering down both sides; they ricocheted, split and then splintered into the sea. The noise reminded me of the Alps under a midday sun, when the heat has melted the bond between the rock and the ice. Amongst the sounds of stone-fall, another noise drifted through the air; it was a familiar voice: the defining pitch of a scouser.

'Juliaaaan . . . Juliaaaan!'

I looked out to the north, and fifty yards away was the next tourist boat, with a new set of passengers, including my mum, brother and Debbie, who waved and shouted enthusiastically, informing everybody that I was her brother-in-law.

At the far end of the crest, Mike psyched up to take the 60ft jump, but the face was casting shadows over the water and we couldn't ascertain from our position if the water was deep enough. I was glad; it was too high anyway, and I didn't want to puncture a lung with the jump. We descended the south face, checking the security of every hold with dogged concentration. Descending was harder than anything we had previously encountered. At the water's edge, we jumped in and swam through a gentle current in order to reach the base of the second Needle. My confidence started to soar; one Needle completed - just two to go. We made good time along the crest of the second Needle. It was perfectly flat, although only a foot wide in places. Nearing the end of the ridge, the chalky spine started to curve gracefully into an overhanging, knife-edged cornice of chalk. Mike was ahead and words started burbling out of him. Knowing Mike reasonably well, this was his way of controlling his fear - more burbling meant he was becoming more scared and the situation more dangerous, making him more excitable. Every time he completed a loose section, he would shout back to me in relief.

'Bloody hell Ju, this is loose as shit . . . suicidal . . . madness!' amongst other words. I could tell he was having fun and enjoying the experience nevertheless. I followed, and understood what Mike had gone through - the whole knife-edge was actually loose and moving, and any excessive lateral pushing or pulling movements would cause the whole spine to tumble off into the sea, with me after it. The only feasible way to climb it was to push it downwards into itself and shuffle along. My concentration was intense, and my body was alert to the slightest movement of rock. Progress was painstakingly slow. If The Needles had been made of granite, the ridge would have been a mere scramble, enjoyed by many and climbed in seconds. But no, this horizontal spine was the easiest and most humbling climbing experience I'd ever endured. Mike's take on it, as quoted in the newspaper the following week, summed it up all too evidently . . .

'When you are climbing on this type of rock, you will either come out unscathed, like we did, or you'll probably die. We're two of the few people who would take that risk I think . . . '

At the end of the crest, the cliff tapered steeply down towards the sea. Mike once again contemplated the 70ft jump, but again the shadows masked the true depth of the water. It was a stupid idea. Mike descended the crumbling, white arête to a small foothold at 50ft. Here he considered another jump, and seconds before he leapt, I shouted down to him: 'Look Mikey! There's a good ledge to jump from a little lower down!' I hoped that my words were going to persuade him to down climb a little further – if not, then I knew I would have to jump after him and risk injury. Thankfully, Mike took notice of my concerns and descended further, to the small ledge at 30ft, before leaping into the sea. 30ft was still high enough for me to feel my stomach hit the back of my throat when I plummeted into the sea after him. We were now faced with the most intimidating section – the 100m swim between the second and third Needle. As legend has it, the currents between these Needles are sometimes so powerful that they wash people up on the French coast! Our standby boat drifted in, boosting our morale, and Mike took advantage of some refreshment; some water and his favourite food – a malt loaf.

I declined food as I tried to work out the direction of the current before aligning my bearings, sticking my head down into the opaque abyss and swimming as hard as I could. Every so often I would pull my head up to check my orientation, but the surface of the waves spat in my eyes. I felt pathetic against the force of the sea, but I struggled on manfully to the third Needle. I drip-dried contentedly on a ledge at the base of the third Needle, watching Mike swim the channel, seemingly unperturbed.

The third Needle was the squattest of the three. And the climax occurred at the very end, when the final crest ended abruptly at an overhanging wall that faced the island. Mike looked at me and I looked back at him - we both knew we had reached a cul-de-sac. A 50ft jump into a 4ft deep pool, surrounded by bone-breaking blocks, wasn't an option, even to Mike. The only solution was to make a descent by the north slab, which had its fair share of green sea slime and flaking holds. I anticipated breaking holds on every move, bracing myself, waiting for the slide and fall into a very shallow, watery grave. Luckily, none of the holds gave way at crucial moments as I clawed my way down, agonisingly slowly. This final descent on the slab was the hardest part of the whole traverse. I thought it to be more gripping than most 'extreme' slab routes I had soloed. At 25ft, I reached a point where the best option was to swivel and jump. My body broke the surface and my feet hit some blocks under the water just as I came to a stop; I wouldn't have wanted to have fallen from any greater height. I surfaced, rather worried, and waded out over an irregular array of crumbled rocks – the remains of the collapsed archway that once formed between the third Needle and the island ridge, less than a century ago. It is said that these famous Needles were named after this archway – the true 'eye of the needle' – but nature had inevitably destroyed it. When I reached the security of the island, I felt overwhelming relief as I waited for Mike. We were joyous for a few moments before we started discussing our escape plan. A solo of *Skeleton Ridge* had been mentioned, but we were both drained of commitment. So we carried on traversing around the headland into the Alum bay, exploring some caves and tunnels as we took the long swim back to the beach.

The sun hovered on the horizon like a dull, orange orb. Its final rays were dissolving fast into the atmosphere, and it was a fitting conclusion to a memory that would probably last longer than the Needles themselves.

The Otter's Breakfast Table

A beach of eggshell-white sand curved in a graceful arc, forming a crescent moon, honed to perfection by the invisible forces of nature. An apathetic sea washed over the fine grain with a gentle rhythm, the interface forever in motion like liquid glass. Further out, the water radiated with turquoise tones, sensual, but just an illusion. Behind the beach was a squat, irregular landscape dominated by random splashes of colour. Above this, a deep blue sky was scented with a whiff of smoky-white cirrus. Moored idly on the calm water was a solitary, white-hulled yacht, its sheets beating the mast with a gentle chime in the breeze. A couple stood on deck – the first humans I had seen for a week. They were naked to the elements. I watched them dive through the sparkling glass and take a short swim before climbing back onto the deck. I gazed at the naked woman, becoming aroused at the feminine form as I looked down from my rocky perch above the bay. I had the longing for company and intimacy, but for now the island would have to suffice.

I followed a sharply twisting sheep-trail that wound its way down onto the beach where I wiggled my toes in the fine, dry-dusted sand, allowing the grains to filter between my toes, tickling them with a strange sensuality and a feeling of peace. As I approached the water's edge, the water glinted with speckles of dancing light, so deceiving that it fooled me into thinking that I was in the Seychelles, on the fringe of the exotic Indian Ocean. I ran into the sea, breaking the serenity of the water, and dived in. Reality struck immediately; the water was shockingly cold, and I spent ten minutes running up and down the beach after my swim, trying to warm up before returning to my tent that was pitched amongst the machair on top of the dunes. A strange wound in my ankle wept with a thick, yellow fluid. I tried to mop it up with a T-shirt before dousing the hole with the only natural preservative I had: honey.

From up high, the warlike skyline stunned me: shipyard cranes and oil rigs – a tangled mess of steel obelisks stretched across a hazy horizon, looking like the spooky aftermath of a nuclear strike. The heavy pollution and the incessant noise were driving me insane. Forget pretty windmills and tulips – this was Rotterdam, the heart of industrial Holland. Freedom could not have been further away. What was I doing here?

I took a breather from my work and looked down into the bottom of the vast, concrete dry dock, 150ft below, where workmen were running around like busy ants. Above me towered the top half of the drilling derrick, from which I was hanging by two ropes. Living surrounded by this world of noise and machines, I felt like a cyborg embryo, attached to its steel mother by two precious nylon umbilicals. I wiped sweat and metal dust from my brow, pulled my goggles back over my face, and re-started the angle-grinder which kicked in with its usual centrifugal jolt and the deafening screech that never failed to startle. I had one final bolt to cut through, holding the cladding to the main derrick frame. The bolt was out of reach, but I managed to stretch out horizontally, gripping the angle-grinder dangerously with one hand. My abdomen and shoulders burnt with pain; the grinder was nearly through. I persevered. The bolt started to glow amber as it heated. I began to adjust my position in order to miss its flight trajectory. As I was doing this, the molten missile flicked off and disappeared. I waited for the sound of it hitting the pipe deck far below, hoping that it wasn't going to bounce chaotically and hit someone unawares. Suddenly trauma ripped through my foot! The bolt had gone down the throat of my rigging boot and my skin started to sizzle. My initial reaction was to drop the angle-grinder and rip my boot off, but I couldn't let go of the grinder because there was a chance that it might pivot on its safety lanyard and slice through my ropes, leaving me to fall 100ft to the pipe deck, and to be potentially impaled on metal tubes.

Amidst a typhoon of pain, I pressed the blade hard against the metal frame to stop its rotation, and at the same time I shouted for Luci – my team-mate – who was on the walkway on the inside of the derrick. She poked her head outside the structure, rather concerned and bemused, wondering what the fuss was all about. I stuck my boot through the safety rails and screamed:

'Pull my boot off! Pull my boot off!'

Luci wrestled with my boot, pulled it off, and screamed as flames licked out into the air – my sock was on fire, and all I could do was laugh in agony. My foot was singed black and yellow, and the stench of my burnt flesh, together with the sight of my own bone, made me wretch uncontrollably.

Luci was great to work with: she was fun and unique. There weren't many petite, forty-one-year-old mothers that could be seen abseiling from oil rigs in such grimy, industrial shipyards. Every morning, we would walk down the length of the shipyard. All the men would gaze at her because she was wearing rig boots and a pair of jeans cut off keenly at her thighs, a bit like Daisy Duke. I felt as if I were in the company of royalty! When we arrived at our small ropes container on the dockside, Luci would say: 'Can you stand sentry by the door, Spidey?' as she changed out of her clothes and into her overalls.

Work is what you make of it, and it was fun in Holland. Striking up relationships with the characters you work with is an integral part of the job. Colleagues come and go, travel and work all over the world, but somehow you always know where they are through the grapevine. Although the world is vast, the rope access community is quite close-knit. I could feel the wilds calling me again. I told Luci that I couldn't be arsed with working anymore and that it was time for me to find some freedom, and I think she was a little sad to see me go.

Erraid is a small, partially tidal island off the Isle of Mull on the west coast of Scotland. It is a long drive from the mainland to the very tip of the Ross of Mull peninsula from where tourists do daily tours to the famous islands of Iona and Staffa. Just to the south of this lies the lesser-known paradise of Erraid. I had first visited the island the previous summer, with the mildly obsessive climber, Gary Latter. I was curious about the quaint granitic rocks I had read about, as well as Gary's rumours of superb arêtes to climb and the promise of deep water soloing. Erraid is an island composed entirely of granite, and the island has been blessed with gorgeous and unforgettable, white beaches.

The first rock climbs to be recorded on Erraid were on two tiers. The upper tier is a gently overhanging wave of granite, forming a miniature amphitheatre with a lush green meadow at its base whilst the lower tier forms a small cove above tidal shelves and boulders with a wee smugglers' tunnel. Word has it that they were first discovered by climbers who sailed by in their yacht during a summer holiday. Thereafter, Gary climbed many new routes whilst guiding school groups. He was very taken by the place, which is not surprising, as Gary devotes most of his time to rock climbing in and around the remote corners of the Highlands and Islands, always in search of that perfect venue or climb, and he always has an unblemished optimism with regard to the climbing and weather in Scotland. The enchantment of Erraid's granitic rocks had also lured in Colin Moody, a local climbing activist who works on one of Mull's fish farms. His pioneering pace was slower than Gary's, or mine, but perhaps he didn't think anyone else would bother to visit. But it wasn't about pioneering climbs - it was the sheer enjoyment of existing somewhere so magical.

Seeing Erraid's golden granite for the first time, I was smitten. Climbing became addictive; the days passed by, route upon route. In the late afternoon on my very first day, my knuckles were ripped and bloodied, and my body sore, limp and dehydrated. Instead of stopping for the day and recovering, I continued up 'just one more climb'. On this 'last' solo, reaching for the top, cramp suddenly buried itself into my muscles. My numb fingers split open. I just let go, and all that remained was a 30ft fall onto sea-sprayed, barnacle-encrusted rocks . . . in the instant my fingers popped, my toes slipped onto a foothold, giving me a split-second chance to grip on again instinctively, before reversing to safety.

For the remaining couple of days, we turned our attention to the deep water soloing wall which we named *Paradise Wall*. Here, the most perfect granite cracks rose straight out of turquoise waters on gently overhung granite. We departed with raw skin, dehydration, withered arms and, most of all, precious memories.

I drove into the car park – the remains of a sheep pen, part outlined by crumbling stone walls. There were some rust-like skeletons of old tractors, hens and geese and a few straggly-coated sheep nonchalantly eating the lusciously green grass, or rubbing themselves up and down relics of old cars. Some fishing nets were strewn over the wall – bleached, aged and tattered – whilst pink fishing buoys were cast away on the ground like motherless orbs. It was all very nineteenth century. But this shit-scattered pen was a sight for sore eyes, for this was the end of the road . . .

There was no sign of life from the adjacent croft house of Knockvolagan, and there never seemed to be a problem leaving a vehicle. I stuffed my camping gear – sleeping bag, tent, thermarest, book, food, cutlery, climbing boots, chalk bags, spare clothes, jacket and food – into my rucksack and carried five litres of water in my hand. I set off down the track and out onto a beach of white sand. The tide was out, and the beach extended seaward like a ripple-covered prairie. I turned right and walked over the 100m long neck of sand that links the Isle of Mull to the Isle of Erraid. The next twenty minutes were spent crossing featureless and undulating bog and heather, weaving a lost trail between knolls, navigating by a loose sense of direction. Finally the vista opened ahead of me, and the sight down to the lonely beach was one to be cherished forever. I felt good as I once again approached one of my favourite spiritual haunts. I dumped my gear on the flat area of grass atop the dunes – a perfect campsite. A stream trickled by only a few metres away, although it dripped with green slime and swam with water-boatmen larvae. This time I had brought water to drink. I pitched the tent before walking down the beach towards the sea where I was eager to swim and wash away the sweat and memories of the Rotterdam Shipyard. Afterwards, I wandered round the bay to a pleasant granite platform – a small dais above the sea. Here I sat for a while, admiring the deep-yellow lichens and the shapes of the black inclusions in the rocks, the beautiful turquoises of the sea and the glaring off-whites of the sand.

It was here in the 1870s that Robert Louis Stevenson spent his childhood, relaxing and absorbing the beauty and aura of this very bay – *traigh gheal*, the Gaelic for white beach. It inspired him to begin his famous novel – 'Kidnapped'. The bay is named after David Balfour, the youthful hero of the book. I encountered the same views, the same solitude and the same natural beauty, but nothing had surely changed in over a hundred years. But in the outside world so much had changed: a number of wars had been fought; the motorcar, the aeroplane, space travel and the computer had all been invented . . . all of that seemed so irrelevant here; Erraid is timeless. It is an escape - a place to be free.

The burn from the shipyard still stung. It ran its length up the back of my ankle and was beginning to tingle due to the tightening of the skin as it dried out after swimming. I assumed that sea water would do it some good and keep it clean. I wanted to climb, so I pulled on my boots, only to find that the boot rand cut tightly across the wound. I cursed, but soon resolved the problem by cutting a chunk out of my rock boot with my penknife.

Once my boots were on, I climbed down to the barnacle zone and became entranced in a sea level traverse. I gazed intently down to the water and to the brown fingers of kelp that floated aimlessly, swaying in the water to the motion of the tide like giant, brown tagliatelle simmering in a saucepan. Further out, a seal popped his head up like a whiskered periscope, having a look. I reached a smooth, granite chockstone that had perhaps been thrust there into the rock in a massive storm. It had been there for hundreds of years, perhaps thousands. I used its jammed security to pull through the overhang and onto a delightful flake crack that soared positively upwards. Time drifted away . . .

Lazy shafts of sunlight danced across my eyelids, awakening me.

I had slept in on the rig! Why hadn't my alarm gone off?

My mind was confused. Something was wrong, but I couldn't ascertain what it was.

Where was the light coming from?

My cabin on the rig had no window; it was merely a cell in which to sleep between shifts. Then my brain re-engaged as I tilted my neck backwards to peer through the cloth window towards an inverted picture where the sky was the sea and vice-versa. I was at peace once more, realising that I wasn't at work or dependent on time and alarms. Shining wisps of light danced across a shield of granite - these were merely reflections of a shimmering sea. The sunshine forced me to rise, but as I tried to get out of my sleeping bag, I found that I couldn't - the weeping burn on my ankle had stuck to the fabric like toffee. I had breakfast - muesli and water - before grabbing some gear and running down to the beach for my morning swim. I felt great; I had no rules to obey, no deadlines, no boiler suit, no hard hat, no safety glasses, and no one telling me what to do . . .

After a refreshing swim, I started trying to deal with a niggling, knotted muscle in my back. I couldn't reach it, so in frustration I scooped the stone out of an avocado, placed it in a sock, and rolled my back around on it atop the machair. A strange improvisation, perhaps, but it had the desired effect. Later, I wandered over to some rocks across the bay where I happened to look down a 40ft high, clean-cut corner of granite. There, half in the water, half out, was an inclined tablet of stone, onto which popped an otter holding a crab in its mouth. The otter used the stone to help him crack open the crab's shell whilst his front paws worked expertly on the delicate task of extracting the flesh. After his meal, he cocked his head ever so slightly, shooting a glance at the greatest predator of all, and in an instant he was gone, lost in another world below the surface of the sea. The only sign of his fleeting existence was a collection of smooth, radiating ripples that soon petered out, and a husk of a shell that would be carried away by the oncoming tide. I put on my boots and climbed down the corner before hopping onto the tablet of rock alongside the crab's remains. In front of me was a beautiful concave wall of granite, golden in colour, seemingly flawless and impenetrable. I could see two flake holds a distance apart, but absolutely nothing else. I weighed up my own arm span and decided to trust myself that I could reach between them, and then excitedly began to chalk up. An initial groove of rock succumbed to some exquisite moves. I reached out to the first flake hold and swung dangerously onto it. I was alone now; I couldn't go back. To my right was the next flake hold - the only one in a blank sheet of virgin granite. If I couldn't reach the hold, then I'd end up on the breakfast table too. My arm stretched out and my fingers curled neatly around the hold, then my second hand followed. My body was now out of balance, and my feet tore across the rock in a scraping arc. I tensed up to hold the swing, and there I hung, transfixed by the uncertainty of the way ahead. A hold on the overhanging arête lured me. I grabbed it and then realised ... I was there, stuck. Life had suddenly lost its colour and had turned ugly, very ugly. I glanced around, looking hopefully for a positive suggestion, but there was none. Then I looked down, and directly below me was the otter's breakfast table, all ready to break my bones. I searched desperately for a solution before the strength in my arms gave out – out of the blue it appeared. If I tucked my feet up high enough and sprung back horizontally for 8ft, I might just land in a few feet of water. With that knowledge, my body, muscles and mind relaxed. I continued up the overhanging arête, grinning from ear to ear.

I went for a wander and to explore the island further. I found myself fighting my way through waist-deep heather, giant bracken and some strangely scented shrubs that scratched at my legs. Unexpectedly, I came upon civilisation in the form of a quarry and some cottages, and the magic somehow dissolved. The island felt tainted in a strange kind of way. I learned that the quarry had been cut for the materials to build the cottages that were in turn built to accommodate the lighthouse keepers.

Thomas Stevenson, father of Robert Louis, was the engineer who designed the 145ft high Dubh Artach lighthouse that sits ten miles to the southwest, off the coast of Erraid. It was built to protect ships that might have strayed too near to the shores. Three miles out lie the Torran Rocks - a set of fierce, granite protuberances that lurk in the water. They had been responsible for over two dozen shipwrecks and the loss of countless lives in the mid 1800s. In fact, in the novel, David Balfour himself became shipwrecked on those very rocks.

I continued around the coast, endlessly seeking out rocks and climbs, passing by some granite islands and hidden inlets – cosy shelters for mooring yachts safely out of the ravages of the south-westerly winds. I walked away from the sea and stumbled upon the stinking carcass of a dead sheep, the head bent back, the vertebrae broken, the ribs poking through the fleece, the eyes deep, hollow sockets, and the mouth frozen in an expression of simultaneous agony and placidity, a cohort of flies dancing around the woolly nucleus in orbital spin. I hastened on and arrived on top of a flat, heathery hillock where I sat and stared out towards the shape of Iona. Unlike Erraid, Iona has an Abbey that was built in the 6th century by Saint Columba - it is rife with tourism.

I made my way down from the knoll, heading westwards towards the sea again, still in search of some climbs. I was in luck, as I came upon a 25ft high granite slab, littered with multi-coloured intrusions. They had shapes that seemed to form ancient murals of animals and fish, and one red intrusion in particular looked like a pig; I called it the 'strawberry pig slab', named after a fish and chip shop in Wilmslow, Cheshire. Having enjoyed the tenuous nature of the routes on the slab, I scrambled round to Erraid's most impressive feature – the remains of an ancient, geological tragedy. A black, basaltic dyke had cut through the mother granite many millions of years ago, eroding faster than the granite, leaving an 8ft wide and 70ft high chasm of atmospheric proportions, on top of which was jammed a ten-ton, spherical, granite boulder. One can walk across the top of the chasm via the boulder. On first acquaintance, the chasm is breathtaking; it's not what you would expect amongst such tranquil surroundings. The walls of the chasm are smooth, and the curving corners on the east wall are like elevators to the gods. I could not pass these by, so in another one of my 'moments', I started soloing the finest corner. A few feet from the top, the holds ran out as the corner steepened and sea grass had overgrown it - I frantically rubbed away at the grass, baring enough holds to assist me in extricating myself.

It was fun roaming and exploring, finding boulders and small crags in abundance. Even nature's creatures weren't that averse to humans residing here on the island - a cheeky, black mink popped his head up, with a mackerel bigger than itself in its mouth, and nonchalantly scurried along the granite pavement whilst I sat a few feet away tying my bootlaces. By late afternoon, I wandered back to the beach, exhausted, took a swim, and re-proofed my burn with honey.

Scotland is a country where you have to view two good days weather per week as a blessing; I had now experienced almost a week of clear blue skies. I felt spoilt by the continental weather – it had made me somewhat lethargic. I remained naked most of the time, gaining a golden, leathery skin; even my climbing was taken at a more sedate pace, and I began to feel like a castaway. I had neither seen nor talked to anyone since I had arrived. I decided to go and climb at the upper tier – the first of the areas to be pioneered by other climbers. When I arrived, the heat radiating from the walls made me feel woozy, so I lay down in the grass and took in the view. There were a couple of unclimbed routes to be done - one powerful, one dangerous - but I wasn't in the mind set for that type of motivation. Instead, I decided to climb one of Gary's routes - *Covenant*: a 30ft high, overhanging crack which wouldn't be out of place in the Yosemite Valley boulders. The rough, crystalline crack tried to puncture my flesh as I climbed swiftly to reach a little respite above half height. The crack then thinned and baffled me; I started to lose strength and belief in unison. But since the ground was soft, my subconscious surprisingly gave me the go ahead to continue. I swung onto my fingertips and committed, pulling like fury, before belly flopping over the top.

I was in no mood to leave, but my ferry ticket was due to expire, and I didn't have enough food or water to last me past breakfast. After supper, I decided to walk to the top of the knoll and catch any breeze available to avert the midges. There I watched the final flames of a west coast sunset, and I sat engrossed in the timeless view that surrounded me. To the south, the isles of Colonsay and Islay were just distinguishable, floating shadows of crust upon the sea. Only the dark shapes of the Paps of Jura held some presence. To the southwest, the Dhu Artach was just an illusion of my imagination - I knew it was there, but a slight, twilight sea haze obscured it. To the north was Iona, to the east sat the fortress of Ben More – Scotland's last volcano – rising in solitary defiance, a wisp of cloud protecting its summit like a halo.

The following afternoon I pulled up at Fishnish. The ferry had just left, casting its wake in the calm, black water. Luckily it wasn't the last one of the day, so whilst waiting for the ferry's return, I crouched on my haunches in front of the car's wing mirror and shaved my head around my topknot. A short queue of cars built up behind me, and I could sense the incredulous stares. I felt untouchable and so distant from the realities of life and families . . . I had truly lost all burden of care.

Nothing seemed to make sense. It was like bereavement, and I was sad and baffled. I drove east through the mountains where the skies gradually swelled with cloud and turned to grey. Spits of rain landed on the windscreen. I was back amidst the grey, sodden spirit of Scotland I knew so well.

So where had I been? Was it a dream? Had I just been fast-forwarded from the mid nineteenth century in a time machine?

I negotiated the winding road ahead, casting a glance in my rear view mirror, and there I saw it, in the distance, beneath the greyness - a slither of bright, mango-hued light shining - the fading sunset of a far away Avalon.

Rumours of Rain

The constant drone of crickets and insects became a background monotone. I was curled up on rough ground in a lightweight sleeping bag, sealed tight from the fresh air and the mosquitoes. My own humid breath stuck to me as I fought off sleep. Time passed and I must have dozed off now and again, but suddenly unfamiliar voices tore into my consciousness: 'Get up! Get up!'

I ignored them, pretending that they were voices in a dream, but the shouts were followed by kicks into my ribs. I came to rapidly and recalled that I was in the hills of Turkey. Scared, I unravelled from my bag and stared up at the dark silhouettes of men with guns over their shoulders.

Oh God . . . bandits! We are in the shit!

The familiar voices of Mike Robertson and Gavin Symonds cut in, trying to appease the situation. They had been roused before me. When I realised that the men with guns were, in fact, police officers, I relaxed. There were a number of locals all gathered in a group, speaking Turkish I assumed. Then there was silence until one officer asked: 'What are you doing up here on the mountain?'

'Sleeping!'

'Why do you not sleep in a hotel?'

'We haven't got a hotel . . .

'Why not?'

'We like sleeping outdoors.'

'Why here on the mountain?'

'We are travelling and don't have a hotel . . .'

We recognised a local fisherman from whom we had hired a boat earlier that day. We exchanged glances of recognition, and he turned to discuss with the others that we were indeed the three lunatics who had been climbing the sea cliffs without ropes and jumping into the sea. There was a marked pause, and I could feel the atmosphere and tension drain like water through a sluice gate as humour lit up their eyes. An officer came over and said:

'We are really sorry, but the local farmer had seen you arrive and thought you were terrorists. He contacted us. We are sorry.'

We looked at each other.

'Terrorists!' We burst into laughter.

'The farmer has said you can sleep on his veranda.'

'Can we not sleep here?' Mike asked.

'No, you shouldn't be sleeping out in the mountains; there are snakes, very, very dangerous . . .' he answered imperatively.

Not wishing to give the farmer any further cause for concern, we were directed to some waste ground not far from town. Once we had settled down again for the night, we chuckled amongst ourselves: Snakes! Very, very dangerous! Terrorists!

Six months later: For hours, Mike Robertson and I had been driving along dirt roads that carved through hot, arid desert, leaving only dust plumes in our wake. We headed across flat plains with stunted bushes and distant mesas. Kimberley was now two hundred miles behind us, and we were heading west towards the Cederberg and the fiercest heat wave of the year. I took a moment and sat pensively, watching the sun drop towards the western horizon, knowing that at its next rising in the east

I would reach 'the big 4-0'. I grinned smugly - I knew that I had beaten the odds simply by getting this far.

Early the next morning, the sun sparked the eastern horizon and the hot wind whipped the temperature up to 30 degrees . . . and rising. The natural, random shapes of the Cederberg boulders sizzled under a tortuous sun: reindeer antlers, wolf heads, bird beaks and whale-eye sockets all weathered in stone. The sandstone was hard-baked, pebbles gleaming, radiating heat. Dry, orange tears spilled, black and grey streaks too; tiger hide. Geckos padded silently over the rock faces, throats rasping, searching for shade. Green shrubs lay scattered, leaves whistling, rattling, flowers too: parched purples, blues, reds and yellows, shrivelling, yearning for moisture.

We went in search of some fun, some moves to tune in our bodies. Under a roof we found chalk marks imagining a path, textures of impossible adhesion . . . we shook our heads. For those with limbs of penne pasta, joints of a locust and tendons of rubber, then ultimately a possibility? It was a fanatic's art, and all we could do was to stand back and admire. Hundreds of more plausible holds were discovered, mere mortal grips, arêtes, slabs and walls, caught between light and shade in this remarkable landscape.

Whoops of delight; another hard-won score was settled between bouts of shade. A fall here and there with no crash pads gave rise to aching joints and ankles. A few pouches of water hidden in the bedrock were just able to accommodate human immersion, cooling, refreshing . . . frogs accelerating to the deepest depths. Dragonflies appeared, hovering and disappearing. Midday was too hot – a time to rest blistered fingers and toes, get back to camp, into the hammocks and a book's fiction for a while before a snooze. And then suppertime: cheese, watermelon and finally a cool beer as the night crawled in and the heat diminished. So this was the lifestyle of a boulderer?

Four days were not long enough to explore a lifetime's tenuous movement; it was time to move on. We left nothing but a dusting of chalk. We were mobile ghosts vanishing into a vast, African landscape. We turned north and west and set off to the coast and the wine and flower region of Namaqualand. The Atlantic swell collapsing upon the rocky shoreline of pebbles and crushed shells was powerful, confident and so very cold; a refreshing contrast to the abhorrent heat of the Cederberg.

A seventy-mile track followed the coast, past salt lakes, shipwrecks and huge manmade mountains of dirt - the diamond mines - where massive trucks and diggers worked away like extra-terrestrial insects. We turned back inland only to be faced with intense heat and an infinite landscape of hills, archaic rocks and flora clinging to survival. In the distance, a granite dome rose up, smooth and brave above the remainder of the continental crust. We sought permission to discover its possibilities and went off-road in search of it, across a land of golden grass, dust, sheep droppings and tight bundles of thorny bushes. The dome was 300ft high, with an in-situ eyrie at half height, complete with Eagle, tucked precariously in one of those buttock-smooth grooves. The rock was colourful, radiating granite with a coarse, exfoliating skin. There was a time when I would have made a beeline dash, boots in hand, and set to the dome with that crazy coolness I once had, but my blizzard-type drive and commitment for pure recklessness had been sapped by the years, by survival instinct, and now by the intense heat. I seemed to grow more inquisitive about the unperturbed, bright red grasshoppers with shiny black and yellow striped underbellies. The urge to climb wasn't my primary motivation; it made a relaxing change . . .

In the morning, we climbed some beautiful, untouched boulders with serene views near to the camp – exploration at its simplest. Later we sought the appeal of a 150ft dyke that cut through a smaller dome. The holds and rock were so hot we moved like two space-bugs chasing each other up the incline of a celestial wok. Once sufficiently fried, we slewed the tyres northwards towards Springbok – the final outpost before the Namibian border.

Namibia: the pistons cranked across an empty hinterland, passing the odd gnarled tree, sand, rock and dwarf-like hills. We drove by the Fish River Canyon and on to a strange, solitary lake surrounded by encroaching desert where we camped for the night. In the morning, Mike went off to photograph the sensuous ripples carved into the sand whilst I went in the opposite direction, alone with my thoughts. Before leaving for Africa, I had not been in the greatest state of mind. I was a bit shaken, having had a brush with someone with a materialistic, manipulative and cruel persona. I was reeling from it. I found travelling with Mike was a good tonic; he was a good friend, deeply caring and understanding, and also knew when to just let me be.

Later that day we finally arrived at the sand-soaked village of Sossusvlei. Early the following morning we spilled westwards out of the village and onto the National Park road. It was 60km long and disappeared into the darkness, but in time the sky began to ripen in colour, revealing shapes that rose out of the plain like the mythical dragon's teeth warriors. When the light intensified on the horizon, the near-invisible shapes began to transform into sensational dunes 2,000ft high, tantalising and in need of touch. We walked the mile across the dead-flat desert plain to reach one. Their ridges curved in sensual and surgically precise arcs, the contrast of light and shade extraordinary.

Dehydrated but satisfied, we continued to the end of the road and then did what only mad dogs and Englishmen do: the heat was fierce, my throat dry, and the sand burned my feet, making me hop and dance. The path consisted of a few disorderly footprints that were slowly being disguised by the combination of hot wind and dust. There was yet another rise - we began to feel duped. The view that we sought was obviously a mirage, or a figment of someone's over-imaginative mind. Finally, the next rise flattened out, and there down below hovered the most magical sight. Although the midday sun bleached the colours, it did nothing to destroy the pure pleasure of the experience – a circular, white salt pan held fast in the bosom of a rust-pink coloured dune. Out of this mirage rose a dozen ancient, charred trees, their ebony branches twisting awkwardly into the burning skies. On one branch stood a sole magpie, beak ajar, cooling down painfully. Where was its water, its food? What a beautiful, stark life; what a very cruel life . . .

The small swimming pool in the campsite at Sossusvlei was the only oasis in town. It cooled and satisfied. The mercury rose to over 40 degrees the following day. It was time to head for the Skeleton Coast. The two hundred mile journey took us through the eccentric settlement of Solitaire where the rainfall in November accounted for over half the year's precipitation. On the approach to Walvis Bay, we drove into the mist where the cold, Atlantic air hits the hot, dry air of the land. The mercury went into free-fall, and when we eased out of the truck and onto the beach, it felt a bit like Brighton. The temperature was 19 degrees. Shipwrecks abounded - this was the Skeleton Coast, haunted by fogs and ghostly wrecks.

After a brief spell of civilisation - a supermarket and an Internet café – we slewed inland once more in search of the Spitzkoppe and rumours of unblemished, granite domes, baking beneath an African sun. The fresh, cool air soon fizzled out and some peaks started rising up in the distance, fuzzy in the haze. We came upon some granite plinths and boulders – the periphery of the main geology – towering hundreds of feet above the plain. Up ahead, a woman stood by the side of the road. Was she mad, a hitchhiker in the middle of nowhere? We slowed down and found that she had some tables with crystals on display. We stopped and went to investigate. There were amethysts, tourmaline and other stones that I hadn't seen or heard of since I had studied them, eighteen years ago at university. Her four children sat behind her under a makeshift canvas tarp. We bought some stones and then enquired about the boulders. We gave her kids orange juice, watermelon and some coloured pencils, and gave her a couple of cans of Carling Black Label which she opened and drank on the spot. There was obviously no six o'clock watershed in Africa . . . The boulders were shaped like massive, tourmaline crystals – 20ft high, protruding from the ground amongst relics of old cars and the woman's house that was made from flattened-out Total oil drums. It was all quite surreal to us. The boulders offered quality arêtes, slabs and other thin features on small, subtle edges. It was too hot, so the day was passed under the canopy of a nearby acacia bush until the air had cooled. Only then did the mental and physical punishment begin.

The following morning, we moved on into the Spitzkoppe National Park where gold-red domes punched through a flat, grassy plain. It was inundated with boulders, some huge, some not so, as if they had fallen from the moon itself. It was too hot to appreciate them, so we followed our crude map in search of the elusive watering hole at the far end of the park. The watering hole was a type of elevated jacuzzi, carved into a cleavage of granite, with the best view on the continent - overlooking the savannah and granite domes. We had to share the water with tadpoles, and our view with the eagles that cut acute circles above us, looking for a kill. I began to relax, immersed in health and wellbeing, but not for long. I was drawn to a perfect looking 800ft, granite dome a mile away, with a vague, black line slicing it in two. I could feel the cogs turning as my inner drive returned . . .

I left Mike reading his book and headed out across the plain towards the dome. No boots, just a foray. It was too hot to do anything during the middle of the day. When I approached the dome, it started to dwarf the surroundings - it was huge. I located the base of the water-worn dyke line and to my astonishment there was an inscription on the rock: *Rumours of Rain 20* (20 being the grade of the climb) and above it was a line of metal pins dissolving into a vast sea of inclined rock. It was a slab, easing at 200ft with absolutely no holds or features. Just characterless, bare, granite smearing . . . it was tempting though. Intelligently, I walked round the back of the dome and scrambled upwards to see if there was a way off the top. Soon I had my answer: an impasse near the summit – a 20ft overhung step of crumbling rock, looking impossible to descend without a rope. However, on the way back, I spotted another line that might be possible; it only went half way up the dome and traversed off round the side. The inscription said: *Desert Storm 20*. The steepest section looked to be about 50ft above the ground. I was quite psyched to try it the following morning.

Back near the watering hole, Mike was studying something in the bushes. He called me over to take a look at the chameleon he had spotted whilst he was reading. It was very well camouflaged in the branches, its skin changing colour, its movement slow, decisive and almost hydraulic in nature. Its feet were like velvet oven-gloves, opening and closing along the branches, eyes like barnacles, spinning full circle in their sockets. Butterflies hovered in their numbers, and then in a split second one just vanished – plucked from the air by a foot long invisible tongue. I sat and watched the chameleon's progress for hours, mesmerised. Africa was a mix of beautiful life and death; I was quite disturbed by the simple brilliance of nature.

In the morning I went in search of *Desert Storm* to quench my thirst, or whatever it was that needed quenching. The cool morning air, the uncanny calm and the Namibian desert were all rather romantic. I sat down at the base of the granite dome, laced my boots, and started smearing my way up the slab in my usual, optimistic, confident rush. I seemed to wake up at 50ft where the slab steepened. I stopped momentarily beside a bolt. I began to study the smears more carefully and saw that the surface of the granite was exfoliating, just like my confidence. What was happening to me?

I didn't know. I didn't want to be there, here, anymore . . .

Over many years, I had become used to managing the fears of soloing in the mountains, but since my paragliding accident, I had begun to feel the true level of my own mortality. It was frightening. I looked at the bolt, longing to clip into it and be lowered off on a rope. But Mike didn't have a rope to rescue me. I thought about poking my finger through the bolt head and hanging on until my ligaments were stripped from the bone. I tried not to think about where I was – in the middle of Africa, miles from civilisation. I had absolutely no choice but to climb on. Cunningly, I used smears directly above the bolts so that in the case that my foot slipped, it had a chance of catching on top of the bolt, and I had a slim chance of being able to regain control. Another bolt passed by, I tried hard to ignore it . . . and the next and the next . . . and then I was up onto the easier-angled slab. It was a massive canvas of rock, without a single hold, that seemed to go on forever. The climbing grew easier and my fears subsided. At the top, I really began to wonder if I was getting anything from these long solos in the mountains. Was this a turning point for me?

Mike and I found ourselves discreetly at loggerheads in the Spitzkoppe; I wanted to stay longer and climb and Mike wanted to continue on. Eventually I saw sense. I was simultaneously happy and sad to be leaving the park, but the Kalahari beckoned . . . I rallied as I realised that there were, after all, adventures and misadventures yet to come.

The Dark Tide

The distant, primal groan of a rutting stag echoed in the night. Strangely, it was heartening to hear; it proved there was life out there. I was on my back, staring blankly into the dark expanse of the sky. My limbs were strapped tight, and some tubes were hanging out of my veins. I tried not to dwell on the pain too much, so I disengaged and waited for the next groan, and its resultant echo, to bounce off the sides of the glen and multiply.

Another sound began to counter that of the stag's random efforts; it was faint at first, but then the unsympathetic beat rose steadily to a crescendo. It was followed by a strobe light, marking my position on the hillside. The peace of a warm, autumnal night was suddenly shattered, and any misconceptions of my predicament had been totally obliterated . . . this was real. I looked up at the helicopter's almost invisible belly and the circular, grey glaze of the rotors against the black of the night, inching ever closer to the silhouette of the cliff. An RAF paramedic was lowered to me on the end of a thin, snaking cable. Stretchers were changed, and I was hoisted away.

The helicopter's navigation lights started spinning perfect orbits; they weren't of course - it was my stretcher that was spinning. The downdraught from the exhaust was hot and comforting as I ascended into the darkness attached to what looked like a very thin wire. I had visions of being snagged under the belly and the wire snapping

... but without much ado I was in, the door pulled to, closing out the sound of the rutting stags and the impassive countryside. The helicopter banked away ...

Having soloed one final route on the little-known grit outcrop of the Rollick Stones, I ran back along the rim of the peat-choked moor of Bleaklow, hoping to descend to the valley before it became pitch-black. When I arrived at the car, I stood there, vacant, disbelieving as reality sank in. All my belongings - climbing gear, clothes, camping gear - everything had gone. I didn't have many belongings, I was as free as anyone could be, but I felt violated and angry. Theft was rife at the 'beauty spots' of central England. I loved climbing on the gritstone in the Peak District, I was now only a few routes shy of my goal of a thousand grit solos, but this was the final straw. It was time to seek crime free climbing destinations.

Two months later, I headed out to the substantially less prone to crime surroundings of the Outer Hebrides to enjoy the lacy, white beaches, nineteen hours of daylight, and the idea of some deep water soloing. It was a little crazy as the prevailing southwesterly winds can inject lethal power into the Atlantic swell, so much so that 100ft cliffs can be consumed quite readily by the ocean's spray. Undeterred, I went in search of a perfect deep water solo amongst the Lewisian gneiss geos. I later enquired about hiring a boat from the small pier at Valtos to take me to the island of Pabbay Mor. I was pointed in the direction of Paul and Alison Tyler's house, having been informed that Paul was in the local Coastguard and had a rib. Paul was out when I dropped over, but Alison lent me one of their kid's sit on top kayaks and handed me a brand new lifejacket. She offered me some tea, and we had a chat in the kitchen as if we were old friends. Hebridean hospitality is staggering! Later that day, Paul took me round the coast in the rib. I managed to get a good look at all of the deep water soloing possibilities, however, nothing truly sparked my imagination until I went to search for *Mega Tsunami* on the small isle of Bernera off the west coast of Lewis. Cubby had mentioned that his route could be a possible deep water solo; I discarded his tip-off as far-fetched - it was recorded as being 100ft high! As I wandered around the erratic coastline so typical of gneiss, a leaning prow came into view, thrusting out over the sea at a tightly acute angle that resembled the bow of a ship . . .

Mega Tsunami?

At 60ft on a high tide, it was a viable solo option and the most stunning piece of deep water solo architecture in the country. I exploded with desire, but I couldn't get myself to commit to such a high deep water solo without someone else around if it all went horribly wrong. Was I becoming sensible with age? However, by good fortune, Daniel Laing turned up after an epic journey from Aberdeen; young and psyched, as soon as he arrived he soloed his route, *Minor Ripples,* under a setting sun. The following morning, with Daniel as a subconscious safety net, I committed to the square cut arête as it rose plum-straight out of the water, beautiful rock . . . The higher I climbed the steeper it became, as it punched me out into orbit over the sea. Just when fear started to mess with my mind control and stamina, better holds were reached, and there was nothing left but euphoria and 60ft of pure space beneath my feet. Later that afternoon, we discarded the deep water soloing, grabbed some ropes, and set out past the Uig sands – where the Lewis Chessmen were discovered - and to Mungarstadh and the Screaming Geo, our sights set on *The Prozac Link.*

The Prozac Link is the easier and therefore more popular variation to the original line of *The Screaming Abdabs*, a Cubby creation from 1988. They are the absolute businesses as far as adventurous sea cliff climbs go; with individual pitch names – The Yosemite Crack, the Traverse of the Gods, and the Moonlight Cooler – no other routes had names with such theatrical infamy. Not even the fascinating and atmospheric climbs at Gogarth on Anglesey could be classed or christened with more style.

I had once thought about attempting *The Prozac Link*, but when I first caught a glimpse of the geo, the idea of a solo made me quake uneasily. The architecture and the line the route takes are truly inspirational to any visiting rock climber. The Lewisian gneiss rock is twisted and contorted with a diverse array of colours: yellows, orange, black, greys, pinks and creams - it looked like a Herculean marble cake, very edible. We set up an abseil point and made our descent, spinning in free space. On the sea-washed ledges, the walls hung around us as though forming a natural coliseum. The abseil ropes were pulled, and there was no option but to climb out – game on. I fiddled with my knots longer than I should have because tying a figure of eight knot was no longer a regular occurrence for me. In fact, I hadn't tied into a rope for two years. I located the start of the Yosemite Crack and set to – it was steep and wet and the conditions were humid. Placing gear was strange – this nut, that nut, wrong size, too small – it sapped my energy and my jams slipped. I was exhausted when I reached the first welcoming belay ledge. I plugged in a belay of sorts with clove hitches – they were easy to tie - and then pulled the ropes in tight.

'Climb when ready!'

I heard a muffled reply, and the ropes came in leisurely. Daniel obviously wasn't having too many problems. He was eighteen, and although he came across as laid back and easy going, underneath the disguise he was incredibly psyched. I saw it in his eyes as he belly flopped on the ledge - he really wanted to succeed on this route. *The Traverse of the Gods* was his to lead, and he went for it, without any hesitation, in his fashionable rolled up jeans. The wall above the arch hung like a huge mural, striped with blacks, rusts and peaches. There were holds - big holds, big exposure - protection was seemingly sparse. Daniel took his time fiddling with small wires and cams. I left him to his absorption and started to daydream, as one does on a belay, methinks . . . subconsciously paying in and paying out by judging the tension in the rope; it becomes a natural instinct after many years of practice.

I began to grin as I watched one of those small, rock-dwelling sea shrimps moving towards my Rock 3 - a small, metal chock, wedged in a crack as part of the anchor belay. The shrimp was obviously not happy with the new arrival taking up his crevice and seemed to be squaring up to the metal wedge to which I was attached, with serious aplomb. The ropes tugged a little; I paid out a little. Daniel clipped in his runner and shot off in search of the gods. My turn . . . the security of the rope from above felt like a novelty. I took my time and enjoyed the exposure in a stress-free state. Behind Daniel's belay was a roof, the rock all coloured, kinked and buckled like hardened plasticine. I had a quick, inquisitive glance at the belay before I set off through the roof – no gear, but positive holds - 30ft further - still big holds, but still no gear. I was learning that I had forgotten how to find protection. I wedged against a block, cramped and tired. I just wanted to let go and rid myself of all the paraphernalia; to go for a swim in the calm, turquoise pool below me to wash away all the sweat and humidity. However, the situation forced me to hang in there and continue leftwards, to an awkward web of a hanging belay by some flakes and fangs. Before long, Daniel was fast approaching the belay. It was tight, ropes everywhere – a mess. Geared up, he climbed leftwards to an impasse and looked upward in disbelief at the quartz stippled, crux wall. Once he had fixed a good cam, he climbed on with real determination and presumably also with a generous helping of fear. I was suitably impressed when he disappeared from sight, ropes dangling in sweeping loops, silence, and the wake of a basking shark 150ft below. The Screaming Geo wasn't screaming, but Daniel probably did when he reached the grassy plateau atop the cliff. The ropes went tight and that was my cue to follow.

As the summer progressed, my formerly obsessive thoughts of soloing long 'extremes' in the mountains were fading. I didn't seem to be driven anymore. Perhaps this was because nothing was inspiring me at that moment, or perhaps I was becoming dutifully bound to my older age – a mid-life crisis perhaps. But I assumed that it happens to us all, when the youthful drive, immortality and carefree spirit all too quickly dissolve into middle age, mortgages, pension plans and arthritis. I thought I was immune to it all - a gerbil that had jumped from its spinning wheel of 'life'. I was still single, and the previous winter I had been voted one of Scotland's 50 most eligible bachelors in the 'Scotland on Sunday' newspaper! I was elusively eligible perhaps, but my lifestyle did not make it easy for me to settle in any way and I had grown to be comfortable with my own company.

It was a damp, calm morning as a light mist hovered along the upper catchments of the River Spey. To either side, an assortment of rugged hills dipped their brown, heather-clad slopes towards the broad, pastoral banks of the river's lazy meanders.

High up on the flanks of the hills, random strands of dense, white fog slowly nudged their way around the mottled contours, forever tightening like giant cummerbunds. The colour of the landscape and the chill in the air certainly hinted at an autumnal day. The chill in the air didn't bother me; I was due to fly out to Spain the following morning with the quiet mannered Ken Palmer from Devon. We both claimed to be unfit, although an 'unfit', strong sport-climber like Ken would still be in a different league to a 'super fit' me: it was never about difficulty, but more about the fun, adventure, and not least the much needed warmth and sun before the onslaught of winter. So for my last day in the Highlands, I decided to rest and fly my paraglider. By the time the afternoon arrived, the mists and dampness of the morning had evaporated, the air had warmed and there was little wind. Further down the valley, a squat, castellated knoll sat guard above the river's broad, fertile banks. I guessed that it would be a suitable place for a short flight - I sweated my way up its overly steep slopes.

On the summit, it was peaceful in the warm sunlight, and the 20ft high cairn and cross that crowned the summit looked surreal as the light glanced across its stone symmetry, casting an elongated shadow in the heather. Far to the south I could hear a rutting stag's retort echo from some unseen, heather-rich glen.

I searched for a good take off zone amongst little craglets and cliffs, but there was little that suited, apart from a neat, heather-clad strip on the knoll's shady east side. I laid out my paraglider, went through my checks, and launched down the hill. I had to abort when I realised that I wasn't going to clear a 7ft high deer fence. Frustrated at this, I went in search of another take off area, not wanting to walk back down the hill with the paraglider on my shoulders; flying was a far easier option. Just around the shoulder to the south, I found a good slope, albeit a little short, terminating in a 10ft drop to a tiny ledge, and then a further 100ft drop down a fractured rock face into a bowl of scree. I stared deeply down into the hollows, shuddering at the thought of falling down there. I calculated. I knew it was too short, but only marginally, so I carried on. I turned up the slope, knowing in the back of my mind that my risk assessment held no water whatsoever. However, I had made up my mind and I was no longer worrying about it. Excitedly, I threw the paraglider off my back, flattened out the wing and neatly organised all the lines. After a few minutes, I was clipped in and ready. With the A risers clamped and taut in each fist, my legs pedalled like fury down the slope, my arms bringing the risers up, and the paraglider gradually began to lift neatly into the still air. I could feel the tension in my lines through the harness. All was good. Then, within seconds, the slope had run out - the paraglider wasn't quite above me ... I checked ... I calculated ... I checked again ... I needed another metre or two! Too late ... the slope had gone - I was on the edge of the cliff. Since the paraglider now had forward speed, my best chance was to continue and to hope that it had inflated enough to lift me away. If not, then I would at least have a chance of landing on the lower ledge ...

I was in the air, and then pain hit me as my feet thumped into the ledge ten feet below. My ankles buckled, the glider lines slackened, and it began to pass over my head – all bad! Adrenalin was injected into my bloodstream at lightning speed, turning one second of 'real' time judgement into thirty seconds of imaginary time ...

Collapse the glider!

'I can't! The forward momentum will pull me off the ledge in one big downward arc ...'

Shit, what do I do?

'I'll have to jump and hope for the best'

Jump!

I jumped immediately, knowing that a micro second could mean the difference between life and death. My eyes shut tight in the faint hope that the paraglider would re-engage and this would be just another one of my near miss incidents. I was totally in the hands of fate.

Instead of that smooth, sweeping feeling of flight and the weightlessness of a successful launch, I heard noises, bad noises, and felt the rush of air and my skin being torn as I whipped past rocky fangs. One of my legs was tangled in the lines and my organs were floating around inside me.

Shit, I'm screwed!

I was prey to gravity now, feeling like a field mouse clenched between a buzzard's talons. I understood the circumstance - the cycle, the 'natural selection' - and began to accept my fate honourably, as there was nothing more I could possibly do. This time, it was over.

A dark tide rose up and entombed me in its powerful, watery fist. My mind and body shut down. The tide was taking me to a place where nothing existed – to absolute zero. I knew that, but somehow I didn't care. For the first time in my life, I was at ease in the dark catacombs of the tide and it felt warm and homely, a little grey but simple; there was no pain or fear, and I didn't need to think or feel in control. I realised then that letting go of that control opened the gates to a zone of true peace and inner harmony, I finally began to relax . . . and then . . .

Pmmphhhh!

Shock waves resonated through bone on impact. The dark tide vanished and I was left an empty, broken shell. My mind re-engaged - ready to sort out pain from fear, and the shock of whatever injuries I might have sustained. Paralysis didn't bear thinking about. I couldn't breathe; my lungs had collapsed, and I thought I was suffocating. I began rasping for air, the intake slow and painful. My eyes reopened: rocks surrounded me; sharp edged, cold, lichen-clad stone that could quite easily have cleaved my skull open. I glanced down over the scree-fan, through sunlight and shade to low, evening shadows, and then onto some golden-tinged leaves of the autumn birch, the grasses of the glen, a lost ravine and a red figure cut into the far away hillside.

My breathing was slow as my lungs began to fill again. I was still motionless. Part of me wanted to get up and move, dust myself down and go home, but part of me didn't want to move because I didn't want to find out that I couldn't. I wanted to shout to the red figure in the distance to say that everything was ok, but I couldn't move my jaw. Slowly, my senses started to return and trauma began to fire through my whole body. My left leg was bent backwards, caught in my paraglider lines, my harness was digging in tight to my thighs, and my ribs were beginning to melt with pain. I flopped back, flayed out in the scree, sharp, ragged rocks poking at me from all directions, and then my body began to flush with the cold sweat of shock.

I managed to reach out and free my harness buckles before falling back again, limp, trying to ascertain the extent of my injuries. Thinking I was ok, I forced myself to stand up and begin descending the scree slope. I pivoted and made small shuffles over some tomes of schist on my burning ankles, and my ribs throbbed with fury as if a hole had been blown through them with a shotgun. I turned all rubbery with shock. I could not sit back down, or move forward, and for an age, I just stood there, frozen in pain. I was a mess! I needed painkillers or morphine so that I could at least reduce the agony and descend the hill without the embarrassment of being rescued. I had pills in the glove box of the car, but that was a mile away.

An hour later, a small air ambulance arrived, circling the hill before dropping off a paramedic. Some questions were asked before an intravenous needle was stuck into my veins. Within half an hour, two more paramedics arrived from the direction of the road with a stretcher and oxygen. The story down in the glen, amongst the locals, was that someone had tried to commit suicide by jumping out of a glider!

After my helicopter ride to Raigmore Hospital, I was unloaded and wheeled into the operating theatre, surrounded by many professional faces; doctors and nurses - questioning faces of concern and worry, all routine, paperwork and notes. I wasn't worried; I felt ok. The doctors gently checked for neck and spinal injuries whilst a cute nurse was pulling at my right arm to insert a drip. Then someone with large scissors took to my clothes; my favourite fleece was snipped and ruined. The X-rays were painless and then there was a long pause. Finally, a female doctor stood over me and asked:

'It says here in the paramedic's notes that you fell over 100ft!'

I wasn't sure if it was a question or a statement, perhaps a bit of both, but there was bewilderment on her face.

'Yeah, I guess so,' I offered.

'You don't have a broken bone!' she forced out, letting her disbelief be known.

I smiled at that, and wondered if I was indestructible after all, but I reflected on my luck and was annoyed with myself for being so gung-ho with the paraglider, a risk I would never have taken whilst soloing. I wondered how many of my nine lives I had now used up. I didn't believe in the superstition anyway, but I did believe that if I stopped all my dangerous pastimes then some terminal illness would kill me instead. That just wasn't my etiquette. I was discharged from hospital the following day, feeling rather relieved and very fragile. I was about to find out in the next couple of months that I had lost some of my carefree courage – a quality I had which many climbers sort of envied. I rang Dari up and left a message on his answerphone. He returned the call the following day, sounding a little confused, and after making sure that I was ok, he asked:

'So, if you were airlifted off the mountain, then who was there with you? You never take a mobile phone with you, and if by chance you did, there is no way you would use it to call a helicopter. You would either crawl down the mountain by yourself, or just curl up and die.'

Dari knew me better than I knew myself. My mind replayed the whole episode, and I paused at the red figure cutaway on the far hillside.

I wished the red figure had never been there at all.

Soul Of Silence

Except our own thoughts, there is nothing absolutely in our own power.
René Descartes.

The beauty of travelling alone is that you have complete freedom of choice. When I left Yosemite, I had six weeks of travelling stretching in front of me – a journey with no specific itinerary. Quite literally, I had an open road. I had with me a twenty-year-old guidebook to Joshua Tree that had never been opened. The approaching winter meant that it made more sense for me to head south, to Arizona and New Mexico, rather than north, to Wyoming and Montana. I had heard that Bishop, a small town on the eastern side of the Sierras, was a preferred climber's hang out and that there was good bouldering in that locale. Bouldering had not been a preference or a *force majeure* in my climbing career. For me, it was similar to 'sport climbing' in that it short changed you on adventure and 'the experience', and bouldering also tended to dish out a plentiful supply of muscle, tendon and joint injuries, making it eminently avoidable for a soloist.

Completely out of character then, I found myself now purchasing a tiny, second-hand bouldering pad and a fat guidebook to bouldering around Bishop. I think at heart my newfound subconscious reasoning was that if I bouldered, I could increase my strength and refine my technique without frightening myself, thereby increasing the likelihood of going home in one piece. Flicking through the guide, it became apparent that the Buttermilks stood out as the place to go.

Buttermilk Drive is a sandy, bumpy track that winds up into the foothills of the Sierra, rising to an open boulder-field at 6,500ft. Camping is tolerated, if carried out with discretion. In contrast to CAMP 4 at Yosemite, there are no rules and regulations, no bears to consider, and it costs nothing. Sitting at the foot of Mount Humphreys, 13,992ft, and Mount Tom, 13,658ft, it has an almost alpine feel to it too. Perfect!

The main boulder field is galactic - a random mixture of sizes and shapes that look like deposits of asteroid fragmentation. The Grandpa and Grandma Peabodies are the biggest - reaching up to 40ft in height, they aren't truly 'boulders', more like climbing propositions. 'Bouldering' was taking on a whole new meaning to me, and I started to relish the idea of finding a balance between bouldering and soloing. It is termed 'highballing': bouldering with fear, or alternatively, soloing with the marginal possibility of breaking a bone. The boulders are formed of granite with interesting textures, coarse in some parts, and with a smooth patina in others. Every style of climbing exists here, and I soon discovered that the Buttermilks are home to the highest concentration of world famous problems - the likes of *Evilution, High Plains Drifter, Iron Man* and *Checkerboard*.

During November, with the impending drop in temperature, the Buttermilks begin to gather a crowd. Climbers from all over the world can be found walking around, imitating Nepalese Sherpas, carrying stacks of pads on their backs. Some of these problems are too high to be constantly falling off without a deep, cushioned landing. My pad was neither deep enough to protect high falls nor broad enough to cover all bases. Occasionally, I would improvise and use a cut up, five-litre water container as a shovel, heaping up gravel to soften the landings.

I felt at home in the Buttermilks. Sunshine brought warmth during the day, but as soon as the sun fell behind the mountains, the temperature plummeted below zero. After two weeks of bouldering, my fingertips were raw and both ankles were mashed. It was time to move on and head south for Death Valley.

The contrast between the alpine snows of the Sierras and the hot desert sands of Death Valley, barely fifty miles apart, could not have been more marked. The mercury began to push 77F (25C) even now in November. The landscape changed dramatically. The serrated, granite mountains became plains, rising again into hills with colourful strata and then, intermittently, into a mix of plains, hills, dunes and salt pans. In amongst the cacophony of all of this immense, geological faulting lie the lovely towns of Stove Pipe Wells (no more than a shop and an archaic fire engine) and Furnace Creek, the lowest town in the US, with a golf course, a hub of palms and a 'world record' temperature of 134F (57C), recorded a century ago.

I continued on to Badwater Basin - a large salt pan that is the lowest point in America -282ft below sea level. Salt pans are strange phenomena - they have a feeling of space, serenity and horizontality, similar to the sea, but tangibly calmer to the spirit. It was getting dark, and the next town was seventy miles away. Wild camping was not permitted within two miles of the road in Death Valley National Park, or so it proclaimed in my National Park guide. So, with my tent and sleeping bag duly packed, I began to walk towards the centre of the salt pan, passing a lone, guileful coyote. After an hour's walk, I made my pitch; the salt was smooth, flat and comfortable. With the tent doors open, I found myself staring into untainted space. The stars were crisp and real, pulsing with a distinct glow, and there was absolute silence, not even a breath of wind on the fabric of the tent. I could hear only my own thoughts. I was, for one night only, the lowest inhabitant of North America, enjoying the best room in the world, a room in a five million star hotel, surrounded by peace and heavenly mystery; no money could ever buy this.

I continued south and on to the Mojave Desert; hundreds of miles of open sky and a cooked, arid landscape – it fascinated me. I turned up in a sprawled out clutter of a town called 29 Palms, on the periphery of the Joshua Tree National Park. In marked contrast to the town, the park was like a utopian garden, littered with the ubiquitous ten feet high, warped and wiry yucca plants – the Joshua Trees - and an extensive diversity of coloured shrubs and cacti, all set amidst a lunar landscape of granitic rocks and boulders. The campsites blended in and were well managed, but contrary to the opinion of my old guidebook, they did now cost dollars for 'a site'. The way I eventually evaded the fees was to go 'back country' camping, requiring that I filled out a form in the designated car parks and then walked into the open desert along small trails for a minimum of one mile, all in order to pitch my tent.

I found myself exploring the many stockpiles of rock here, wandering around the desert for hours, simply trying to take it all in. The rocks themselves looked enchanting, but the surface was a little gritty, and the flakes quite creaky. One day I stumbled upon a beautiful, golden rib with a number of bolts in it. I searched through the guide to find the route's description and decided to give it a go. At the very top, with a high right foot move, my tender ankle buckled. I lost my balance momentarily and only a frenetic knee-jerk reaction saved me from the long, long journey down to the desert floor. I sat on the summit, gazing out over the extraordinary desert oasis, a sapped soul with a cold sweat and a thousand yard stare. Inexplicably, I cannot remember the name of this route, and I gave my guide away when I departed.

I no longer had any urge to go and solo. I did, however, want to go home with some good climbing memories of Joshua Tree. By chance, I had overheard someone say a route named *Slashface* was 'the best boulder problem in America', and that it was somewhere near the famous finger crack of *Equinox* which itself was half an hour's walk from the road. I set out into the desert from the Geology Tour Road with my pad under my arm, without an inkling where I was going or what I was looking for; maybe I would stumble across a rattlesnake - it was worth a foray, and I had nothing to lose . . .

After having located and climbed the beautiful 'highball' 25ft wall of *Slashface*, I set off again, heading east towards Arizona across repetitive, endless desert. I put the car in cruise control and set it to 60mph, curled my legs up into the half lotus position on the seat and began to massage my ankles with Tiger Balm for the next hundred miles or so.

When the sun began to set, I decided that it was time to stop and eat. I found a tin of corn beef hash that someone had given to me in CAMP 4. I wasn't sure why they had been so generous, but I soon found out. I opened it up - beef flavour Pedigree Chum smelled better. I stuck in a fork and ate it.

I ran round the rim in the dark. It was cold, and I was impatient as I waited for the finest geographical phenomenon in the world to show itself. It was like waiting for a giant, prehistoric monster to wake up, and at 7am it did. Rays of sunlight streamed in, awakening the Grand Canyon. The width and breadth were absolutely staggering; band upon band of strata, stacked one upon the other, each one defining an epoch and its own fabulous story of tectonic mayhem. I stared down into the hollow and a mile below I could just make out the culprit responsible for all this destruction - the River Colorado - a crazed, devilish serpent, twisting and turning, devouring two billion years' worth of rock in a mere ten million years.

It was surprisingly overcast and quiet – and it was Thanksgiving. I headed on towards the deserts of Utah and Monument Valley. Caramel-coloured towers poked their way out of the desert plain, unjustified and random. This was Navaho country, and I fully expected John Wayne to go riding past with saddlebags and spurs. It was hard to take it all in. The River Colorado is more infantile here as it sweeps through the sandstone walls of Canyon Creek. I got lost looking for Indian Creek – the world's premier destination for crack climbing. I had no map and no directions. I probably could have found it if I had persisted, but I didn't feel like climbing. I turned up the music and continued driving, absorbed now in the beat of the American dream.

I stopped and hung out for a few days at the rather secluded and elevated haunt of Joe's Valley, somewhere in the middle of Utah. The temperature here was immeasurably colder than in Joshua Tree; the boulders were smaller, the sandstone more pleasurable on the fingers and the grades better for the ego. I left to rejoin my journey feeling that I needed to be thawed out. The state line changed - Utah to Nevada - but the landscape was still the same – continuous desert without variation. I arrived at the town of Ely where I gave the car an oil change, had a much-needed shower and washed some clothes in the back room of a gas station.

The next place on the map was the 'silver' town of Tonopah, nearly two hundred miles away; there was only the odd farm or two en route. The roads at times were die-straight, and I tried to guess how many miles it was to the horizon - it was always grossly foreshortened. To break the journey, I turned off at a sign to the Lunar Crater. I watched a herd of Mule Deer tearing across the desert floor in front of me, kicking up dust in their wake; I felt that we might be the only life forms that existed – I might just as well have been on the moon.

Finally, on arrival in the White Mountains on the state line between California and Nevada, I drove up to 11,000ft to see the gnarled, rust coloured, ancient bark of the Bristlecone Pines, the oldest trees in the world at nearly 5,000 years of age, growing out of a harsh, weather beaten, magnesium rich, limestone meadow where nothing else seemed to grow. The vastness and diversity of America had been a geographical education.

I returned to Bishop and the Buttermilks. I wanted to deny it, but as a matter of fact I had become more excited about bouldering here than I had ever been. I joined up with a group of Brits, the more pads the merrier of course, but these weren't just any Brits. I felt a little demoralised when the two girls burnt me off on *The Checkerboard*. They made it look simple, and I fell a few times without success. I couldn't use my height as a get out clause - Hazel Findlay was quite a bit shorter than me. She was an absolute pleasure to watch, with the natural climbing ability of a well-oiled lizard. Katy Whittaker was taller, and had the grace of a swan, with such delicate fingers that never seemed to fail. I was in awe of the younger generation, with their ability and technique. And then, to cap it all, I watched Ryan Pasquill on *The Mandala*; very tall and very slim, he was all arms and legs. To an untrained eye, his climbing style looked awkwardly random, but his skill was immeasurable. They inspired me to get stronger at least; soloing doesn't promote power.

My birthday had come round again already. I was feeling sorry for myself because I had fallen sideways onto my hip and had missed the pad. My aches and pains were accumulating; I now had pulled tendons in my knee, my shoulders and my elbows and bruises everywhere else. I was a mess, and the weight of another year on my tally wasn't doing my head any favours. However, there was still a 25ft high problem that I wanted to try – *Secrets of the Beehive*. I borrowed a few extra pads and the evergreen, travelling Scotsman - Trevor Wood - to come and spot me. After a couple of tries, I reached the big hold a few feet from the top. The last move would be 'easy' if my arms were fresh; however, I was far from it and all I could do was dangle from my fingers and feel them uncurl involuntarily. I looked down at the pads way below, screaming at Trev to move the pads in line . . . out *a bit . . . right a bit . . . out a bit more . . . agh . . .* my fingers let go . . . an anxious second or so passed before I impacted into the centre of the pads. My ankles crumpled and I hobbled back to camp in a little pain, although happy enough with my efforts given the circumstances.

That evening, when the sun went down over the Sierra to the west, the full moon rose above the White Mountains to the east. Eight of us had decided to celebrate my birthday in the hot spring in the middle of the Sierra plain at 8,000ft. It could fit more people than that snuggly, and there was a tap on the inflow pipe to regulate the temperature. I was presented with a cake with one candle - nice touch. The moon slowly shifted across the sky and illuminated the landscape with subdued light. The air temperature was 4F (-15C); by midnight there were only four of us remaining, including a random local who turned up and started a conversation about politics, third world economics, religion and feeding the world.

I began to stare at the stars and the vast openness of space, pontificating about all the soloing I had undertaken. Thousands of routes - miles of verticality - in which one loose hold, one rogue cloud precipitating at the wrong moment, or one split-second lapse of concentration could have been fatal. I examined my hands in the moonlight - they were small, perhaps delicate even, and they had favoured me by holding gravity at bay for more than quarter of a century now. I mulled over the unspoken rule of soloing: 'If you don't stop, it will one day kill you'. Luckily, my innate, subconscious, clinical risk assessments had averted the laws of probability thus far. Looking ahead, I knew that I was not going to stop soloing, although I had mixed it up a bit to incorporate the safer art of deep water soloing which has undoubtedly helped to prolong my existence. Like a squirrel hiding his food, I always had a small supply of climbing projects stored away in my psyche, waiting to come to fruition. If I didn't have these, then my life would be empty. They were almost like my girlfriends. It was no longer wholly about the climbing though, it was about the purity of simple existence in the beautiful places where the climbs are to be found – that is what matters more to me now. As the debate around me and under the moonlight intensified, I drifted away to the scene of my most treasured project. I visualised the tiny holds, the sequences of choreography required to link them, and the fear that would undoubtedly percolate through me on the long, blind move for the tiniest of edges, 50ft above a boulder the size of a hay bale. All of this intertwined with the sentinels of the Caledonian pine, the thrash of melt water carving the bedrock into delicious curves, and the young bracken shoots rising out of the ground like bass clefs to the tune of spring. I was far away now, happy with what lay ahead, lost in myself, once more a soul of silence.

At the rising of the Sun, between the dew of the heavens and the richness of the earth, two powers struggle for domination (Circle: ancient, strong rocks, a gentle reminder of the vulnerability of mankind). © Inge Nic A' Bhraonaigh